Inspirational Dissatisfaction

Steven Kind

Published by Steven Kind, 2021.

INSPIRATIONAL DISSATISFACTION

First edition. October 29, 2021.

ISBN: 979-8201031435

Written by Steven Kind.

Table of Contents

I dedicate this book to my wife Susan for stopping me from driving off a cliff.

A special thanks to Kraig, Cher and Nicole for their editing help.

Also to my friends in the sober community who's encouragement kept me writing.

The Letter

The flash of the cursor mocked my inability to formulate a single word. I didn't know how to approach this idea beyond knowing to whom I would be writing. I was given an exercise which seemed initially to be a simple task.

I didn't know where to begin. What would I write? What would I say? How could I possibly put into words what I have experienced to bring me to this point in my life?

"Write a letter to someone you trust and explain why you have decided to help others recover from addiction."

On the surface it felt like an easy task. I expected to sit down, write the letter and move on to other things. I knew I was going to write the letter to my oldest brother, Arn. He was by my side at many of my worst moments and has seen me struggle to find peace. He has been there to help me pick up the pieces in the aftermath of the chaos I had visited upon myself.

I was dumbfounded for quite some time until I decided to just start writing. Let it flow. Do a dirty first draft and go back over it after it's done. The moment I broke through that initial barrier, the cursor refused to stop.

Arn,

I am writing this to you because I want you to know who I am in a very real sense and because the events of the last year have made it difficult, if not almost impossible, to have face-to-face interactions. I think you are the brother who gets me more than the others, and I am so grateful that you don't just see me as the black sheep, the troubled one, or the loser. I know that I am seen in that way by the other brothers to some extent. You have, somehow, been able to simply see me as an individual with a different perspective.

I have come by who I am through more trial and error (and success) than most people I know. I do not possess a four year college degree, which I know makes me standout from all my brothers right off the bat. I have, however, received a fair amount of education in various ways. My formal education came from various institutions. By formal I am talking about the type of education required to gain the credentials to follow a career path. I went to MSU for 3 quarters and excelled in the area of sociology. I loved it! I had two professors who felt I had a far more advanced grasp of it than most first year students and encouraged me to pursue an education in that field. So why did I stop? I didn't want to go through four years of college to become a social worker, police officer or sociology professor. The field has very limited professional applications and none that I could see myself as striving for. When I did find something that truly piqued my intellectual curiosity, I quickly learned that there weren't any schools in the area that were providing the type of education needed to enter that particular field. Website design and internet marketing was in its very infancy. I took two weeks of HTML at the community center, one year of graphics and one year of programming at South Central Technical College. Not exactly the traditional curriculum but it gave me the skills I needed to start my web business (a business which had two sales years in excess of $600,000). In *addition to that education, I have done the classwork needed to attain my Realtor's license, my insurance sales license and my facilitators certificate to be allowed to start SMART Recovery here in Mankato. I am an avid reader and study a wide variety of subjects. Despite all of that, I still feel that I am perceived by my brothers as the undereducated one.*

My education involved the school of hard knocks. I learned how to defend myself and my family by getting far too much practice. It's not that I'm a hothead; it's that I have been in endeavors that have placed me where the wild things roam. From a few scrapes in high school and truck stops (and a few purveyors of adult beverages near those truck stops) to working with bikers out in California, I have had to stand my ground more than once. Now that may seem to suggest that I put myself in harm's way, but the truth is, I wouldn't trade those heart pumping adrenaline rushes for anything. Most of those fights ended up in long-term tight friendships or, at the very least, deals being struck and business moving forward.

There are very few people out there who can say that they can quote basic insurance law or real estate law, drive everything from straight trucks to double trailers, work with sales people, bikers, recovering addicts and others and truly say they had a blast doing all of it. I am somewhat of a chameleon in that way. I have forged long lasting friendships through just about every type of experience I have lived.

So what landed me where I am today? I have made some bad choices. Many bad choices. A little bad luck, but mostly bad choices. One of the bad choices I made was to sell pot and other drugs when I was in Jr. High. Stealing liquor from dad's liquor closet, valium from the drug cabinet and selling street drugs for a profit led me to my first big consequences. These were just the first issues in a long series of deleterious problems. I didn't take those consequences and stop doing them. Instead, I found better ways to do the same toxic garbage. Being arrested for selling pot in 1985 stopped me from getting into the Army and put me on probation. This was what led to me getting my CDL (not a bad thing but not what I really wanted). I think I have shared with you in the past that the only reason I began driving truck was to get off probation early. The chameleon in me was able to con my probation officer into believing it was a dream of mine to drive semi. I never had that thought prior to seeing it as a means to an end.

I have been in serious situations an almost unfathomable number of times which put my life, and indeed the lives of those I care about, in serious jeopardy. Many of those situations would have put me on a completely different track had I not been able to avoid their consequences. It brings to mind one situation that stays in my head to this day.

After trimming marijuana out in California and living on the side of a mountain with no electricity or potable water for six and a half weeks, I found, through the connections I made while out there, a way to make some money. Trimming, in and of itself, actually cost me more money to do than what I earned by doing it. I left California with zero dollars and had to transport over 50 pounds of marijuana, several pounds of hashish and about a dozen *pounds of pot butter in order to have enough money to get home. The opportunity I saw, however, was to go home, find an investor, return to California and purchase several pounds of pot and hash to resell back home at a huge profit. In Mankato a pound of pot was sold for around $3,600. In California, I was able to buy several pounds of extremely high grade pot from a few of the farmers at between $1,000 and $1,200 per pound. Some of the biker clubs could bring that down to $850 to $900 per pound. I usually went with the farmers or the Native Americans on the reservation because they were much easier groups to work with. So I was averaging about $2,500 per pound pure profit. That was if I sold it back home by the pound. When sold in smaller quantities, that profit went way up. Splitting the pound into quarters brought in $4,800 per pound. If it was sold as ounces it was $6,000 per pound. As far as the hash, I was actually given trim from the farmers for free. I arranged to drop that off at a friend's house in Cali to turn into hash...I supplied the free trim, he made the hash and we split it 50/50. That would amount to about 3 ounces of hash coming back with me. When arriving back home I would turn the hash into tincture (alcohol infused hash) and turn the tincture into hard candies. There was another $3,000 profit. It all sounds good until you consider a few of the drawbacks.*

On one of my scariest trips back from California, I was in my Toyota Camry with 17 pounds of pot and about two ounces of hash in my back seat. I would put the product in a big green bag (it was a bag for hauling product in a legitimate sales role) and put it directly behind me on the floor between my seat and the back seat. On that particular trip, I was coming out from Reno heading east when a sheriff's vehicle pulled out on the highway behind me and started mirroring me off the back driver's side while going through the canyon. He followed me for several miles, during which time I noticed the emblem on the side of his truck said K-9 unit. I happened to be on the phone (hands-free of course) with Sue. When I started to get caught up to the car ahead of me in my lane, I tapped on the brakes to slow down and that's when the lights came on to pull me over. I was terrified. I honestly thought that may have been my last moments of freedom for the remainder of my life. Because Nevada is huge in the area of private prisons, it was one of the worst places to get pulled over. Kickbacks to officers who feed the private prisons are a well-known hazard associated with Nevada. I had to take some deep breaths and try and calm down by reminding myself that I had done everything possible to prepare for this eventuality. When the sheriff stepped up to the passenger side window I rolled it down. I didn't have to worry about HIM smelling anything because the bags the pot and hash was transported in were vacuum sealed and bleached. If he got the dog out of his truck it would be an entirely different story.

"Where are you coming from?" the Sheriff asked.

"I have been at the A&E programming convention in Reno for the last week," I said.

The sheriff then asked me a series of questions. "Where was the convention? When did you get into town? Where did you stay?"

As I said before I had prepared for this eventuality. I had my fake itinerary including hotel booking (book the room in advance, print, then cancel), convention information (there's always a convention in Reno, I just looked them up in advance) and convention pass (easy to get the logo from the convention and put it in a laminate) printed out and sitting on the passenger seat, opened, with some notes on a scratch pad (to give a reason for the book to be open). I worked for a Marketing firm in Mankato that printed logos on everything from hats and shirts to coffee mugs and pens. I had these items all over the back seat and also on top of the bag where the pot was stored. Directly on top of the pot bags was a line of monogrammed hats. I answered his questions including telling him that I stayed at the La Quinta (perfect for the salesmen on a budget).

"Did you stay at the La Quinta over by the athletic field?" he asked.

"No," I replied. "The street outside of that La Quinta is under construction and it's a mess. That is the one I usually stay at when I come to one of these conventions but because of the mess I stayed at the one by the airport."

He asked for my license and went back to his truck. The longest few minutes of my life was waiting to see what was going to happen next. If he came back without the dog I figured I would be ok. I was hoping that my knowledge of the area and my response about the hotel might have done the trick. After what seemed like hours, he came back to my car without the dog! He gave my license back and told me that the reason he pulled me over was because I had got too close to the car ahead of me. He warned me that I should refrain from doing that in the future. He sent me down the road. I swear I shivered and shook for several hours while the gravity of that situation sunk deep.

I avoided a long prison term by the skin of my teeth. Was I prepared? Yes. Was I ready to answer tricky questions? Yes. None of that would have mattered if he just decided to bring his dog out for a quick once over.

That was an example of just one of the many crazy and dangerous situations I put myself in. The profit was not worth what could have happened had I been caught. On top of all that, the money that was stashed at my place (can't really put that in the bank) was stolen one night while Sue and I were home and asleep. I will never visit that kind of danger on those I love again!

After all of that, it was a couple of DUI's that made the lightbulb come on above my head. I won't go into the detail of those DUI's. I had no business being behind the wheel at even a fraction of the level of intoxication I was at. I used to say I was such a good driver that I could drive drunk without issue. That was wrong. All it would have taken was the decrease in my response time, cutting a corner short or any one of a thousand other things for me to have hurt or even killed somebody.

It is odd to say but I am angry, ashamed and grateful for the last DUI. Angry because I was accused by the officer of things that didn't happen (the officer's own video proves that he was lying). I am angry because the judge didn't throw out the case on the grounds of a lack of probable cause (again shown in the video). I am ashamed that I drove, not just that time but many times, after being far too intoxicated. I feel ashamed because my actions caused Sue and I unbelievable financial hardship and damaged trust from those I care about (including you). I am grateful that the events of that night put me in a place mentally and emotionally to re-evaluate my life and its purpose. I am grateful that after being a heartbeat away from losing the love of my life over my alcohol addiction, my relationship with Sue is stronger than ever. I am grateful that you have given me another chance to prove myself to be trustworthy. I am grateful that I have new purpose in my life. I am now able to reach out and help others find their path to recovery.

I know there are many out there who get great help from AA, NA and other 12 step programs but I also know that there are many for whom the religious aspects of those organizations are a turn off. I tried AA and NA SEVERAL times. They only worked for a short period because the precepts simply didn't work for me. There are many out there who will never get help if they don't find some alternative to trying to pray away an addiction. It simply doesn't work when they don't have faith in the power of an outside force to do so. The 12 step programs are absolutely the right fit for many people. I am grateful for their existence and have seen those programs work for countless numbers of people. It is my personally imposed mandate to help people find the right program for their recovery. Whether it is AA, NA or a secular source, I just want to help people find a place to experience the peace I have discovered in my sobriety.

When I finally allowed the cursor to take a breath, the letter was done. I had barely looked up from the keyboard for over an hour. With the exception of a few grammatical errors, spelling mistakes and sloppy sentence structure I was done. I went back, did my spellcheck and fixed some grammar. I read it through, edited a couple paragraphs that needed some clarification and hit save.

I opened up my email and addressed it to Arn. In the subject line I wrote "My history, future, self-reflection and motivation." I started questioning if it was a good idea. How will Arn take it? Am I revealing too much? Does the letter really have to be sent or could I simply use it for self-reflection? Is there truly anything to be gained by sending it?

I hit Send.

It was a couple days later that I received a phone call from Arn. He was impressed with the contents of the letter. To my surprise he commented on how well it was written. Considering I was just spewing it out at a rapid pace (once I was able to start at all) I was not expecting to get that positive feedback from him. We discussed the letter and he wished me luck with the future I was eyeing as a Peer Recovery Support Specialist.

Before the conversation ended my brother said something that I really wasn't expecting. "Have you ever considered writing a book?" he asked.

"Actually years ago I started a fiction novel and never finished it. Cassie (my oldest daughter) has been encouraging me to take it back up," I replied.

"I'm not talking about fiction," he said. "I remember the stories you told me about the crazy things you've gone through. You should write a non-fiction book about the crap that has brought you to this point in your life."

After finishing the conversation I started thinking about his suggestion. The idea of writing about myself had never occurred to me. I have to admit the idea didn't seem completely crazy. The things that I have lived through, the places I have been and the situations I have found myself in are a little outside of what most would consider normal. I started reflecting on my life and couldn't think of where I would even begin.

Do I go back to the first time I ever smoked pot in the summer between 5th and 6th grade? Do I talk about stealing booze from my dad's liquor closet in junior high or selling the valium I had stolen from his medicine cabinet? Do I start a bit later with the sex, drugs and rock and roll of my High School years?

All of those options were possible and they could all be considered part of what brought me to this chapter in my life. If I started on Day 1 of my drug use, I would have enough for an entire book before getting through my over-the-road driving days.

I had to narrow it down.

When did the fun of my drug use begin to change from mostly fun to seriously dangerous? That would be a good starting point. I racked my brain for the answer. I didn't want to write a book that was all doom and gloom. Drinking and doing drugs does not start with horrific consequences. That comes later. Not for everyone but certainly for me. When most people first decide to try any mood altering substance the goal is to have fun. I enjoyed many days of inebriation and the consequences were pretty minimal. So when did it change? At what point did my life go from, life with a side order of drugs, to drugs with a side order of life?

It hit me like a lightning bolt. What event put my life on this path? Meeting Carl.

Meeting Carl

When my business needed a shot in the arm I reached out to a college student who had been making some inroads in the local internet marketing game. While attending college Mike started a site that took local businesses and put them next to college kids with credit cards. Brilliant! My business was website design and internet marketing but was missing the mark with any sort of real local component. Through a mutual friend, Charles, we were set up to meet. The best part in my mind about that first meeting was that there was a shared interest in truly good marijuana.

We were pot snobs. Unabashed, down to the core, serious weed connoisseurs. The first meeting involved about 60% business and 40% war stories and bragging rights over tales of smoking such exotics as Maui Wowi (which eventually became the name of my cat), Alaskan Thunderfuck, and Thai Stick. We also talked about the current standards that we liked. We were both fans of Jack Herer, Cinderella 99, and Purple Urkle. It was a match made in the smokiest parts of heaven. Mike and I decided to become partners and went forward with a merger between his startup and my pretty well established company.

The partnership came along with an introduction from Mike to his dealer, another weed connoisseur by the name of Carl. The first time I was introduced to Carl, I was not alone. Charles, Mike and I were treated to Carl's "collection". Carl took down a large box as big as a small refrigerator and opened up what I can only describe as a smoker's Nirvana. I don't recall how many different varieties of pot were in that treasure trove - memory is not a smoker's strong suit - but I would guess there were at least twenty large labeled mason jars filled with beautiful bud.

It was a game changer. He not only had an encyclopedic knowledge of each strain and its history, he had two volumes of cannabis encyclopedias to back everything up. After giving us the tour of his cannabis cornucopia Carl leaned over to me with a sheepish look.

"Steve, if you could mix any three strains of those I have available, which three would you chose and why?"

I was not hesitant in my reply. "I would start with the Hindu Kush to get a good Indica in the mix. I would follow that with some Durban Poison to add a potent Sativa. I would top it off with some Purple Haze for the flavor and added kick!"

"Great answer," Carl said as he collected the three jars I had just mentioned.

He took out a large grinder and put a good sized flower top from each of my selections into it. Once grinded, he said as an added treat, he was going to add a little something extra. That's when the tackle box came out of the closet. When Carl opened the tackle box I wouldn't have been surprised to see a genie emerge, or a unicorn, or any other mythical source of happiness considering the tour so far.

What came out was better. It was varieties of high quality hash; hard blonde, soft brown, soft black, oils, and more than one of each. Christ, somebody pinch me! I was salivating as Carl added some blond and black hash sprinkles to the ground weed, rolled them together into two perfectly hand rolled joints and proceeded to put some oil on the finished masterpiece. After waiting about 15 minutes for the oil to dry, it was time. Time to smoke which, to that day, was the most perfect concoction I had ever seen.

It is hard to describe how excited I was to be smoking the perfect joint with fellow weed aficionados. To say that I was stoned would be akin to describing an ocean as wet. No description would suffice to actually relate the experience in terms I am able to convey with any sort of accuracy. It was sublime.

Carl and I became fast friends and I, of course, became a client.

Cali with Ally

I had slung my share of drugs in the past; white cross, mushrooms, acid and the occasional pharmaceutical were always part of my wares but I was always partial to, and consistently stocked, with pot. From junior high through high school and in the years following, pot was always a favorite for me and my friends, who were of course, my clientele. Coming in contact with Carl truly expanded my inventory and allowed me to not only sell the dank green but to get pre-orders of available varieties. I was able to charge prime dollars and get enough pre-orders to not only cover the cost of my voracious appetite for good smoke but enjoy a tidy profit along the way.

After more than a year of enjoying the cannabis connection, Carl approached me with some news and a proposition. Carl had purchased a plot of land in Northern California and was going to start a marijuana growing operation. It was still illegal on a federal level, but in California it was allowed on a state level. Carl had devised a way to grow a limited amount of weed (substantial to his enterprise but small in comparison to the neighboring sites) and stay enough under the radar to make it work.

"Steve, I need somebody to drive a pickup truck and a U-Haul trailer out to California and deliver it to my guy in Redding," Carl said. "There is nothing illegal involved, it's just my furniture and household items. I can cover all expenses for the drive out, cover the cost of a ticket to fly you back and give you $1,500 for your time."

I immediately loved the idea. I loved to travel. I loved driving. I've always loved visiting new places. Hell, I was always up for an adventure. I was working at a job selling promotional materials on a strictly commission basis, and it was not bringing in very good money. I was in!

My younger daughter Ally (who has since changed her name to Dwella) who had never flown before and had never been west of Colorado, showed some interest in going with me. It may sound confusing but Dwella, who was named Ally at birth (She hates that name), will from this point forward be referred to as Hondo (the nickname I gave her growing up and still call her to this day). I was excited for her to join me. I made arrangements to get two return tickets. That cost me out-of-pocket for the additional flight but Carl agreed not to split hairs on the other expenses. It was decided. Two for the road!

Hondo, who was already excited to make this trip, was taking Thursday and Friday off from school (she was in 9th grade at the time) and I had Carl order two return flights for the following Monday morning at 7:00 AM. That would give us a couple days to get out to California and a day and a half to relax before heading back. Everything was set, or so I thought. Carl was unable to coordinate everything by Thursday morning so our departure was moved forward to Saturday morning. That not only allowed zero time for relaxing, but gave us a little over 36 hours to go 2,000 miles. That was, if we wanted to get any sleep before boarding the flight home.

The day to go west arrived and my wife drove me and my daughter to Carl's place. When we arrived I saw what was to be our conveyance sitting out in front of his apartment. The pickup was a large white truck with multiple storage compartments along the bed. The middle of the truck bed was stacked so high that the view from the center mirror was completely blocked. The bed portion of the truck was covered with a plastic tarp and strapped down with a combination of bungee cords and rope. Hitched to the back was a large six foot by twelve foot trailer. I have always hated the instability of U-Haul trailers and I was beginning to feel a bit queasy at the prospect of taking this combination on an almost 2,000 mile trip. As a man who has hauled 80,000 pound truckloads over mountain passes on slick winter roads, you would think I would be quiet, calm, and ready; I was not. U-Haul trailers are not generally equipped with high-dollar sway bars and the high winds on that particular day were daunting. Add to that, rain storms were in the forecast covering about the first 500 miles of our journey. But a trooper I was, and my daughter was ready for the big trip.

As we made our way to the highway that cuts around Mankato (the Minnesota hometown I was born in, raised in, and live to this day) I started getting familiar with the truck. Windshield wiper control? Check. Light control? Check. High beams? Check. Cruise control? Hmm, where the hell were the buttons or switches for the cruise control? They were not on the center of the steering wheel. They were not on the shifter. They were not on the steering wheel tree. Where the hell were they? After several minutes of attempting to find the cruise control, I decided to call Carl on my cell phone and have him direct me to the switch.

"Hey Carl. What's up?"

"Not much, what's going on?"

"Just getting rolling, but I can't locate the cruise control."

"I'm not sure if there is one. I just bought the truck a couple weeks ago, so I have not located all the controls."

I frantically searched for the elusive controls. As you have likely guessed, there was no cruise control installed in the truck. That's not a problem when you're going to the store but when you're hauling a swaying truck and trailer on a road trip of 2,000 miles, it's an issue. With the understanding that it was going to be less than ideal conditions, we trudged on.

The winds began to pick up and before getting 20 miles out of town, the canvas topping had begun to unravel. More wind. More unraveling. I pulled over and tried my best to get the load covered once again. The threat of darkening skies made it a priority. The last thing I wanted was to get Carl's furniture drenched with rain. After securing the load with the limited resources at our disposal we pulled back onto the road and continued rolling. As the wind picked up, the canvas went from unraveling to flapping around, and soon it was ripping. We had not ventured more than fifty miles from home when we found ourselves hauling a load with streamers snapping and thrashing in the wind. When we arrived at the outskirts of the next town we stopped at a store and secured more tarps (Both plastic and canvas. Two layers are better than one right?) and a couple of ratchet straps. Thankfully it had not started raining yet so the load, though uncovered, had remained dry. I took the little victories where I could find them.

The rain held off but the winds picked up to 50 or 60 miles per hour. The canvas didn't stand a chance. By the time we cruised though Sioux Falls, South Dakota, fewer than 150 miles from our starting point, the canvas once again began its violent dance and let loose. The ripped tarps were so bad that our only option was to pull over and remove them completely so they didn't cause any additional damage or get caught in the tires. We made it to a rest area and removed the shrapnel that once was my newly purchased canvas and plastic covers. I had been keeping my speed well under the speed limit. The canvas wasn't the only issue I was confronting. The instability of the loaded trailer was its own additional little piece of hell. But now, as we pulled away from the rest area, we entered a whole new level of frustration.

The first drops hit the windshield with a splattering sound. This was not the mist of an afternoon sun shower, this was the indication of a torrential downpour about to let loose. With the truck bed now exposed, we had to get to some kind of shelter quickly to ride out the storm.

The tank was getting low so we pulled into a gas station and as I was filling the tank the clouds opened up and the downpour began. We had our first piece of good luck so far. The overhang kept us and the load from getting drenched. We sat there about 15 minutes after the rain had stopped just to make sure that the waterworks were not going to lull us into a false sense of security and open back up. With the luck that had accompanied us thus far, it seemed like the right call.

The rain remained at bay and the next hundred miles went by without major incident. Of course the wind was no fun. Every time a truck passed, or in the rare instance that I braved passing one myself, my hands gripped the wheel so hard I thought it may require surgery to separate them. The sun began to disappear and both Hondo and I started to think about getting a bite to eat. At that time, one of her favorite places to eat was Perkins. I remembered from earlier travels there was a Perkins on the other side of Rapid City. We pushed on and made Perkins our next stop.

The meal was good and surprisingly uneventful. My nerves began to calm down for the first time since leaving home. We finished eating, paid the bill and set out on the road. The wind, though still there, had calmed down and we were getting ready to leave the Interstate for a two lane road across Wyoming. Growing up in Minnesota I am very familiar with the sight of deer running across the road but there was way too much possible road venison that night. I kept on my toes and managed to go carcass-free the whole way. The reduced speed of the two lane road seemed to take forever and, though it did slow us down, no major incidents occurred. Hondo and I were both very tired but caught our second wind when the sun began to rise. Moments after sunrise, we got gas and ate some breakfast at the Denny's in Rock Springs, Wyoming before continuing on our journey.

Hondo and I were enjoying the scenery. That area of the country is a beautiful and fast changing landscape. Even from the limited views allowed by staying on Interstate 80 the view quickly changed from the brown and rust colored rolling hills and rocky cliffs of western Wyoming to the steep grades of the "Three Sisters." I'm not sure if truckers originally named the Three Sisters but it is three back-to-back long pulls up and down a fairly straight stretch of road east of Evanston Wyoming. That roller coaster ride opened up into the canyons while entering Utah. The canyons were beautiful and curved downward at a slow pace until we were swallowed up by large mountains, which then opened up to the Echo reservoir and a flat green valley that stretched for miles. After we passed through the valley, the climb began. Following another canyon area, the twisting climb brought us up the side of the mountains and into the ski resort area of Park City. I could smell the money. I would venture to say there were no hidden trailer courts in the area. After passing through the resort area, the long decline into Salt Lake City started. The grandeur of that area is hard to put into words. As we came down the pass into Salt Lake City we went from oohing and ahhing at the mountains around us to, BAM, metropolitan traffic! Four lanes became five lanes, became split highways, became dual exit lanes, became single entrance lanes and went back to five lanes. Salt Lake City was one of those places that I felt I had better keep my head on a swivel and watch the signage, or we would end up going the wrong direction and never be heard from again. As quickly as the mountains ended and the city began, the city was behind us and the Great Salt Lake was in front of us.

It was beginning to get difficult to say what was more urgent at that time. I was fading fast. Both Hondo and I were getting very tired, but hunger was competing with the need for sleep. I knew at the beginning of our trip that I was going to have to cover the entire distance without getting any shut-eye. As an ex truck driver, I had been on my share of long hauls with little or no sleep but, 2,000 miles in a swaying rig with the safety of my daughter at risk was something new. Hondo had decided she wanted to try to stay awake for the long journey as well. I looked over and saw that she had become somewhat rejuvenated by the changes in scenery we had just traveled through.

"How are you doing?" I asked.

"I'm getting pretty fucking tired, but I'm doing okay," she replied with a grin. It may shock some that she, a ninth grade girl, slipped the F word in there. I was not shocked. My wife and I have never put a stigma on using foul language to emphasize a point. Hondo was fluent.

"We are coming up on a truck stop just around the next bend," I said. "We could get some fast food or sit down to eat. We could skip eating for now, but it will be about another two hours before we'll get another opportunity to pull over. The salt flats start right after the truck stop area, and there are no services until we get to the other side."

Hondo had to go to the bathroom and figured we should get some food to get us through the next stretch. We decided to sit down and have some breakfast.

I ordered coffee and the breakfast buffet. Hondo had pancakes, her favorite. I would have taken the coffee in the form of an I.V. drip if it was offered.

"How much farther is it to Redding?" She asked me while stretching and rubbing her eyes.

"We are a little under two thirds of the way there; I would say about 675 or 700 miles to go," I replied.

"Really? God that's still a long way!" She exclaimed with some serious eye rolls.

"Well Hondo, you really don't need to stay awake the whole way. After the Salt flats we're going to be going through Nevada. There are some interesting areas going through there but most of it is pretty repetitive once you've seen a little bit of it," I explained.

"Fuck that. I want to stay awake if I can," Hondo smirked (Like I said, fluent).

I loved seeing her determination, and I loved the idea of her keeping me on my toes. We filled the truck with gas and I filled my mug with some truly awful coffee. We got back on the road. About 30 miles after leaving the truck stop, the Great Salt Lake had disappeared and we were on the edge of the Salt Flats. Miles of white flat land stretched as far as the eye could see. There were rock formations and the occasional bend in the road but, for the most part, it was a very flat and straight stretch of road. I was going about 65 miles per hour but being passed as though I was in park. When I was a trucker we used to call this stretch of Interstate 80 the Mormon speedway for a reason. Either running to Nevada to get some gambling in or running back with their tails between their legs, there was always a constant flow from Salt Lake City to Wendover (nicknamed Bendover) Nevada, the first town across the state line. Between the high-speed vehicles and the continuous truck traffic, I kept awake and alert. Every passing truck whooshing wind against the side of my unstable ride and every racing car flying past made me feel the need to keep ever vigilant and ready for anything.

After about thirty-five miles of watching Bendover slowly draw closer, we finally entered the rocky terrain of the approximately 420 mile gauntlet standing between us and California. Immediately upon entering the state of Nevada the land became a combination of rocks, sagebrush, and miles of sandy brown and tan landscape of unforgiving country that stretched for long distances between glimpses of civilization.

"Dad, that sign says don't pick up hitchhikers. Prison area," Hondo said while looking over at me with bloodshot and weary eyes.

"Yeah, you will see many of those as we cross Nevada. There are a few private prisons along the side of the interstate," I replied.

"What do you mean private prisons?" Hondo questioned. "What is private about them? That's weird."

"Most prisons are run by either the federal government or state government. These prisons are actually owned by private individuals and corporations and they are run like a business," I explained.

"Why would anyone own a prison?" She asked.

"They make a lot of money. Personally, I think they are a bullshit concept and shouldn't be allowed to exist." My reply came with obvious disdain.

"How do they make money?" Hondo asked with some confusion. "Do they make the prisoners make things to sell?"

"No, their main source of income comes from the state paying them to house the inmates themselves. The inmates *are* the product." I did not cover up my disdain for the system.

"That's bullshit!" She said, proving she is definitely a lot more like her old man than she might want to admit.

Rocks and rough country gave way to more rocks and more hard country. We began a long climb and I pointed out that we were down to about 500 miles left on our journey to Redding.

"We're only about eight or nine hours from hopefully pulling into the hotel in Redding." I said, expecting to hear a little bit of relieved response.

There was no response at all. Hondo had finally given in to the ever-present pull to get some sleep. She was sitting with her head bobbing to the beat of the slats in the road. I swear she had a bit of a grin on her face. I was happy, and admittedly a bit jealous, that she was enjoying her slumber. I know she wanted to stay awake for the entire trip but I couldn't get myself to interrupt her sleep. We had about another 150 miles worth of fuel left. It might have only been a nap, but I felt it would do her a world of good. I decided to push the limits of the fuel tank to give her some time to snooze. Winnemucca would be our next stop.

As we approached Winnemucca, I attempted to wake Hondo up.

"Hondo, we're going to stop for fuel if you want to go to the bathroom or get something to munch," I said.

No response.

"Hondo," I said as I tapped her on the knee.

"Don't do that Raina!" She said as she swatted my hand away. "I don't care Raina, it's not up to you." She said with a little anger in her voice.

Raina was the name of one of her best friends and was obviously the subject of whatever dreamscape she was floating in.

"Wake up Hondo. We're stopping for gas."

She slowly and reluctantly opened her eyes. She was dazed and having a bit of a struggle grasping the reality of what was going on. It took a minute but she finally sat up and shook off some of the cobwebs, as we were getting on the off ramp into town. She had to readjust her eyes as it was extremely bright out that afternoon. Midafternoon in the desert didn't comport with her Raina dream.

"Where are we?" She asked.

"We're in Winnemucca, Nevada," I said.

"Where the hell is Winnemucca?" She asked me.

I knew the crux of her question wasn't so much a matter of geographical significance. The subtext was how much farther did we have to go?

"We're getting pretty close. We're about 160 miles from Reno and then it's only about 200 miles to Redding. I'm hoping to get us to the hotel by about ten o'clock California time so we can get a full seven or eight hours before we have to go hit our connecting flight in the morning," I said hoping that would put a smile on her face.

The smile didn't come. She was hoping we were farther along.

"How long was I sleeping?" She asked.

I told her she had gotten about two and a half hours of sleep. I asked her if she was dreaming about being with Raina. She gave me an odd look.

"Why do you ask that?"

I told her what she said to me when I tried waking her up. Finally the smile I was looking for crept across her face. She thought what she said was funny but didn't recall what she had been dreaming.

We got gas, went to the bathroom, grabbed some snacks for the road and set back out. We made our way through the rocky terrain and followed the interstate through the winding canyon that twists and turns its way into the Sparks and Reno area. When I asked Hondo if she wanted to stop and get a bite to eat, she curtly said no. She just wanted to get to California. We proceeded while keeping an eye on the prize of arriving at our destination. My hopes were to get to the top of the pass that leads into Lassen National Park before losing the sunlight. I have never been on that stretch of road and wanted to have a decent visual, both for safety reasons and simply to see the beauty of the park. The trip had gone without major incident for the last several hundred miles. I was beginning to think we would not only get there on time, but perhaps even a little earlier than my estimate.

I knew our luck was not going to hold. It didn't. After crossing the state line into California, we entered into an agricultural inspection station. When it was our turn to roll through, we were asked several questions from the woman at the booth.

"I see you have Minnesota license plates. That's a long trip. What is your reason for visiting us today?" The woman asked.

"I'm helping a friend move out to the Redding area," I replied.

"Do you have any fruits or vegetables in the vehicles?" She asked

"No ma'am," I stated

She asked me to wait a moment and went into the booth. A few minutes later she returned with a bit of news I really didn't want to hear.

"Please pull the rig forward and park off to the right in the inspection area," she said as she pointed to the concrete slab set up for inspections.

Her and one of her male associates then came over and asked us to open the back of the trailer. We did. That's when the fun started. The inside of the trailer was absolutely packed! It was so full, in fact, that it was difficult to open. Once I managed to get the door open, they wanted us to take out a recliner and a table that was set on its side, so they could get a better visual of the load. This was easier said than done and took some arranging just to get the legs of the table free to be able to be removed. The whole time this was taking place, the sun was beginning to set behind the mountain range. After they had taken a quick look, we were told we could put everything back in and proceed on our way. Shit. How the hell was I going to get this back in and get the door closed? It was like playing Tetris to move everything around enough to get the items back in the trailer. I was never very good at Tetris. It was a nightmare. Once it was all situated I tried closing the door. No go. I moved things back out and made another attempt, then another and another. It was a good hour before I was finally able to get the door almost closed. I had to ask the man at the station to help me by pushing against the door enough for me to latch the door. The sun was gone.

We made our way down the road and before long we passed through the town of Susanville. Immediately on the north end of Susanville we began a long and snaking climb. It was a bit of a surprise how quickly the ascent took us from town directly into the mountains and forests of the high sierras. As we climbed, we were able to see the lights from the valley below grow smaller and more distant. Within about 15 minutes we were in almost total darkness on winding two lane roads. Did I mention I had a swaying trailer attached to the truck? Through almost the entire trip thus far, I was familiar with the roads from my trucking days. This particular stretch of road, however, was unchartered territory for me.

With the trailer pulling and pitching behind me I was treated to the challenge of navigating through hairpin turns posted at 25 miles per hour, then up to 55, then 35, then 55, then 30. My legs were getting a workout jumping from the accelerator to the brakes. It was wearing on my tired and fraught nerves. About 40 miles into the nightmare of a highway we hit a steep grade. As we descended at 40 miles per hour a deer jumped directly into our path ten yards in front of us. I hit the brakes hard and felt the whole rig pull to the right. The load shifted and tugged us toward the ledge, which I could only assume would have been our doom, had I gone off the road at that point (confirmed later on subsequent trips).

Along with the tug, the brakes hung up for a brief period and then released. We missed the deer by mere feet but then the brakes began to feel very soft and spongy. Something was not quite right and we still had a ways to go to get to the bottom. I kept the speed low and applied light pressure to the brakes. I was happy to make it to flat land a couple minutes later. Flat, not straight. We were back to hairpins and saw two more deer. Luckily these deer were not daring me to hit them. They were in two separate locations on the side of the road. My nerves were shot. I just wanted to be done. Every mile felt like time had slowed to a crawl. After what seemed like an eternity I finally saw the lights of Redding drawing near.

My instructions were to go to the Northside Motel 6 to meet with a man named Don. I had his cell phone number and I had directions to get me to the motel. It was around 1:00 AM when I called Don's cell and told him I was minutes away. He said he would be waiting to meet me in the parking lot and said that Carl had already booked a double room for me and Hondo.

My directions to the motel were spot on, and minutes after calling Don I was pulling into the parking lot of the Motel 6. Don was standing at the entrance and waved me over to him.

"I'm Don. If you want to pull around this way I'll show you a spot you can back the truck into for the night," Don said.

I pulled the truck around the building and backed in as directed.

Don was a man in his late fifties with a look about him that said he had been around the block a few times. I would find out in the future that my summation was very accurate. He obviously had some weary miles on him but seemed like a nice guy. After I parked the truck Don came over, shook my hand and lit up a cigarette.

"Carl thought you would have been here earlier tonight. Did you have any problems?" Don asked.

Thinking back through the myriad of problems we encountered, I decided I would give him the short version. "Got stopped at the inspection station coming into California and they made me open and partially unpack the trailer. Other than that, there were no major problems."

"Yeah they can be pricks," Don stated as he exhaled a cloud of cigarette smoke. "Here is the key to your room. I assume you want to get in and get settled. I know you have an early flight in the morning."

I said goodnight to Don, unpacked everything me and Hondo had in the truck and went to our room. That was the last I saw Don on the trip. He disappeared in a haze of cigarette smoke as he walked to his room.

It was 2:30 in the morning. Time enough for about a three hour nap. Hondo and I settled into our beds and crashed hard.

The 5:30 AM alarm came way too soon. My attitude was bordering on hostility. I don't remember what I was dreaming or even if I had dreamt at all; all I know is I wanted more of it. That was a day that I had already been dreading, but as odd as it may sound, the idea of starting it off as a walking zombie could actually be considered a good thing. I went to the shower and did my best to prepare for the day. My eyes were already bloodshot and they were not helped by the couple of pulls I took off of my one hitter (a convenient small pot smoking device). Ah yes, smoking pot in California. It seemed righteous. I stepped out of the bathroom and Hondo stepped in. I went into my shower bag and pulled out my pharmaceutical cocktail of valium and two sleeping pills.

Taking downers could be considered counterintuitive. I had no sleep and was already feeling like a corpse that hadn't realized he had crossed over, but damn I hate flying! That day was going to be an extra special circle of hell for me because our itinerary included taking a prop plane from Redding and flying into LAX. No biggie. Los Angeles airport is just one of the largest and busiest airports in the country. From there we would board a commercial jet and head home. My nerves, the ones I still retained, were on edge.

While waiting for Hondo to get out of the bathroom, I went down and grabbed a couple sweet rolls, some orange juice and a cup of coffee from the complimentary continental breakfast. After she came out of the bathroom Hondo ate the roll and drank the juice

I had picked up for her. You could tell she was exhausted from the trip and lack of sleep but she was also excited to begin the journey home.

The cab arrived and took us to the outskirts of Redding and up to the terminal. Naming the damned thing terminal is not helpful for those of us who fear it may be exactly that. We got out and checked our bags and waited for about a half hour before the boarding began. The plane was very loud and the seats felt like vibrating massage chairs. I had flown on small prop planes before and they were fairly loud but this was a whole new animal for me. Hondo was excited. We taxied to the end of the runway and paused. For me it was like the pause looking over the ridge of the first drop on a roller coaster. It was the pause while waiting for the steep drop and the instant regret.

The engines grew louder and the plane rattled as the brakes released and the rush began. I wanted to close my eyes but I was transfixed looking at Hondo with a big, semi concerned, shit-eating grin on her face. She was enjoying it, and I was actually enjoying watching her reaction to our takeoff. I don't know if it was the downer cocktail or watching Hondo, but it was actually the least panic-stricken launch into the wild blue yonder I had ever experienced.

With the possible exception of a few minor rumbles of turbulence, the flight went quite smoothly. The two of us were looking out the window watching the scenery of the beautiful state of California unfold beneath us. Hondo had the window seat and was taking full advantage of her view. She was digging it in a big way. I loved seeing the smile on her face and lost myself in that enjoyment. That is, until we began our approach at LAX. I hate the takeoff. I hate the landing. Okay, I hate it all. Hate it as I may, it was a pretty smooth landing, and I felt no major need to kiss the ground when we disembarked from the plane. Another first.

Our next plane would not depart from LAX for three hours. Not enough time to really do anything in Los Angeles but way too much time to be stuck at an airport terminal. With the added burden of having to go through security again if we left the building, we decided to pass the time at the airport. We made our way to the Starbucks and got coffee. We took our time drinking our ten dollar cup of Joe and then did some window shopping at the little gift shop. High priced, low quality items were there to prove you were in Los Angeles. I was not that anxious to prove anything. As we were winding down to only about an hour left to wait, I found a spot to grab a cocktail (a literal cocktail, not pharmacological). I ordered a Bloody Mary and used it to wash down the last two sleeping pills. I know, I know, bad idea. In my mind the bad idea was hurtling across the sky in a metal tube. I looked at it as a good, sound, medicinal treatment.

Once seated, we were again at our taxi position ready to ride the next roller coaster. Every time I takeoff in a jet, I get anxious, queasy and intensely focused on how much I hate being there. That time was again an exception. Hondo was obviously excited and I found myself getting excited watching her take it all in. It was exhilarating rather than dreadful. I was actually enjoying the takeoff for the first time in my life. The thrill of watching Hondo all but removed my normal fear. We climbed to cruising altitude and the dual cocktails began to take effect. As the inflight movie started to play, I went to sleep and stayed blissfully close to comatose. I was groggy as I regained consciousness. I barely remember descending into the Minneapolis airport. I, again, did not dirty my lips kissing terra firma after leaving the plane.

I was numb as I floated through the terminal with Hondo, retrieved our bags and stepped out to the car where my wife was waiting to pick us up. Our adventure was over.

The Sales Pitch

Carl had been out west for about eight or nine months. It was at the end of July when I received a call from California with a request.

"Hey, Sir Carl!" I said as I answered the phone. "How are things going out west?"

"Not bad, Duder. How are things back home?"

Duder was the moniker that Carl affixed to everybody he talked to. I always hated it, but what are ya gonna do? The weed he sold made the label worth wearing.

"Holding the fort down as usual," I said.

"Duder, I am in kind of a bad spot," He said with an obvious **ask** lurking behind the statement.

I knew Carl well enough to reply with just a bit of skepticism. "What's going on? What can I do to help?"

"Well, you know I've been doing the grow out here, and I am coming up on harvest time. The problem is, I need trimmers. I thought I had six people lined up, and now three of them have cancelled," he explained. "Without having enough trimmers, we'll never be able to get the crop in and trimmed in any sort of workable time period."

"What is it you're asking? I mean, I have never trimmed before, and I can't just head out there at the drop of a hat," I replied.

This is where the Carl I knew, the used car salesman in tie-dyed clothes, went into his pitch. "It's really easy to trim, and you can make some pretty serious money doing it." He was pouring it on thicker and heavier as he went. "You wouldn't have to be out here until mid to late September, so you have plenty of time to get prepared. There will be three others heading out at the same time, so you would be able to ride out with them. I'll even give you a little bit of travel money to help get you out here. You know, like a hundred bucks to cover meals on the way out."

Intrigued, I asked the obvious follow up. "How much does it pay?"

"If you work a full day, like sun up to sundown, you should be able to make between $500 and $700 a day. I also have a neighbor in Redding who would pay about the same if you want to do more at night. That pay is pretty much dependent on an ounce staying at current prices, but I don't see that going down anytime soon. If you could make it out I would truly appreciate it," he said, putting the final touch on his sales pitch.

"How long would I need to be out there?"

"Well, Duder, it should only be about three or four weeks from first harvest until all is trimmed. If you decide to do it, you would have to stay out at the site until it is all harvested." he said.

"Wait a minute. You want me to stay out in the hills where the pot is growing?" I inquired.

"Yeah that's the only way it could work. In order to get it all trimmed in a timely manner, it requires starting at the crack of dawn and trimming until sundown. You may even have to trim by camp light." The slick salesman had one last statement to get me to drive the car off the proverbial lot. "I need somebody I can trust, and I thought you would be that guy. Can you help me out?"

"Wait a minute," I said as a new question dawned on me. "You said I would be staying out at the grow site. Are you not going to be out trimming with us at the site?"

"No, man. I have to be at the house in Redding to stash the pot after it's been trimmed. I also need to turn the spare trim into butter and hash," Carl replied.

"Jesus man, that's a lot to think about, and I sure as shit can't give you an answer until I talk to my wife." I said.

I was thinking about the money that Carl was offering and the calculator in my head was entering all the pertinent digits. Even at the low end of $500 a day for three weeks, it would be over ten grand! Add to that the money working for his neighbor, and we have some serious dough on the line.

"I have to line up one more person minimum, and want to have some commitment by next week. If you say you can make it, I will count on it. I know I can trust you to follow through if you commit," Carl said.

"Okay man. Let me talk to Sue and I'll call you back in a day or two," I said.

"Sounds good. Later Duder." He said and hung up the phone.

I was both excited and perplexed. Why would anyone turn down an offer to make that kind of money? First accepting, then cancelling sounded very odd to me. Was it the idea of living on the side of the mountain for that long that had deterred three of the original crew? Was it some kind of falling out with Carl? Was it just bad timing?

Whatever it was, I had to look at my personal cost benefit analysis. It was very enticing for me to try and replenish a bank account that had dwindled down to the point of overdraft fees and constant below zero balances. That qualified as a serious plus. I also looked at it as a chance to have another adventure. Another serious plus. The idea of preparing for weeks on the side of a mountain in northern California seemed daunting, but it also sounded exciting. The scales tipped toward another plus. As I pondered the offer, my next thought was what I would say to my wife. Sue was used to me being very transient in my career paths in the past, and although it wasn't a career, it wouldn't surprise her in the least to hear that I had another get-rich-quick scheme up my sleeve. I decided to just lay it all out on the table and see what she had to say.

I told Sue about the compensation and the details of the arrangements as I knew them to be. She was more than a little hesitant about the whole idea and needed to think about it for a while. I knew the pressures of our financial situation would weigh heavily on her. I also knew that the idea of me being gone for that long would enter into her calculations. What I had not thought about was what she hit me with in response.

"How are you going to be able to afford all of the things you will need to stay out there for that long?" She asked. "I mean, gas and food to get out there are minor expenses. Have you thought about the costs of getting all the camping gear and supplies you're going to need when you stay in that environment? What do you eat out there? Do you have to cover three or four weeks of meals?"

"Shit, you're right. I am going to have to think about this in more detail," I said.

Her question not only had merit, it was crucial to my ability to respond to Carl. With no money in our bank account, how was I supposed to get everything paid for before leaving Minnesota? The first thing I needed to do was to get a rough idea about those expenses and get some further questions answered by Carl (not the least of which was why the others cancelled). I began to create a list.

According to Carl I would not have to worry about traveling out there so that did not make the list. What did make the list was the cost of a decent tent (when I camp I don't exactly rough it), a cot, basic survival gear, food, cigarettes, beer, scotch and a little extra cash just in case. The list would grow as more necessities occurred to me, but it was a good start. With just the initial list, we estimated that I would need in the neighborhood of $1,500.

That was a neighborhood I didn't live anywhere near. But as with everything else in my life, I didn't consider it a nonstarter. I may not have the money available, but if I was going to bring in a minimum of ten grand in cash, I may be able to get a short term loan. With my horrible credit rating, it would have to be a personal loan. I thought, if nothing else, I could hit Carl up for an advance.

That was the list of tangible items I would need. Now I compiled another list. A list of questions I would need to ask Carl before I could move forward. Armed with my list, I made the call out to California.

After a couple rings Carl picked up the phone. "Hey Duder!"

"Hey man," I said. "I have been talking with Sue, and I have a few questions for you before I can commit to heading out there."

"Okay, what have you got?" Carl asked.

"First thing is this, when I am living at the site, will I need to bring cooking supplies, a cooler etc.?"

"No. While you are staying at the site the food will be taken care of. If you remember Don, the guy you met when you delivered my supplies out here, he will be making sure that everybody has food. He will get supplies and be responsible for cooking them for you. We will also have a large propane grill out there for your use," Carl stated.

"Oh okay," I was happy to check that expense off my list. I went to the next question. "You said there were six people coming out, but three of them backed out. Why did they change their minds?"

As is the case with any good salesman, he was quick with his reply. "They were not able to take that much time off from work. When I first talked to them, it sounded like that wouldn't be a problem, but they said they thought it would only be two weeks at the most. Once they found out it could be up to four weeks they had to decline."

Not the satisfying answer I was hoping for, but it seemed plausible. My inquiry continued. "If I decide to do this, who is my ride out there and how much room will they have for my equipment?"

"Actually I think the other car is going to be full," Carl admitted. "I do have another person coming now so maybe the two of you can come out together. I think you might even know him."

"Really? Who is it?" I asked.

"Do you know a guy named Lucas with long dreadlocks who goes to the festivals out at Harmony Park?" Carl asked.

I was pretty sure I knew who he was talking about. Harmony Park was a music venue that put on several camping weekend hippie type events every year. Lots of drugs, lots of music and lots of me enjoying it all. As a matter of fact, Carl and I had gone to one of the events called harvest fest where we sold copious amounts of hash tincture. As I mentioned in the letter to my brother, hash tincture was hashish that was dissolved into Everclear alcohol (usually about ninety-eight percent alcohol). A single teaspoon of tincture and you were stoned for several hours.

"Yeah, I know who Lucas is. What kind of a vehicle does he have?" I inquired.

"Well, I don't think he will be supplying the ride. I'm sure he would pitch in some money for gas if you can drive out," Carl said. "Do you think you could use one of your cars for the trip?"

"I'm not sure," I said. "That's something else I'm going to have to discuss with Sue. My last question for now is this. Could you advance me some of the money you will be paying me for the trim so I have enough to cover my costs?"

That's when Carl gave me an answer I didn't want to hear. "I can't advance anything and I can't pay you in cash after the trim is done."

"Then how do I get paid?" I asked

"You get paid in pot. For every pound you trim, you get to keep one ounce. You can easily trim a pound and a half to two pounds a day. When you get back to Mankato you can sell it and get your cash," he said.

I was not happy about that prospect. That meant I would have to transport the pot back, right in the middle of trimming season. That was a truly scary proposition.

"You have given me a lot to think about man," I said to Carl as the conversation was winding down. "I'll talk to Sue and call you back tomorrow or the day after."

"Sounds good, Duder. Talk to you soon." Carl said and the phone went dead.

So in the space of one day, things had changed. On the plus side, I wouldn't have to worry about food, I'd have a vehicle so I'd be mobile if things went south, and I would have somebody I knew staying with me. On the minus side, I would have to use my own car for the long trip out, I was not getting paid in cash so I would have to sell to get paid, and I would have to transport the product back with me through a law enforcement gauntlet. It was a lot to bring to Sue.

Obviously, the biggest roadblock to saying yes was arranging the finances to get supplies for the trip and expense money while out there. I hit on an idea. A friend of mine, Big Mark, who owned his own home remodeling business, was also a fan of the cannabis. I would ask him if he would be interested in getting a discount on some killer weed, with the catch being, I would need the money prior to leaving but he would have to wait to get his smoke until after I returned. Sue and I decided that we had to get over that first hurdle if we were going to commit to the gig.

I went to work and contacted Big Mark. He was interested but could only come up with $1,800. With travel expenses and a couple more items to add to the list I needed a total of three grand. I was twelve hundred short of that mark. I contacted a few more people, and with deals struck for discounted weed, I had my stake secured. Upon my return from California, one pound and two ounces would be used to pay back my benefactors. It would hurt the bottom line, but I figured with three weeks at an ounce and a half to two ounces a day, I would still have enough left over to make the trip well worth it.

After a long conversation with Sue, the trip was a go. I called Carl and told him I would be willing to commit, and I immediately began making my preparations.

The Preparation

Getting prepared for spending weeks on the side of a mountain required some serious preparation. Where to start? I figured my first step had to be to get familiar with the kind of terrain and wildlife I should be prepared for. I got online and started looking for the basics. I ordered a book on northern California survival and viewed everything from topographic maps and weather averages, to plant and animal information. All I needed was some basic information about the specific location where I would be setting up camp. I had asked Carl where the grow was and he said about thirty-five miles west, southwest of Redding. According to the topographical maps, it was going to be very mountainous, and the roads heading in that direction appeared to be two lanes of nonstop curves.

The average high and low temperatures in September in that area were between fifty-five and seventy degrees. The averages in October were between forty-five and sixty-five degrees. Ok, so taking the averages and assuming the mountains could get a bit cooler, I planned on bringing a lot of clothes, including some heavy winter stuff, just to be on the safe side. Wardrobe, check.

California has a wide variety of plants that are poisonous to consume. I sure as hell was not planning to forage for food. I did, however, want to avoid those plants that could be toxic to the touch. I learned about the Poodle-dog Bush which looks very pretty, with long purple rows of flowers that look similar to lilac bushes, but differ in two ways. First, they stink. Second, they can cause blisters that last for weeks if touched. Ok, so don't smell the California Lilacs. Check.

As a former boy scout I already knew to avoid Poison Oak. What I didn't know was just how prevalent it was in that area. Carl told me there was a pit bull out at the campsite for protection. That meant I had to be careful, of both the dog, and Poison Oak oils that might be on the dog's fur if it decided to roll around in the dangerous weed. So, pack calamine lotion just in case. Check. The only other one to be aware of was Stinging Nettle. Stinging Nettle can cause some irritation beyond the original sting but calamine lotion is all I would need. Check and check.

Then it was on to wild animals. I knew there were a plethora of animals in the mountains of northern California, but I needed to know which ones may cause a good stay to go bad. California has many things that stalk, slither, bite, and sting. Those were my main concern. Bears. Black bears to be specific. I had no desire to bring any firearms, so added to my list was bear spray. Bear spray was also good for use on two other local predators, mountain lions and wolves. So bear spray? Abso-damned-lutely, Check!

California also has a few types of rattlesnakes. Most common are the Diamond Back and the Red Diamond. Avoidance was the best bet and a machete has always been one of my favorite camping tools. I packed my machete. More of the things on my list to simply avoid were black widow spiders, tarantulas, recluse spiders, law enforcement and the feds (sorry, I couldn't help it). There are also scorpions but a majority of those were fairly innocuous in the area of the camp.

There was a lot to consider, but among the things that go bump in the night, the list was pretty comprehensive. The next step was to reach out to Lucas and make a plan for departure time, route, and expense sharing.

After visiting Lucas we decided the best way to test our camping supplies would be to leave a few days early and set up camp along the way somewhere. That would give us a chance to test the equipment and see if we were missing anything crucial. The last thing we wanted was to get set up in the middle of the California wilderness and discover holes in the supply list. We decided we would leave on September 18th and take the route that would take us through Yellowstone National Park. While in Yellowstone we would set up camp for a few days and get the feel of the equipment.

Though Lucas and I had some shared friends, we had not really known each other. We had some of the same connections in the pot game (Carl for one), we had both gone to Harmony Park for music festivals and being from the same town we knew a lot of the same people. Actually doing things together had just never happened. Over the weeks leading up to our departure I stopped in a few times and chatted and, of course, smoked. I even bought a little smoke from him during that period. He was a pretty cool guy and I got to like him in a short time.

One thing, however, was really starting to bother me. The dreadlocks. I am not anti-dreadlocks, and I honestly thought Lucas had some awesome dreads. The problem was, upon our completion of trimming out in California, I didn't like the idea of those dreads making our car the one to be pulled over. They screamed "pothead in the car!" Though it was an uncomfortable thing to bring up, I felt I had to. To my surprise, Lucas was thinking the same thing. The first thought was that he not join me on the return trip. That hardly seemed fair. I would then have to transport his portion of the pot while he flew or took a bus back home. I also didn't really want to take the trip without some company. After broaching the subject and a ten minute conversation we moved on to a little smoke session and left it at that.

About a week before we were planning our departure, I stopped up to Lucas' house to enjoy a little smoke. I knocked on the door and somebody I didn't know opened the door. I was surprised because I rarely saw anybody else at his place. I had to do a double take. It was Lucas without dreads! Who the fuck was this guy? He was clean cut and sporting a baseball cap. He looked like an all American boy. Not a hippie, not a pothead, his look now screamed "nothing to see here!" I was shocked, relieved, and impressed by his commitment to the journey. We had a good laugh and a good smoke.

As the day to depart was closing in, my supply bill was adding up fast. Tent, cot (I didn't skimp on the either of those), small propane heater, mini cooking stove, new hatchet, a reinforced air mattress, tent repair kit, medical kit with a good supply of calamine lotion, portable folding table, two folding camp chairs, cooler, three types of flashlights, two lanterns, bear spray, a hunting knife, and a few miscellaneous last-minute additions.

A couple of days before leaving I received a surprise visit from my older daughter Cassie. Knowing that I would not be in town for my birthday, she brought me two gifts. She brought me a book to read, and a blank diary style book with no lines to journal my journey (nice alliteration huh?). She always knew how to pull at my heartstrings and this gift was no exception. Like her younger sister, she is fluent with the darker side of vocabulary. On the first page she wrote; Dear Dad, First of all, HAPPY FUCKING BIRTHDAY! I wish you were still going to be in town on the 26th, but that's alright. We'll party once you're back and soon after that we'll party twice as hard in Vegas! Anyway, I thought I'd get you a couple sanity-saving gifts. Choke is one of my favorite books by one of my favorite authors. It's the same bad ass that wrote Fight Club. I got you this blank book right here so you may track some of your wild adventures, save your excellent ideas, draw your gremlin and maybe even start up that novel again. I hope you thoroughly enjoy your time in Cali. I'll miss the hell out of my best friend! I FUCKING LOVE YOU! (so don't get mauled by a bear, dammit)

♥ Cass

It's hard to put into words how much her words touched me. Expletives aside, it was, to me, beautiful prose. Oh, hell the expletives are part of the charm. I loved it! I had the last pieces to add to my supply list. Something to bring with that would remind me of home and something to read.

The night before the big day, was reserved to have a nice meal with Sue, and prepare for the journey. Lucas and I decided to head out early in the day so the packing was done, for the most part, that night.

It was decided that for the trip I would be using my wife's car, a Nissan Maxima. It would be best on gas consumption. Although the gas mileage was a definite benefit, the size was not. With all the purchased provisions packed in, the clothing, sleeping bags, pillows and other equipment added on top, it was, well, a bit claustrophobic.

I went to bed early that night and spent much of the first hours staring at the ceiling. Was I making a mistake doing this? Was I truly prepared for everything this trip entailed? Did I get everything packed? Would the remaining money be enough to last me for the full three or four weeks? Every thought going through my mind was conspiring to stop me from getting the rest I knew I needed. Lucas and I had decided that we would drive nonstop until we got to our camping spot in Yellowstone. We would be driving about 950 miles straight. Actually, I would be doing all the driving. I make a bad passenger. The plan was to take our time, do an overnight run, and arrive in Yellowstone early the next morning. Sleep was desperately needed, and at that point, eluding me. After hours of mental gymnastics, I finally drifted off.

Heading Out West

The day had finally arrived and I was filled with a cascade of conflicting emotions. I was nervous about the overall project. I was excited for the new adventure about to unfold. I was scared my funds were insufficient to cover the expenses. I was looking forward to getting to know Lucas better. I was wondering about the others I would be camping with at the grow spot. Oh, and I was tired. I think I may have managed to get about four hours of sleep, and the sleep I got was less than deep.

I brewed a pot of coffee, loaded the last of the gear in the car, and sat down to have a little breakfast with Sue. My deep love for my wife made this a hard morning to deal with. I knew I was going to be gone for at least a few weeks. I gave her a kiss and a long hug. I grabbed my cup of coffee for the road and set out to go get Lucas.

I pulled in to Lucas's place and stepped up to his deck. He was ready to go, standing inside his screen door, before I had the chance to knock.

"Ready to go?" I asked.

"Yeah, let's get going," Lucas said.

Lucas had a couple of bags, a small tent and a couple other small Items. I helped him grab them and had to move a few things around to get enough room freed up in the car to place his stuff. The Maxima was packed to the gills. The trunk was full, and the back seat was packed almost to the roof. We made one last stop at the Kwik Trip before heading out of town to refill my coffee and top off the gas tank. We sparked up the joint I had reserved to mark the beginning of our trip and off we went.

As we made our way west of town, I couldn't help but flash back to the trip with Hondo heading out on this same route. As we were approaching the town where Hondo and I had to stop to secure new tarps and ratchets, I told Lucas about that trip. We had a good laugh and were united in the hope that our luck this time would be much better. Lucas had actually grown up in the area we were passing through, and I got to know a little more about this man I would be spending the next several weeks with.

Lucas is a very quiet guy. He is one of those rare people, who don't feel the need to talk, unless he truly has something worth saying. Often there would be silence from him, then, out of the blue, he would say something that made me laugh. His lack of nonstop chatter made those pearls all the more funny.

I, on the other hand, have no problem with speaking continuously. Don't get me wrong, I don't just chatter, I like to keep the conversation moving and rarely am without something to say. We were an odd pair, but it worked.

We had good weather and clear sailing. With the exception of a couple stops for gas, we just rolled west through Minnesota and South Dakota along Interstate 90. As we were traveling through the Rapid City area, the sun began to retreat over the black hills. The scenery went from several shades of lush green hills to black silhouettes in a matter of minutes. We pulled over and grabbed more coffee, more gas, and stretched our legs at the western outskirts of Rapid City.

After a long day's drive we finally crossed the state line from South Dakota into Wyoming. I related to Lucas how glad I was that we had encountered no problems on the trip so far. It was a far cry from the last time I had driven over the same roads on my windy trip with Hondo. Somehow the universe must have known I was getting too comfortable because that's when it happened.

Bang! Screeeeech! "Shit! What the fuck is that?" Lucas exclaimed.

"I have no clue," I said. "Something is seriously wrong."

Something had let loose under the car and was immediately dragging underneath us at seventy miles per hour. I hit the brakes and made my way to the side of the road.

There was very little traffic and the night had no moon. It was damned near pitch black. Lucas joked that this was like one of those horror films which always involve the travelers having to run from psychopaths wielding butcher knives.

We grabbed a flashlight and got out of the car to inspect the damage. The car was riding low due to the weight of all the equipment which made it hard to get a decent visual. After a few minutes of inspection we finally confirmed that the muffler had broken. Normally that wouldn't be too tragic but it had broken in a spot that would make it difficult to rehang and dangerous to drive. The muffler was hanging in such a way that forward momentum could push what remained attached into the bottom of the car. We were screwed.

That was when we noted one of the supply categories I had overlooked. Car repair tools. The only way to get the car off the ground would be to jack it up. The jack? The jack was under all the shit in the trunk, under the floor panel, next to the donut spare. Even if we jacked it up, we didn't have the tools to tie the muffler up or even remove it. Screwed, glued, and tattooed (an old saying meaning shit out of luck).

We went back into the car to discuss what we could possibly do, and see if there were any towing services near our location. According to the information on the cell phone, the closest town was Sundance. No services. Next was Moorcroft. No services. Our best bet was Gillette, which was over fifty miles down the road. There was no way we could afford to get a tow truck, so then the question became, how could we get things rigged just enough to get down the road?

As we were contemplating our next move, an old style pick up pulled over to the side of the road in front of us and parked. The dark figure that emerged from that truck was, well, ah, you remember the horror films Lucas and I had discussed? Shit. The figure was huge and actually wearing a cowboy hat and a long black duster. Stephen King could not have written a more sinister looking character. Lucas and I looked at each other with a mirrored expression. We were both wondering if this indeed was the psychopath we had talked about.

"Oh shit man. What the hell is this?" Lucas asked. "This is too weird. That guy's fucking huge!"

"No shit! Is he wearing a duster?" I said.

As he approached, Lucas stepped out to meet him. Lucas had balls, I'll give him that. I readied my hunting knife, you know, just in case. As the towering figure drew closer, Lucas walked up to greet him. Close up he was every bit as intimidating as he was from afar.

"Are you boys having car troubles?" He asked.

"Yeah," Lucas replied. "The muffler broke apart and we're not going to be able to go anywhere until we get it secured. It looks like it's broken in a really bad spot, right in the middle."

"Oh man, sorry to hear that." The man said. "Do you have a jack to get it up enough to take a better look?"

I chimed in "We do but it's buried under a ton of stuff in the trunk. I don't suppose you have one we could use?"

"I actually don't have one handy, but I do have some boards in the back of my truck that you could drive up on. That might bring it up enough to get a look." He offered

"Hell, it's worth a shot. Thank you," I said and offered my hand for a shake. "My name is Steve and this is Lucas."

"Pleasure to meet you. My name is Jebediah," He said as he shook my hand and turned to shake Lucas's hand. "I'll grab the boards and be right back."

Sadly, both Lucas and I were still playing it on the cautious side. Given the situation it was beyond kind of him to stop, but being out in the middle of nowhere, we watched him closely.

Jebediah returned with some two by fours and put them behind the tire. I jumped in the car and backed up and onto the boards. It worked. The car was raised enough to get a better look at the damage. Lucas and Jebediah were outside the car discussing the best way to rig things to make it down the road. Then Jebediah walked back to his truck and returned with some wire. He then went underneath the car and did all the work to secure the muffler.

After rigging the muffler enough to get down the road, the three of us talked for a bit, and we found out that Jebediah worked for the railroad and was on his way home when he saw us on the side of the road. He then offered to follow us to Gillette to make sure we got there safely. I tried to give him a few bucks for helping us out and he refused it. Psycho killer? No. Actually one of the kindest people we could have asked to meet that night.

The car was loud when we were idled on the side of the road, but it was deafening as we made our way onto the Interstate and brought the speed up to about sixty miles per hour. Christ, we needed to get it fixed before our hearing became another casualty. I couldn't imagine living with the noise much longer. True to his word, Jebediah kept with us the fifty plus miles to Gillette.

It was about midnight when we rolled into the gas station in Gillette. We quickly learned that there would be no luck in finding a place to fix the muffler in the area, at least not that night. We decided to purchase some supplies in the convenience store to attempt to secure the muffler enough to continue on the trip. Again we were confronted with the less than tasteful fact that we needed to jack the car up. We didn't want to do the archeological dig which would be required to get to the jack. Instead we decided to drive the car up on a curb across from the store. With the car so heavily loaded, it was easier said than done, but we managed to get the car up enough to work with. While Lucas was attempting to secure the muffler, a local cop rolled up on us in his cruiser.

"What are you boys doing?" The officer asked

I stepped over to the cruiser as Lucas continued to work on the car. "Our muffler broke a little ways down the road and we're just trying to get it secured so we can safely get down the road."

"I can't let you work on the car that way. That is a serious safety hazard. You will need to drive back off the curb," he said.

"I understand," I said trying to bide a little time. "But the only jack I have is buried under a tightly packed trunk."

Being a cop, he couldn't resist the follow up. "Why is the trunk packed? What are you hauling in there?"

"It's camping gear," I explained. "We're heading to Yellowstone for a camping trip," I thought it best not to explain that we were heading out to California to trim pot.

He stepped out of his cruiser and walked over to the car. He looked into the back seat and saw sleeping bags, pillows, Lucas's tent and other camping gear. Luckily, he did not see the remnants of the joint we had smoked earlier sitting in the middle ashtray in plain sight. I was not aware it was there until that moment.

"Well, I'm sorry guys but I have to insist you drive off the curb immediately." He said.

Just then Lucas came out from underneath the car "We're good to go," Lucas said. "It's secured."

You could see the cop was not thrilled with that outcome but thought better than to hold us up any longer.

"Drive safely," He said as he got back in his patrol car and took off.

We once again got back on the Interstate. The car sounded like a Cessna (small prop plane) as we wound it up to sixty-five. Lucas took out his phone and started looking for places to get the muffler fixed in Buffalo (the next town of any size), and Sheridan (the next town after that). He dialed several numbers and either got an answering machine, no answer at all, or somebody telling him they couldn't do anything until morning. It was about 1:30 in the morning so we were about to give up and pull over for the night. That's when Lucas actually talked to somebody who said they could look at it right away. We were shocked and delighted. If we could get the muffler repaired right away, we could still be in Yellowstone by late morning. The shop was located in Sheridan and Lucas got directions. What a stroke of luck...or so we thought.

After twisting and turning through downtown Sheridan we were getting frustrated with the directions. Lucas made another call to our would-be mechanics. They answered on the first ring. Lucas got the directions. We had actually passed right by their place twice. We wound back to their location and there he was with the large garage door open waving us in. This was no regular shop. We pulled up and a very skinny man came out and introduced himself.

"I'm Rodney," he said. "Are you the guys with the busted muffler?"

Who the hell else was he expecting at 2:30 in the morning? I would have thought his first clue would have been the sound emanating from the car. What the hell had we got ourselves into? Rodney was wearing ratty clothes and looked wired as hell. Tweaker! Shit. That explained why the shop was open in the wee hours of the morning. It was then that we noticed the two other guys and one woman standing inside the shop. Each one more tweaky-looking than the other. I've searched my vocabulary for a better description. Tweaky sums it up better than anything else I could come up with. The whole group looked like they hadn't eaten anything for weeks. They all had emaciated bodies with horribly unwashed clothes draping off their skeletal frames.

We decided to play the cards we were dealt and had them take a look at the car. Rodney went underneath and looked around. While Rodney was looking under the car, we began looking around the shop and noticed several old rusted-out cars in various states of decay. No cars really looked like they were getting repaired. It was a graveyard of junk rusting in place. Within less than a minute, Rodney pulled himself out from underneath the car.

"It's going to tricky, but I think I can weld it," Rodney said with his telltale meth mouth in full motion. "Open the hood real quick."

Without really thinking about it, I did as requested (give me a break, I was tired). Rodney went under the hood and started unhooking the battery cables.

"What the hell are you doing?!" Lucas asked Rodney.

"I need to disconnect the battery before I weld, so we don't get an arc." Rodney replied with bloodshot and shifting eyes.

"We didn't say we were going to do the weld yet. Back up!" Lucas said as he went under the hood and made sure the cables were still firmly attached.

The tension was getting high. I stepped between Lucas and Rodney. I could smell days of Tweak sweat coming off of Rodney. "If we decide to do the weld, how much would it cost?" I asked.

"Two hundred and forty dollars," Rodney said.

"Let us discuss it for a minute," I said to Rodney.

Lucas and I went into the car to talk privately. Rodney stood outside the car and just stared in anticipation of making enough money for a score.

"That's way more than I want to spend, and I don't trust these guys," I said to Lucas. "What do you think?"

I am truly not a car guy, so I was asking Lucas to give me some guidance as to whether this was even a good idea with a *decent* mechanic.

Lucas didn't hold back with his reply. "You're kidding, right? Fuck these guys! Let's get the hell out of here!"

I stepped out of the car and told Rodney we were going to pass on his services. The tension could have been cut with a knife. Rodney's anger, coupled with his lanky frame unable to do anything about being refused, caused the veins in his head to push out and his whole face became flushed. He didn't know what to say. I'm convinced, if he thought he could have gotten away with it, Rodney would have knocked us over the head and taken the car and any cash we had. Rodney had enough of his faculties intact to realize that his spindly carcass would have been no match for me at two hundred and eighty pounds and Lucas who is fit.

While keeping a close eye on Rodney and his minions (even a skinny tweaker can have a gun or a knife) I shut the hood and got back into the car with Lucas. We backed out and went down the road.

"Jesus Christ, did that really just happen?" Lucas said.

"Yeah I know. That was crazy," I replied. "So what are we going to do now?"

"Let's just drive until we find a place down the road to get the muffler fixed," said Lucas.

We left Sheridan and began climbing a steep mountain pass. I was not familiar with the road and was surprised at how steep the climb was. After about fifteen minutes of curves and climbing, the check engine light came on and I noticed the car was overheating. I managed to find a pull off and brought the car to the side of the road. This "side of the road shit" was getting old.

We let the car cool down and stepped over to the edge and looked down. The lights of Sheridan gave us an idea how high we had climbed. It was beautiful. We smoked a couple one-hitters while staring over the edge of the mountain pass. When the car cooled down, we got back in and started the climb once again. Though the car threatened to overheat again, it never made it up to the red line. We crested the top of the mountain and traveled through winding roads with silhouettes of trees and higher mountain ridges. The temperature gauge went back within normal range. I remember being surprised at the amount of time we had been driving without descending. I have driven my share of mountains in the past and usually when I crest a mountain, I begin the descent shortly after. Not on that road! We went about thirty-five or forty miles before we hit a steep grade on the west side. Steep it was. Steep and loaded with hairpin turns and switchbacks.

Once we reached the bottom, the grade went away but the hairpin turns did not. We were running through a canyon. The sun was just beginning to make itself seen in the slight glowing of the sheer cliffs next to the road. What little was visible was truly awe inspiring. Then, just like that, we were on flat ground with straight road. As the sun was rising, we went through the town of Greybull. Nobody was open for business at that early hour so we pushed on.

Less than an hour later, the sun was shining brightly, and we entered the city of Cody, Wyoming, the gateway to Yellowstone. With our heads on a swivel, both Lucas and I were looking for any type of a muffler shop or mechanic. As we got to the west side of Cody, we saw a repair shop and dropped in. The man at the desk said he could look at it in about a half hour. Perfect. It was time to get a little breakfast. Unfortunately, there were only a few food options. Arby's was the only place available in walking distance, so we wandered over, grabbed a breakfast sandwich and a cup of coffee.

When we returned the man told us that the muffler would not be able to be welded or repaired. It could only be replaced. The muffler broke at exactly the wrong spot. Just at the end of the muffler itself and the exhaust pipe. He said the cost to replace it would be $750. It might as well have been ten grand. Not a chance I could come up with that much money.

It was at that point Lucas suggested finding an auto parts store and getting some muffler tape and some wire to try and repair it ourselves (which meant him) as best we could. Two blocks farther west we found the auto parts store we needed and bought supplies. We bought more than we needed just in case we needed to fix it again before getting to California.

I drove the car up on a curb and Lucas went to work. After about twenty minutes, it was in Lucas's words "Good enough to get by."

We pulled out of the parking lot and pointed the car west toward the park entrance. It was certainly not quiet, but it was a definite improvement.

It wasn't very long until we finally made it to the gates to enter Yellowstone. We paid the entrance fee and entered the park. We made it twenty miles into the park when the repair let loose and the sound of the Cessna was back. I also noticed that we were getting very low on gas. It was time to stop and fill up.

We looked for signs for gas. It was quite a while before we saw one. It said ten miles to gas. Unfortunately it also said station closed for the season. What? Closed for the season? Really? Shit! We were getting seriously low on gas. What the hell were we going to do? We kept rolling and eventually saw another sign for gas and it too said closed for the season. We were getting nervous. We really didn't want another "side of the road" adventure. We continued on, with the hope that the next station would be open. I mean there had to be one open somewhere right? Not according to the next sign which again said closed for the season. We pulled in despite the sign because we simply had no more gas left to find another disappointing sign. We pulled up to the fuel island and sure enough, there were padlocks on the pumps. We were stuck. We simply could not continue without gas. We saw a man doing maintenance over by the building and I approached him.

"Excuse me sir," I said to him.

"Yeah, can I help you?" He asked.

"I am completely out of gas and was not figuring on all the fuel stops being closed for the season. Is there any way we can get some gas?" I asked.

"The pumps are all locked up," He said. "I don't think there is anything I can do."

"Is there anyone we could call to get some delivered?" I asked.

At that moment he said "Wait a minute, maybe Ben can help us out." He yelled across the lot to another man, obviously Ben. "Hey Ben! Can you come over here for a minute?"

Ben came over. "What do you need?" he asked.

The situation was explained to him. Ben was the holder of the keys. Finally a little good luck! Ben said he could unlock the pumps and let us fuel up, but because the store was closed, he would have to have cash. He said he would leave the money for the store crew but that there was no way to run a credit card. We put thirty dollars' worth of gas in our thirsty tank and paid Ben. I tried to give him a tip for helping us out. He wouldn't allow it and just said he was glad he was able to help us out.

My nerves were calming down as the Cessna prepared for takeoff once again. With the desperation of a dwindling gas tank removed, I was finally able to truly enjoy the panoramic views unfolding before me. The winding tree-lined road cut through everything from the crystal clear blue water in the park's lakes and streams to the majesty of its mountains. The beautiful mountains morphed from green lush forest at their base to sheer, rocky, unforgiving escarpments, to snow caps that had survived the summer to allow us to take them in. Yellowstone was a fitting reward for having survived the challenges we had faced to get there.

When we paid the entrance fee we were given a map of the park, which we were now utilizing to guide us to the camping areas. We were excited about the prospect of getting our camp set up and couldn't wait to be an actual resident of this beautiful park. We saw three camping areas along the road and decided we would take the first spot we could find. As tired as we were, we just wanted to get to work setting up so we could enjoy a cold one and a little smoke by a nice fire.

As we approached the first of the camps we saw a familiar phrase, "Closed for the Season." Unbelievable! First we were denied access to gas and now we were going to be denied camping? This was not sitting well for two weary travelers who just wanted to come in for a landing. We flew by camp option number one and continued on to option number two. We were expecting to get the same bad luck but, to our surprise, the camp was open. We pulled in and parked at the camp office, which was really more of a log hut, and inquired about availability. We were told there were two sites left but before paying for them we should inspect them, select which one we preferred and come back to pay.

We took the camp map given to us by the man in the office and went to locate our home for the next few days. The first spot was small, out in the open and close to the camp garbage container. It didn't take a rocket scientist to see why that site remained available. We decided it was a definite pass and moved on to the next. The remaining site was surrounded by trees and slightly bigger but was on a bit of an angle and had tree roots jutting into the area where we would need to pitch our tent. Strike two. We decided we would push on and see what was available at the last of the campgrounds, if it was indeed open.

We wound our way down the road. Yellowstone Park became Grand Tetons National Park. It is an area that has to be seen to be believed. The Tetons are the epitome of purple mountains majesty. The rocky cliffs of the Tetons are literally purple, and then dissolve into the white of the snowcapped peaks. We were excited about the option of staying in such an iconic part of the planet. We pushed on in the hunt of a campsite and finally approached the final option within the park which was open, but full. Feeling defeated we knew we had a choice to make. We could double back and go to one of the campgrounds located off one of the other roads in the park, or we could push on and look for something outside the park. We chose to continue forward and Lucas began looking on his phone for options down the road.

We decided to try a campground named Buffalo Valley RV resort. Once leaving the park we would have to drive about ten miles east, which was out of our way, but we decided to go for it. We pulled up to the campground and instantly regretted passing up the opportunity to sleep by the garbage cans or on the tree roots. Don't get me wrong, the campground wasn't filthy or run down but it was a gas station with several flat sites on open terrain behind the building. Not exactly the wilderness experience we were looking for.

We turned around and decided to head toward Jackson Hole to see if we could find something in that direction. As we approached the airport in Jackson, we saw a tiny sign with an arrow that said camping. We hadn't exactly been batting a thousand thus far so we thought we would just throw caution to the wind and follow the sign. The road was thin and beat up but we proceeded, determined to find a place to set up before the sun began to fade. It had been a long day (Okay two days) and we were ready for a cold beer and a hot fire. After several miles of bumpy blacktop we finally made it to the entrance of the campground. It was exactly what we were looking for!

The Trial Run

Coming into the campground and being immediately greeted with a sign urging campers to Be Bear Aware, told us that we had arrived in the perfect spot for our trial run. The land leading up to it was a little on the flat side but the entire campground was densely populated with trees, bushes and a wide variety of abundant foliage. The best part was its location, which framed the Grand Tetons as its backdrop. As we pulled up to the camp office we were immediately ushered in with a smile from the gentleman standing by the door. I parked the car and went in.

"Do you have any tent sites available?" I asked him.

"Yeah we have a few left on the east side of the grounds as long as you don't require full hook ups," he replied. "How many nights are you planning to stay?"

"We plan to stay a few days," I stated "but we're kind of playing it by ear."

"Just so you know, we are in the process of getting ready to close down for the winter months. We're only allowing guests until the end of next week," he informed me.

"That's more than we'll need," I replied. "I see the sign on the road says be bear aware. Is that a common issue?"

"We get our fair share of bears here but the biggest danger, at this time of year, is the moose," he said. "It's mating season and they'll try to jump everything. They've even been known to get overly familiar with vehicles. It's very possible you will see them migrating through the camp. Keep your distance!"

I looked over at the campground diagram on the wall and saw that there was a river running near the camp. I didn't see a river as we were driving in so I asked about it.

"The river runs along the south and west edge of the grounds," he told me. "There are some access areas to get a view but they are fairly overgrown with brush this time of year. Just be careful if you decide to go down there. Bears are often spotted in the tall brush. A lot of people go down there to see the moose that are drawn to the river. I can't stress it enough," he reiterated. "Keep your distance from the moose!"

I thanked the man, joined Lucas back in the car and went searching for our assigned spot. We intentionally took the long way around the grounds to see the other sites, get the lay of the land and scout out a spot to access the river. It was a pretty large campground and there were several open sites. Most of the sites were occupied by tents and pop up campers rather than large recreational vehicles. It was somewhat comforting to know that we would not be the only vulnerable meat sacks available for the bears in the area, or the only targets of overly amorous moose. The grounds were rather rustic and had very little in the way of amenities, although there were a few scattered bathrooms with showers, and bear-proof dumpsters. We did not, however, see any access areas for the river. As a matter of fact, if I hadn't seen the campground diagram we would not have even known there was a river at all.

We took a second lap around the grounds and, this time, we asked a few of the campers if they knew how to get down to the river. When we went to the area that the map indicated the river would be, we confirmed what the man at the office had said. There was tall brush and the paths were so overgrown that they were hard to spot. We noted where the access points were and continued on to our reserved spot.

We pulled in and had to take a minute to take in the view that was going to be our backyard for the next few days. The Grand Tetons! The disappointment of not finding a place to camp inside the national parks gave way to the appreciation of the natural majesty all around us. We could not have asked for a better place to try out our camping gear, see the magnificent sites of the towering mountain ranges, decompress from the stressful journey of the last two days, and prepare for the trip yet to come.

Our plan for this first evening was to get the basic camp set up, smoke a bit of the green, and then venture down to the river before losing the sun. We got to work. Lucas had a two man pup tent and had it up in a matter of minutes. My tent was another thing altogether. I had an eight man tent and what amounts to a full bedroom to assemble. Even the cot that I had purchased required several minutes to get ready. Between the cot with the reinforced air mattress and two layers of sleeping bags, the folding chair next to the folding table, the closet style luggage bag and the dual lighting sources (one lantern hanging from the center of the tent and another on the table) it looked like a bedroom featured in Better Homes & Gardens.

While I was in the process of setting up my portable palace, Lucas pulled out the grill, unloaded his gear from the car, hung up his hammock and prepared the fire ring so it was ready to light when we returned from our hike to the river. We were set and almost ready for the walk but thought it appropriate to toast the occasion with a beer and a bowl. We sparked up the bowl and kicked back with our beer and relaxed for the first time since leaving home. We had a good laugh recalling all we had been through in just the short time we had been on the road.

Anxious to get to the river, we secured the site and began our walk to the other side of the campground to find the amorphous path toward the river. The path was hard to find even after having been by it, and directed to it, earlier. After passing it twice and circling around, we finally found it once again. The lack of definition of the so-called path made forward momentum slow. There were times when backtracking was required to get back on the path we had lost in the brush. From the beginning of the path to the edge of the river was no more than four hundred yards but the trek consumed over a half hour to complete.

Reaching the water's edge was an accomplishment rewarded by the beauty of the river. It's clear blue water meandered slowly through mossy outcrops, muddy shorelines and boulders offering the only hint as to the direction of its flow. It was beautiful and peaceful. It was everything we could have hoped for, with one exception. We were alone. There was no visible wildlife. Our hopes of seeing a moose were not realized. What we had not considered as we ventured to this spot was just how therapeutic it would be. We were dumbstruck by the calm, quiet and, with the exception of the slow swirl of water rounding the rocks, stillness of this picturesque scene. We stood for a few moments enjoying the deafening solitude.

Our moment of Zen was interrupted by the realization that we were beginning to lose sunlight. With the difficulty of making our way through the brush during daylight, we knew we had to start making our way back before the sun disappeared. That realization came a bit too late. The sun did not take it's time in sinking below the mountains to the west of us. We were perhaps fifty yards into our return trip when the remnants of the sun gave way to blackness.

There I was, the guy who over-planned and over-prepared for this trip, wandering through thick brush in the dark with no flashlight and no bear spray. I was not prepared for the dark to descend upon us quite so quickly. If there was any moon at all it would have been shrouded by the canopy of trees above us. It was pitch black. Even as our eyes adjusted to the darkness, there was little hope of finding the direction of the path. We were thankful to be able to see a campfire way off in the distance, so we at least had our bearings when it came to keeping on a consistent track toward the campgrounds. Our ears were listening for any sounds that may alert us to the presence of things to which we may be considered prey. All we heard was the crunch of fallen branches and tall grass beneath our feet.

A loud noise stopped me in my tracks. My heart raced. I stopped moving forward and swung to my right with a pulse of sheer terror tracking the direction of the sound. In the fraction of a second between hearing the sound and discovering its origin, my mind filled with thoughts of bears, moose, or other nondescript sources threatening to lead to my demise. I felt both silly and relieved when I heard the flapping of several pairs of wings. I had stumbled over the nesting grounds of one of the many types of birds that use the heavy brush to conceal their homes. Yeah, that's right; I was scared shitless by a group of birds!

With my nerves still on edge we continued to make our way toward the campfire, which was getting closer at a very slow pace. The crunching of weeds and sticks underfoot continued as we made our way in the direction of the homing beacon of the campfire. A second encounter with nesting birds occurred as we were nearing the edge of the thickly wooded area and, yes, it scared the shit out of me again! Another fifty yards and we finally reached the gravel road that circled the campgrounds. The sound of gravel scraping under our boots was a welcome replacement for the sound of the heartbeat in my ears, the crunch of the forest floor, and the shrill sounds of disturbed birds. We may have only been four hundred yards from civilization, but it felt like we had returned from the other side of the planet. We walked through the grounds looking forward to getting back to our spot.

Reaching our camp in one piece called for a celebration. I pulled out one of the three bottles of wine I had in the trunk of the car and filled a plastic keg cup to the top. It was time to unwind and relax by the fire. Lucas lit the kindling and stepped over to the picnic table to load another bowl for the evening wind down. I took my vat of wine and pulled up next to the fire with my camp chair.

"God damn it feels good to be back here," I said to Lucas. "I wasn't sure we were going to make it back."

"Yeah that sucked. I'm glad we went but I wish we would have had the chance to see a moose," Lucas replied.

"Well we have a few days," I said. "Maybe we'll get the chance yet."

It was then that I heard a more frightening sound than that of the angry birds. Over my shoulder came two simultaneous sounds that freaked me the hell out. It was the sound of something large walking near me and, what can best be described as a grunt. I don't know how I kept my composure, but I slowly looked up from my wine and saw Lucas's face with his mouth dropped wide open and his eyes even wider. It was as though he was frozen solid. I heard another grunt and more movement. I turned my head to the right. My eyes needed a moment to adjust from the flames of the campfire. There was a mammoth figure slowly walking past me.

It was a moose! Its head was dropped low. The rack was gargantuan. It didn't seem interested in me but I locked up every muscle in my body and fought the urge to jump from my chair. I stayed motionless as he slowly walked by, giving way to the second moose trailing behind him. I don't think I took a single breath in those moments as I watched the two behemoths saunter by without knowing, or caring, that they had just about given me a heart attack. They walked by my tent and disappeared across the road.

After several moments of stunned reflection Lucas broke the silence. "Wow," he said. "I guess we did get our chance. Fuck dude, I couldn't believe it when I saw it!"

"That scared the hell out of me!" I exclaimed. "I must have bears on my brain. The second I heard the grunt, I thought I was about to become a bear snack. Seeing that moose where I expected to see a bear didn't calm me down at all. Pass me that bowl!"

We sparked up the bowl and laughed about what had just happened, when out of the darkness a man appeared.

"Did you two see the moose walk by?" He asked us.

"Yeah, he walked right through our site. He was about five feet from me," I said.

"I'm lucky to be alive," he said. "I heard them walking by when I was in my one-man pup tent. When I stuck my head out of the opening, I was looking up at the belly of the lead moose. The second one stepped right on the stake at the corner of my tent. They literally almost stepped on me!"

We offered our neighbor a glass of wine which he gladly accepted. He sat down next to the fire, and we all got acquainted. He had come into the campground the day before on his motorcycle and was taking a couple days rest between long days running his bike across the country. He told us that when he registered for his site, he told the man at the campground office that he wanted to see some moose. He said that the man told him he would give him a site by "The moose highway." The moose highway sits right on the path the moose take between the river area and the base of the Tetons. The moose highway is where Lucas and I now called home.

After a couple hours of conversation and a second bottle of wine, the comfort of my cot was beckoning me. Our neighbor went back to his tent and Lucas and I began to feel the chill as the fire was reduced down to orange glowing embers.

I was a bit drunk and so tired that I fell asleep the minute my head hit the pillow. I crashed deeply for a few hours but was awakened by the cold. I don't know what the temperature fell to but I awoke to shivers and visible breath. I reached for my portable heater and, through chattering teeth, I managed to get it started. It was barely helping, so I turned it off and grabbed two pairs of heavy socks, two sweatshirts, and two pairs of sweatpants. I settled back into my bed, pulled my sleeping bag over my head and fell back to sleep.

When the sun brought me back to the real world, the temperature was still a bit on the cool side but was getting warmer quickly. I stuck my head out from my tent to see Lucas at the picnic table loading the bowl to do a wake and bake.

"How did you sleep?" I asked.

"Not worth a shit," Lucas replied. "I was fucking freezing!"

"Yeah, I was kind of shocked at how cold it got," I said.

"At least you have that mini heater to keep you warm," Lucas raised the bowl offering me the opportunity to spark it up (a true piece of stoner etiquette).

I stepped over to the table and took the pipe from Lucas's hand. "The heater didn't work very well. All of the heat was escaping through the top of the tent. I ended up shutting it off and adding some layers of clothing." As I lit the bowl and took a big drag, I had to ask myself what I was going to do in California if it got too cold to sleep. Obviously, the mini heater was not the answer.

While we passed the breakfast of champions back and forth, we started talking about the priorities of the day. Lucas said he would work on the car later in the day, but we were both in need of munchies and some morning brew. Jackson was only about a twenty-five minute drive, so we decided, rather than stoking the fire back to life, we would make the trip into town.

We jumped in the obnoxiously loud car and cruised at an idle, trying not to wake up any of the neighboring campers. We stopped at the office to get directions to a place where we could get some coffee and a little breakfast. We asked the woman at the desk where the best spot would be in Jackson.

"Is there any other reason you are planning to go to Jackson?" She asked.

"No, not really. Why?" I asked in return.

"If you're just getting some coffee and a bite to eat you should go to Kelly. It's only a few miles down the road, and they have great coffee," She said.

I was glad to hear we didn't have to drive so far. She told us to go to the end of the entrance and take a right (Jackson was to the left) and drive until we saw a sign that said "Kelly on The Gros Ventre" (Gros Ventre was the name of the river Lucas and I had visited). We thanked the woman and pointed the Cessna in the direction of Kelly. After only a few minutes we came in for a landing at the café/coffee shop. It was a log cabin with a gravel lot out front. Across from the café was the Kelly post office. That was pretty much the entirety of the business district in Kelly. There were a few houses near the café and a few more sparsely located off in the distance.

From our later conversations with the café owners we found out that a large percentage of those who resided in Kelly lived in Yurts (kind of a cross between a studio apartment and a tent). While working on making my latte, the barista invited us to join them on Friday for their weekly gathering. We were informed that everyone in the area was invited and that the first attendees, as long as they arrived before 5:00, got their first two beers for free. We told her that we were planning to leave Friday morning but that if we did stay, we would be there. I know this will come as a shock, but we stayed until Saturday.

Over the next couple days, Lucas and I enjoyed the relaxation of camping. The temperature stayed warm enough that we didn't have a repeat of our initial night's stay. During that time Lucas used the muffler tape and some wire to patch up the car. It wasn't 100% but it sounded more like a car and less like an airplane. Those few days were blissfully uneventful. We walked around the grounds, took naps, enjoyed the campfire and kept the bowl hot.

One night while sitting by the fire we had a visitor. Her name was Linda. She stopped over as we were starting the fire for the evening. Too lazy to cook, I was dining on a can of Spaghetti-O's and enjoying my third glass of wine. It's my opinion that Chardonnay is the best pairing for the entire Chef Boyardee line.

Linda was a travelling photojournalist who had heard about some of the sites near the Gros Ventre and had been taking photos all week. She wanted to get some shots of moose and asked if we had seen any. Lucas and I smiled and regaled her with the adventure we had on night one.

Linda was sort of an odd bird. She was rough around the edges. She stood about five foot six inches tall, a brunette unkempt bird's nest for hair and an inviting smile. You could tell she had a vault full of stories to tell. We invited her to join us by the campfire, and she immediately took us up on the offer. The stories began.

She told us about several adventures she had throughout the United States and Canada. She enjoyed wildlife photography as well as taking photos of natural land formations and waterfalls. She especially loved taking photos of waterfalls. She told us to visit a place called Harp Falls when we got to California. She described the falls as beautiful but hard to access. As hard as the access was, she told us it would be well worth visiting. She spoke of many national park trips from one end of the country to the other. She explained how she was checking the Gros Ventre area out because of a recommendation she had from a colleague who told her about a falls area off of a remote hiking trail near Kelly. She planned to visit them on the upcoming weekend.

The stories went on for hours and Lucas and I did not tire of hearing them. She did not partake of the herbal delicacies we were passing back and forth between us, but encouraged us not to hold back. We did not hold back. We shared the last of the wine and several beers with Linda and talked (well, listened) until one or two in the morning. I watched the last of the embers burn out and crashed hard in my tent.

I slept well until the grumbling in my stomach made me bolt up and run to one of the nearby bathrooms. It was not the best way to start the day. When I got back to the site Lucas was, once again, preparing the wake and bake.

He offered me the bowl. "Looks like you really need this," he said.

"Oh God yes!" I replied. "Spaghetti-O's and wine are definitely on my NEVER AGAIN list."

It was Friday, and though we originally decided that would be our departure date, we decided to stick around to enjoy our two free beers at the Kelly Café. We spent the day relaxing and slowly packing the gear we knew we wouldn't need before leaving. I went down to the office and paid for our last night. I commented to the man at the office that the campground was wonderful and hoped I would get a chance to visit again in the future.

It was 3:30 and there were four strong beers left in the cooler. I took it upon myself to make sure they were gone before heading over to the café. Lucas may have had one, I really don't remember. At 4:45 we jumped in the Maxima and rolled over to Kelly.

We walked in the café and the barista (who I found out later, was also the owner) who had invited us had a grin from ear to ear. "I had a feeling I might see you two tonight," she said. "Take whatever kind of beer you like out of the cooler and head out on the deck. The others should be arriving soon."

There was a wide variety of beers to choose from including some that were brewed in the area. I tried a dark beer from one of the local brewers. It was strong and tasty.

We took our beers out to the deck as instructed and sat down. We gazed at the panoramic view, and enjoyed some tasty beer. What wasn't there to love about a night like that? A few people showed up and proved to be as friendly as the owner. Conversations were flowing freely along with the suds.

As far as I could tell, most of the people in attendance had come to Kelly for one of three reasons. The first was a desire to find a place off the beaten track. Several were from larger cities and just wanted a place to kick back, view the natural wonders of Wyoming and get some separation from their normally hectic lives.

The second group, were those who wanted to challenge themselves with the hiking and mountaineering opportunities afforded them in the area. We enjoyed long conversations with people who had been mountain climbing as recently as that day. Their stories were breathtaking. They spoke of long hikes up the base to get to the steep inclines. That would be more activity than I would dream of doing and they had not even made it to the challenging part yet. After hours of hiking, they would finally set their sights on the peak and scale the sheer cliffs to reach the top. Some used equipment to scale the rocky cliffs and some used nothing but willpower and bare hands. It was amazing to listen to these people and hear about their adventures.

The third group, of which Lucas and I were members, was people on their way from one place to another who just happened upon Kelly by accident or providence. We felt in our case it was the latter. Lucas and I were very open about our destination and about our plans when we got there. To our surprise our specific trip caught their attention. They were intrigued by the idea of the adventure they saw in our journey. It was very odd to think these climbers of mountains were so interested in, and dare I say it, jealous of our future destination. We told them of our obstacles on the way out and how we came to be sitting on the deck in Kelly, Wyoming on a Friday night. It was a wonderful evening. We didn't want it to end.

After saying good bye to our fellow travelers, Lucas and I climbed in the car and headed back to camp. It was going to be an early start, so we wanted to get some decent sleep. We sat on the picnic table and smoked the last hits of the day before retreating to our tents.

The morning came too soon. The sun was starting to hit my tent. I rolled off my cot, stretched, and ventured outside. Lucas was returning from the bathroom and said something was going on, though he did not know what it was.

"There are a lot of people out this morning," Lucas said. "Something's going on."

"What do you mean?" I asked.

"I'm not really sure but several people passed me in a hurry while I was returning from the restrooms," he said.

It was then that one of the campers alerted us to what was happening. "There are a bunch of moose in the campground," he said. "I've never seen that many moose all in one spot!"

We had to check it out. We started walking in the direction everybody else was heading. When we got to the other side of the bathroom we saw what all the commotion was about. There were six moose wandering around near the woods by the river. Unlike the moose that had slowly walked through our campsite, these looked to have an agenda. They were walking in a much more determined fashion. They were on a mission.

I remembered the man at the office telling me that during mating season they will jump anything. I, along with the all the rest of the campers, were keeping our distance. Well, all the campers but one. Somebody wearing a red sweat jacket was getting real close. Dangerously close! The red jacket was within a few yards of the moose and only occasionally taking cover behind the trees. Lucas and I were joining in the conversations with the other campers discussing how crazy it was for this person to be getting that close.

At one point the red jacket was between two of the large beasts when one of them took notice. The red jacket turned in our direction. It was Linda! She ran a few yards and ducked behind a tree. The moose lost interest and began wandering toward the trees by the river.

As if on cue, all of the mammoth beings started to retreat toward the river and disappear into the thicket. The procession continued for a few minutes and soon the event was over.

Linda came over to where Lucas and I were standing. "I got some amazing shots!" She said as she raised her camera. "That was exactly what I was looking for!"

The three of us walked back toward our campsite.

"I thought you guys said you were going to leave yesterday," Linda said.

"We were," I said. "It's hard to leave a place like this. I don't really want to leave today, but we have to. Have you been to the falls area yet?"

"No, not yet," she said. "I'm planning on going over there today. Are you sure you don't want to stick around and join me? I could be ready to go in an hour."

"As much as I would like to, I think we need to get on the road," I replied. "We still have to tear down the camp and pack up."

We said our good byes and began the task of tearing down the site. It was about an hour later when we jumped in the Maxima and headed west.

Lucas and I shared the same thought. We were excited to be back on the road, but we were wishing we could have stayed longer.

The baritone hum of the patched muffler was a distinct improvement over its previous screams. We were both reflective of our experiences so far and excited for the adventure that was unfolding ahead of us.

Our travel was thankfully smooth and uneventful. We went west into Idaho and turned south into Nevada until finally hitting Interstate 80. We decided that we would not attempt to arrive in California that night. We were in agreement that getting a hotel room somewhere en route would be the way to go. Getting a good night sleep and a shower before being back in the tent for a long stretch seemed wise.

We decided to stop in Fernley, Nevada and stay at the Super 8. That was an expense I had not budgeted for, but who knew when our next chance to get a shower would be? We decided the expense was worth it. We pulled in about 10:00, got a room, and settled in for the night. Across the parking lot of the Super 8 was a casino called The Silverado. I noted it as a destination for the next morning but decided the night was all about getting some sleep. I set my alarm, and ten minutes later I was down for the count.

When the alarm went off I got up excited for the day and immediately took a long hot shower. I would be on the side of a mountain tonight and I was amped! I decided to work off some of the excess energy by walking over to the casino while Lucas was in the shower. I brought forty dollars cash and left the rest back in the room.

I played the nickel slots and bet very conservatively. I nursed the first twenty for about as many minutes. I moved to another nickel slot and put my other twenty in. I was about five dollars in when I hit a small jackpot for $190. In an uncharacteristic move, I cashed it in. I had just won enough to cover the added expense of the hotel stay and I even had a little left over for lunch. It seemed like a good omen.

Lucas and I wasted no time. We jumped in the car and headed west toward Reno following Interstate 80 through the canyons, made chaotic by heavy traffic. That particular section of Interstate 80 felt like a racetrack. The racetrack gave us a little of everything. Long, arced 70 MPH bends, tight curves posted at reduced speeds, cars passing or being passed, inclines, declines, truck traffic, all competing for my attention.

As we were nearing Reno, the paranoia started kicking in from the bowl we smoked before leaving the hotel. I had told Lucas about the day Hondo and I got stopped and inspected coming into California. Our paranoid minds began wondering if the inspection station did more than just inspect for food or plants. We were getting nervous about the small amount of pot we still had in the car. The logical thing to have done would have been to throw it out the window. After all, we were headed to Reefer Mecca where the crop was ready to harvest and we would have access to multiple pounds of various strains by nightfall. But that would have been logical. That was not us at that moment. Instead we did what seemed logical at the time. We stashed it in the middle of Lucas's tent and just lived with thirty minutes of all consuming paranoia.

When we got to the inspection station we got in line. We were fully expecting to be pulled over because of the Minnesota plates on the car. As we drew nearer to our turn at the booth, our panic heightened. We had thoughts of being detained. What would they do if they found that bud? Arrest? A ticket maybe? Cuffed and stuffed? We had no idea as we nervously made our way to the front of the line of cars. When it was finally our turn, they did something we were not expecting. They waved us by! No stop. No questions. Nothing. The paranoia was gone and we were in California! Life was beautiful.

The Arrival

We had finally made it. All the preparation, all the obstacles, all the adventures of the open road and all the miles were behind us. Well, almost all the miles. We were within a few hours of meeting up with Carl in Redding.

We made our way through Susanville and up the steep grade to Lassen National Park. Though I had been through the area with Hondo, it was dark on that previous trip and I was not able to appreciate the beauty which was now unfolding in front of me. The forest enveloped the road which snaked its way through mountains, ponds and as hard as it was to believe, "Beware of Cows" signs. I remembered all the hairpin turns from my trip with Hondo but this time the mood was different. I was no longer hauling a clumsily swaying truck on the final miles of a two thousand mile trek with no sleep.

I was awake, relieved and excited. The curves in the road were part of the beauty of this day rather than another obstacle in my way to reaching Redding in the middle of the night. The sun was shining, we were nearing the end of our travels, we were in the beauty of the high Sierras, we had a bowl lit and would soon be onto the next phase of an awesome adventure, oh, and it was my birthday. The way the day was shaping up I figured it was a birthday gift from the cosmos.

Lucas called Carl and told him where we were. Carl approximated that we would be at his doorstep by early afternoon.

He confirmed with Lucas that we had the directions in hand and told us he would be there when we arrived.

Lucas and I stopped at a couple of rest areas along the way to hike the trails and take in the mountain air. The last rest area we visited was at the top of a steep pass leading down to the valley below. It was the same steep grade that Hondo and I were on when we nearly hit the deer. I told Lucas about how we slammed on the brakes and damn near went off the road. After walking the trails and smoking a couple hits we got back on the road and started the descent.

Immediately upon leaving the rest area it became apparent that I was lucky to be alive. The area where I had come close to the edge on the previous trip had a steep drop off of several thousand feet. Had the truck failed to stay on the road that night, my daughter and I would not have survived. Chills went up my spine.

We reached the bottom of the mountain and continued on through gorgeous scenery that now included a rapid running stream racing us through the landscape. The whole drive was surreal and fantastic. We passed vineyards and small towns. One of the signs for a vineyard was calling our name and we decided to answer the call. We followed the signs and took a detour off the main road to a narrow blacktop leading back to the gates of the vineyard. We were excited to get our first taste of California wine while actually sitting in California. Unfortunately, we were too early. It wouldn't be open for forty-five minutes. We were in way too big of a hurry to wait around, so we noted its location and decided we would one day return.

Disappointed but excited by the day that we had so long waited for, we drove back to the main road and continued on toward Redding. Pretty soon the forests, streams and mountains were in our rearview mirror and the scenery changed to dry, tall, yellow grass and a sea of cars. We were close.

We came into Redding with directions in hand. South on Interstate 5, west on Cypress Avenue, left on Parkview Avenue, drive past the park, two more turns and we were there. We parked the car, got out and stretched. The neighborhood looked decent enough. Lucas and I were surprised. Carl was an infamous penny pincher. We assumed we would be in a bit shadier part of town. The surprise was a pleasant one and we walked up to the door and knocked.

Carl answered the door wearing his normal tie-dyed attire and invited us in. He gave us a quick tour of the small two-story. When we reached the upper level we sat down and in true Carl fashion smoked a variety of pot and a bit of hash. California was welcoming us in the manner we wanted to be welcomed.

Carl said that his girlfriend Kathy was at school and when she got home we would have a bite to eat before heading out to the site. We smoked and waited. We smoked some more and waited some more.

As we sat in the blue haze of the upstairs area I asked Carl a few questions about the grow spot. "Is Don staying at the site?"

"Yeah," Carl Answered. "He has been living out there all summer tending to the girls."

The girls are the pot plants. They are referred to that way not for any type of misogynistic reasons, but because only female plants produce THC. The girls were waiting for us to arrive.

"He's been staying in a tent all summer?" I asked.

"No. We built a small shed on the property to store supplies needed for the grow and to give him a spot to sleep," Carl said. "It ain't the Taj Mahal but it does the job."

Lucas added a question. "Are the other trimmers out there already or haven't they shown up yet?"

"I thought I told you," Carl said. "They all canceled. You are the only ones who showed up."

We knew Carl well enough to know that it hadn't slipped his mind to inform us of the cancellation of the rest of the party. He didn't mention it out of fear that it might cause us to reconsider coming out. He may have been right.

"No, you didn't tell us," Lucas said. "So it's just me, Steve, and Don that will be doing all the trimming?"

"Well no," Carl replied. "Don is blind as a bat. He can't see detail enough to help with the trimming. He will be the caretaker more or less. He will cook meals and make sure you have the things you need while staying out at the site. Don't worry, the others cancelling just means more money for you."

I jumped in. "I didn't prepare for being here any longer than four weeks. I don't know if it's even possible for us to do it."

"No worries, Duder," Carl said. "If you put in the hours, it should be no problem to be done in four weeks. It's all good."

You could tell by the look on Lucas's face that he was as unhappy about the conversation as I was. We both knew that we had been intentionally kept in the dark until the last minute. Carl loaded another bowl as Lucas and I sat in stunned silence.

As the embers of the pipe were turning to ash, Kathy returned from school. The room had become quiet after the new revelations Carl had dropped on us. It was a welcomed distraction to go downstairs and say hi to Kathy.

We liked Kathy. She was the whole package. She was smart. She was pretty. She was sweet. Best of all she was a hippie chick. When she attended Harmony Park Festivals, she fit right in. Hell, If you teleported her to back to Berkley in the 60's she would have fit right in. She actually made decorated hula hoops to sell when she went to festivals. How hippie is that?

We greeted Kathy, and we were treated to a hug.

"God it's great to see you guys," She said. "Carl said you would be here today, and I couldn't wait!" Kathy is normally pretty quiet. I think she was happy to see some familiar faces.

After sitting down and enjoying some sandwiches, we were ready to head out to the site. I told Carl we needed to stop at a liquor store before heading out. Carl said that it wouldn't be a good idea. According to him, Don should not have any booze near him because he's obnoxious and a bit crazy when he drinks. I informed Carl that it was my birthday, and I would indeed be getting some beer, some wine, and some scotch. I made sure he understood that there wasn't going to be a discussion. He relented, and we went to get my supplies.

After loading up on my liquid party favors, we went to the local Walmart so Carl could purchase a temporary garage to erect at the camp site. The garage would be where we would do our trimming and hang the weed to dry. I thought this would have been done prior to our arrival, but in true Carl fashion, he had been searching for the cheapest deal he could find. I'm sure the fact that he would have extra hands helping to put it up also entered into his erring on the side of procrastination.

Kathy and Carl were preparing to jump in the truck when Carl came over to my window. "Once we get out of town the road gets very twisty," he said. "I drive fast so if I lose you, just stay on the only real road and I will wait for you by the entrance to the reserve. You will go through the little town of Ono. The reserve is about another fifteen miles past that."

With that he jumped in the truck and we headed to the southwest corner of Redding. He took a right off of the main road and on to a skinny blacktop. The posted speed was fifty but Carl hit the gas and was doing ninety right off the bat. I wound up the Maxima and was in hot pursuit!

The road was straight for several miles but then the fun began. Carl's taillights went red and the front of the truck bent toward the blacktop from the force of the deceleration. His truck disappeared around a tight curve as I followed suit and hit the brakes on the Maxima. I was down to fifty when I hit the bend marked at thirty-five. Lucas grabbed the strap above the door and held on. The Maxima hung tight and took the curve like a champ. When the road straightened back out Carl had put more distance between us. He was driving like a lunatic. He was at a pretty good distance from us when the taillights came on again and we lost sight of the truck around another corner. When we approached the forty mile an hour curve we were going fifty. We took the curve only to start an immediate thirty-five mile per hour curve in the opposite direction.

When the road straightened back out we were on a long straight piece of blacktop and there was no sight of Carl. He was gone. I was actually somewhat relived and decided to reduce my speed to enjoy the ride rather than rush through it. The land heading out was not exactly what I had anticipated. I thought it would be lush, green, tree lined mountains. Instead it was mostly flat with an occasional hill and most of the vegetation consisted of tall brown and yellow grass. There were no rustic log cabins. The land was mostly inhabited by small farms and ranches. After several miles of twists and turns we hit a long stretch of flat, straight road that passed by a few more ranches, a dilapidated yard with old rusty machinery and a reduced speed zone. We had made it to the town of Ono.

Ono was a really small town with a handful of homes, a county fire station and a general store. The only cars we saw were parked in front of the general store, otherwise, it was pretty sparse. On the other side of Ono the landscape changed. Taking a long curve out of town the road began to climb what I could no longer call a hill. It was a mountain. Not like the huge mountains of Lassen Park but big enough to qualify as a mountain. Trees began to come into the picture, and it was beginning to look more like what I had expected. We drove though more winding roads and over several mountains. It had been a good twenty-five minutes since I last saw the taillights of Carl's truck. Carl had told us where to expect to see him and right on cue, there he was, parked and waiting by the gates of the reserve.

I pulled in and Carl walked over to the car. "The next several miles you need to be real careful," he said. "It's all unmaintained gravel road and there are lots of areas where the road is partially washed out. If you follow me exactly the way I weave through them, you'll be okay."

He wasn't kidding. We followed Carl up an incline on a curve. Several spots were so washed away that if I didn't navigate and zig zag through them I would have bottomed out and gotten stuck. Ten miles per hour was the top speed for that obstacle course. The car bumped and jolted through as we kept a close eye on the Sherpa in his white truck. We rounded the bend and came on flatter, better road. We were able to pick up the speed to about forty. It was short lived. The taillights ahead came on as we hit another spot where the road was partially washed away. It was only about fifty yards and the speed picked up again. After traversing several small areas of similar difficulty, we turned off from that road to one that was thinner, less maintained and ran along the side of a mountain. There were no guardrails and to our right was a steep drop off. Ten miles per hour was way too fast for this gauntlet. We bumped and jolted the poor Maxima over the rocky path. Suddenly Carl's truck stopped. He parked and walked back to the car.

"I forgot to tell you about the pine cones," he said holding one in his hand that he had picked up off the road. The cone was the size of a small pineapple. "These are sharp and solid. Make sure you don't run one over because they can actually pierce the rubber on your tires."

I acknowledged the new obstacle and Carl went back to his truck. We proceeded while dodging cones, avoiding trenches and trying not to look over the edge. It was less than ten miles since we left the main road but it took twenty minutes to get to the spot where Carl pulled into a small entry area with a gate. I pulled in beside him and he again approached the car.

"After I open the gate I'm going to pull through enough that you can park behind me while I close it," he said.

I stepped out of the car to walk with Carl to the gate and that was when I got my first glimpse of where Lucas and I would be calling home for a while. The site was a pretty large area but from that far away it looked small. Getting to it would require going down the mountain and climbing to the camp on the other mountain across the valley.

Carl opened the gate and pulled his truck through to the other side. I followed and parked. Carl stopped and explained that I needed to take it slow due to the curves, steep grade and the fact that loose gravel doesn't accommodate hard stops well. Sliding could be an issue. We were almost there but I was not able to relax my grip on the steering wheel quite yet.

As promised, the descent was slow, steep and dangerous. We followed Carl at a distance and made our way down the gravel pathway. When we arrived at the bottom we crossed a small bridge over a stream and around a bend.

I had almost forgotten that there was going to be a dog with us at the site. The dog began barking to alert Don that we were approaching. We climbed up about two hundred yards, with the large pit-bull running along the driver's side of the car. We had arrived!

Don was there to greet us and introduce us to King, the camp mascot. King was a big pit-bull with a thundering bark and a cautious growl. I put my hand out for him to get acquainted.

"Don't worry about King," Don said. "He acts tough, but he's a big pussy." Don stepped over with a square flat board and placed it against the back of the car, leaning it against the trunk. "You'll want to keep your plates covered while you're parked. The law enforcement helicopters fly over most days. No need to give them any additional information."

That statement brought the whole adventure into a new realm of reality. We were doing something that could result in serious consequences. I always knew that was part of the deal, but him saying it out loud brought things into a razor sharp focus.

We were given the grand tour. The camp was all angles except for the two areas which had been made flat to accommodate Don's shed and the spot for the temporary garage. There was a long black hose which ran all the way from the creek below to the area where the girls resided. The girls were in two separate areas and enclosed in fencing intended to discourage the local wildlife from indulging. Each plant had its own barrel for the soil and a cage that encompassed it. We entered the first of the two gardens, and I was in awe. The girls were tall, bright green, and beautiful. The buds were bigger than anything I had seen before. I had to get a picture on my phone. The buds were bigger than my hand and I wanted proof that something like that even existed.

As we walked through, we were told the names of each variety. I heard some of my favorites including Jack Herrer and Cinderella 99. Each of the girls had a name, a history, and an aroma sweeter than fresh pine.

We then ventured over to the other garden where the Purple Haze, Durbin Poison and a few other girls hung out. It was amazing!

Behind the second garden was a small flimsy chair with a hole in the middle. We were informed that the flimsy chair would be where we would go when it was time to poop. I wasn't sure I heard him right.

"Just how the hell does that work?" I asked Carl.

"It's not rocket science, Duder," he replied. "You just put a plastic bag in the hole, sit down, do your business and then bring the bag to the disposal pile."

"Rocket science be damned," I said. "I'm two hundred and eighty pounds. That's not going to work!"

"Well, I don't know what to tell you," Carl said. "You'll have to figure it out."

I had assumed there would be some sort of structure with a hole dug in the ground, not a skinny man toilette. This was not going to be easy.

Carl then said we should get to work putting up the tents and the garage. He mistakenly thought Lucas and I were going to set our tents up on the angle. Lucas was begrudgingly compliant. I was not. I would be on a cot with a mattress. The angle of the hill would mean I would be fighting my bed all night. That wasn't going to happen.

"There's no way in hell I'm setting up on an angle," I exclaimed. "I need to plant it on the flat spot by the garage."

"There's not enough room," Carl said. "The garage is too big."

"We have to figure it out because there is no way I'm going to sleep on the slope of this mountain," I asserted, "I need a flat spot!"

Carl was not happy with me. Duder, I said you would be sleeping on the side of the mountain. What did you expect?"

"I expected you to make arrangements for us to stay out here. You should have leveled off another area," I answered. "You thought it through enough to level a spot for Don's shed and the garage. You should have considered the guests you were inviting out!"

That's when the measuring tape came out. We measured the area that had been flattened out for the garage. We came to the conclusion that it would be tight, but it would fit both the garage and my tent. I made it clear that I would rather be on the side of the flattened area that sat right next to the garden. We all set to work on getting the garage set up and staked down. The ground was so hard that a railroad spike had to be driven into each one of the spots designated for stakes before they could be placed in and finished. The six spots where the main poles for the garage would be secured had to be chiseled out. We had to make sure they were all at the same depth to keep the unit level.

While the rest of the crew put the finishing touches on the garage, I began the arduous task of getting the traveling palace erected. It took over an hour but it was set up and ready to take on the elements for the next four weeks.

Don walked over to the tent after seeing all the equipment I had brought into it. He was curious. "Mind if I poke my head in?" He asked.

"No, not at all," I said. "Come on in."

He stepped in through the zipper adorned entrance and started laughing. "Jesus Christ. This place is way better than my shed!" He said. "You mind trading places?" He sat down on the chair next to the small folding table. That's when he noticed my cooler, open with beers on top. "Carl said it's your birthday today. Are you planning to have a few?"

"Absolutely," I replied. "As a matter of fact, now that the tent is up and I'm all moved in, it's time to crack one open. Care to join me?"

Carl had warned me not to offer any alcohol to Don, but I didn't give a shit. Not planning to have a spot for my tent, expecting me to crap on a wobbly chair, and not informing us of the lack of fellow trimmers, was not sitting well with me. I liked Carl and was actually surprised at the events that had taken place in the last few hours. I considered him a good friend, as did Lucas.

"I think I'll wait until Carl leaves," Don said. "He gets pissy when anyone drinks."

I thought it was just Don that Carl didn't want drinking, but then it occurred to me that I had never seen Carl or anyone around him drink. He simply didn't want anyone to drink. Don's behavior was just the excuse Carl used to attempt to stop me from bringing my supplies out to the site. Screw that! I grabbed my bottle of scotch and took a good pull from it. I grabbed a beer, cracked it open and stepped out of the tent with Don.

Carl was packing the last of the tools into his truck, and it looked like he was getting ready to leave. It was easy to read the disapproval of my beverage choice in his face. We said our good byes to Carl and Kathy, and they took off.

Don waited for Carl to pass through the gates before asking for a beer. I pulled the cooler out of the tent and all three of us enjoyed a beer while we watched the last of the sun dip over the top of the mountain. As it was getting dark, Don brought a battery operated lantern and a flashlight out. He turned them on as the last bit of dusk turned to night. We stood there enjoying a couple beers and some cigarettes.

I kept hearing an odd sound. It was like the sound of Carl's canvas flapping around on the last trip out to California. I asked Don what it was.

"Bats," Don said. "Right now there are hundreds of them flying above our heads."

"No way ," I said.

"Yeah," Don said. "Look!"

Don shined the light from the flashlight over our heads. He was telling the truth, though it may have been more than hundreds.

"They come out just after dusk," he said. "That's when they feed on the insects. They'll do this for about a half hour and then they'll pretty much disappear. Don't worry about them. They do this every night and they've never bothered me the whole time I've been out here."

True to his prediction, by the time the next beer was cracked open the bats had all but vanished. With the retreat of the bats and the noise of their wings, the place got chillingly quiet. No cars, no people, no random city noises, nothing but complete silence. It was eerily cool. I commented on it to Don.

"You know it took me a while to get used to that when I first got out here. You know what took me longer to get used to? How dark it gets after the sun sets." Don said. With that he turned off the lantern and switched off his flashlight.

Holy shit it was dark! I did what a first-timer in a photography dark room does. I waved my hand in front of my face. Nothing! It was pitch black. It was pitch black and perfectly quiet.

Don interrupted the silence. "Look up," he said.

I did as he asked and there it was. The most beautiful blanket of stars I had ever seen. It was like I was sitting in a planetarium. There were more stars in the sky than I had ever thought possible. As my eyes slowly adjusted to the dark I was able to make out the shapes of Lucas and Don, but only the shapes. This was an experience I had not considered possible before coming out on this trip. It's an experience I miss to this day.

We enjoyed one more beer and then retired to our beds. It had been a very long and exciting day and I was ready for a deep slumber. The weather was nice so I stripped down to my shorts and a t-shirt and crawled under my sleeping bag. The utter quiet was almost too much. I found myself trying to hear something, anything, but it was dead silent. I had been lying in bed about five minutes when I heard something that made me bolt upright. I heard something just outside my tent walking around and grunting. I knew King was in the shed for the night, and I couldn't imagine his grunt would be that low. Then I heard scratching against my tent just on the other side of where my head was resting. I had two thoughts of what it could be. I thought either it was a mountain lion or the dreaded bear!

Trying not to make too much noise, I slowly got off the cot and considered my options. If it was a large animal and it pushed against or, God forbid, collapsed my tent I would be stuck and defenseless. I figured I had to swallow my fear and get ready to confront whatever it was. I grabbed my bear mace and clipped it to my shorts. I grabbed my machete in one hand and my hatchet in the other. Whatever it was, it was going to be doing battle with some sharp blades and some mace! I went to unzip the entrance and heard the snorting again. The tent rattled. It was definitely pushing against the tent. It was time to for me to nut up or shut up! I unzipped the tent as quietly as possible and figured I would stand the best chance if I surprised the beast by screaming as I lunged out of the tent. I stood by the unzipped door and readied myself. Another grunt! I flipped open the tent flap with my blades ready for action and let out a scream as I rushed out into the dark night and turned in the direction of the last grunt.

I wasn't facing a black bear. I was facing Don, holding King by the collar, laughing his ass off! I was relieved but pissed enough that I wondered if I should still use the machete! It took me a minute or two to calm down and eventually began laughing with Don.

"I'm sorry man," Don said. "I couldn't resist. Besides, I figured you should have a treat on your birthday." With that, Don handed me a big cookie. "I had Carl pick me up some cookies the last time he got supplies. I figured I'd bring you one before you went to bed, but I forgot until I went in the shed. I gotta say you came out ready for blood! With that machete and hatchet ready for action I think your nickname should be Chopper!"

We both had a good laugh, and I had a birthday cookie. Once my heart stopped pounding I went back in my tent and listened to the nothingness until I drifted off to sleep.

I didn't know what time it was, but I was awoken by a scream. It wasn't way off in the distance. It was nearby the camp. It sounded like somebody was in serious trouble. Part of me wondered if the events of the previous day had caused me to dream it. I heard it again! It was scary and whoever was screaming needed help badly! It sounded like a woman's scream, and it sent me into a panic. I had to do something. I grabbed my machete and hatchet once again. This time I threw on my boots and some sweatpants. Whatever was happening to this poor woman, I had to be ready to deal with. I stepped out of the tent, and to my surprise, I saw Don standing off the edge of my tent having a cigarette.

"What's up Chopper?" Don asked.

"What do you mean what's up?" I asked him incredulously. "Somebody is screaming!"

That was the second time Don laughed as I sported implements of destruction. "That's a screech owl," he informed me. "Believe it or not, that screech owl is a few hundred yards up the mountain. It sounds like it's right next door, doesn't it? That's another one of those things I had to get used to out here."

According to Don, I had only been in my tent for about twenty minutes. The owl must have let loose the minute my eyes shut. I said goodnight to Don and went back to my bed.

I threw off my boots, got back down to my shorts, and crawled under my sleeping bag once again. This time, instead of the silence going through my head, it was doubt. How many things was I going to need to get used to while I was out here? Cratered roads in and out, screeching owls, a massive bat population, crapping in a bag, what else? It was then I noticed the smell. A breeze was gently blowing and the tent became filled with the scent of the girls next door. It was wonderful. I drifted off with a smile on my face.

First Day at Work

Thud, thud, thud, thud, thud, thud, thud was the first sound I heard in the morning, and it was the reason my gluey eyes opened in the first place. I didn't have to guess what it was, I knew. Don had covered my license plates for that exact circumstance. I unzipped the large window on my tent to see if I could lay my eyes on them. The heavy thud of the helicopter blades meant they had to be flying pretty low. They were. They were flying low enough that they had to angle up to get to the top of our mountain. I was able to see the tail end as it climbed up and over the top of our spot and disappeared over the trees.

My ears were the first of my senses to be awakened. My sight adjusted enough to be the second sense aroused. Now it was time for smell. Opening up the large window next to the girls brought in a fragrance that turned my rather rude return to consciousness into a welcoming introduction to my first day on the job.

I threw on my jeans, a t-shirt, a flannel shirt and laced up my boots. I unzipped the door to the tent and took the long commute to work. It was literally two steps from bedroom to office.

My senses were now fully awake. The morning was losing its chill to the bright sunlight. The smell of coffee was competing with the aroma from the garden. I stepped through the garage and came out on the other side where Don was preparing some java on the side burner of the grill.

"Another couple minutes and the coffee will be ready," Don said. "How did you sleep, Chopper?"

"Once I got to sleep, I was fine," I said. "Getting there was a bit of a battle. Have you seen Lucas this morning?"

"Yeah he was out with me when the Feds were flying over the site," he replied. "Not sure where he went after that."

A couple minutes later I was enjoying a cup of coffee when Lucas came walking up from the valley. He had been checking out the creek and getting a closer look at our surroundings. He was anxious to start working, and we decided to dive right in.

Don had us each grab a large white bucket and pruning shears and follow him into the garden by my tent. We walked through the various plants until we found one that was so big it was spilling outside of its cage. It was the Durban Poison. We snipped several buds each and placed them in the buckets.

When we got back to the garage Don gave us a basic tutorial.

"First you need to put on your rubber gloves and strip off all the loose leaves," he said. "Then take the small Fiskars scissors and snip off all the smaller leaves that hang away from the bud. That's when you have to go into detail. Remove even the smallest of the leaves that hang off any part of the bud. You will need to do this over one of the cardboard boxes so you are able to collect everything that comes off for Carl to turn into hash and butter." He pulled out a large hefty bag. "Put all the trim in here."

"Where do we put the buds we trim?" I asked.

Don showed us a couple wires that had been strung up along the top of the garage. "It will need to dry for a day or two before you can finish trimming them. Chopper, you hang yours on one line and Lucas you hang yours on the other. After they dry, some smaller leaves will be visible, and you will have to clean those up before the bud is considered finished. At that point you will put everything in a paper bag marked with your name and the name of the variety. Carl will pay you based on the weight of what's in the bag."

We were ready to begin but decided to sample the product before tearing into it. We removed a small chunk of one of the buds and threw it in the pipe. Because it was fresh off the plant it was slow to start but we were determined. We smoked the bowl down to ashes and began trimming. We kept our heads down and plucked, snipped, and smiled. It was as though we were exactly where we were supposed to be at that moment in time. All the obstacles we had overcome to get here were feeling like a distant memory.

After about a half hour, the gloves and the scissors were getting too sticky to continue. I started bitching that it was slowing me down. That's when Lucas told me something I was completely unaware of. He told me that the sticky residue on our scissors and gloves was almost pure THC. When you scrape the scissors and roll the stickiness off your gloves, the resulting ball of joy was called trim hash. I didn't need any additional encouragement. I scraped my scissors clean and it produced a small ball of the sticky substance. I then rolled my gloved fingers together and produced a little more. I loaded the ball of trim hash into the bowl and handed it to Lucas (good etiquette). Lucas fired it up and handed it back to me. It was sweet and potent. Pretty soon my eyes were half closed and I was floating on to the next bud in my bucket. It was truly a bonus.

The sun was starting to beat down on the garage and the flannel had to come off. Don came in to see how things were going. He told us Carl suggested drinking Gatorade to keep hydrated and that he had a few cans of powdered mix. We were game, and Don proceeded to mix us up a batch. The only thing to drink, other than my alcohol supplies, was the gallon jugs of water that Carl brought out to the site. The water for the girls was not potable. Don asked us if we wanted to run the fan while we trimmed. I was perplexed. How could we run a fan when we had no electricity? My curiosity was soon squelched as Don pulled out a small solar panel which he placed out in the sun by the garage. He then ran the chord to the small fan and placed it by the garage entrance. Perfect!

Seeing the solar fan at work gave me another idea. I asked Lucas if he was ok with me putting on some music to trim by. He liked the idea so I went and retrieved my laptop, started the car and charged the computer's battery. Luckily I had amassed a pretty long list of songs over the years that were all sitting on the hard drive of the laptop. We could start the list and have days' worth of music without hearing the same song twice. When it was fully charged, I brought it in the garage, set it on the table and started out with "I Got Stoned and I Missed It" by Dr. Hook. We went back to trimming.

About an hour later the moment came that I was dreading. I grabbed a bag and headed up the hill to the rickety chair designed for the nightmare I was now trying to wrap my head around. I attached the bag, stepped back and took a nice long gander at it. I had the look of a man contemplating the deep sciences. In actuality, physics and physiology would definitely be taken into consideration. Without going into too much detail I will just say that the angle of the hill assisted in my ability to hover. Enough said. Okay, perhaps too much said.

After I returned from my distasteful chore I washed my hands in the creek water and got back to work. Don fired up the grill and put on a few hamburgers. We worked right up to the time the burgers were done and stepped out to have some lunch by the grill. The burgers were just right. Not too done, not bloody, but slightly pink in the middle. I told Don he made a damned good burger, and that's when we heard how he got his practice.

Don had been in prison for a few years and had actually just got out before I met him a year ago. While he was in prison, he was one of the main cooks.

"Do you mind if I ask what you were in for?" I asked.

"No, I don't mind," he said. "I was in for possession and distribution of marijuana. I served five years. My operation was much bigger than Carl's little garden. It was going great until one of the dipshits I was mailing quantities to fucked up. He returned some product and some cash, and it got intercepted. It didn't take long and the Sheriff was at my door. They took my house, my truck, and all my cash. Next thing I knew I was in the can."

Once Don got started he was off to the races. He told us everything from how he started his grow and learned how to cultivate, to setting up distribution networks and growing his business. He even had a couple pictures on his phone from his days of bud and bank. One particular picture he shared was of him standing in his back yard in the middle of several rows of towering pot plants the size of large Christmas trees. They were huge and so was the smile on his face.

When we finished our lunch, we went right back to work. Don followed us in and continued to talk about his life before prison, the business he owned before going into the pot trade, his ex-wife, his kids, and all the toys he bought with the proceeds from growing and selling weed. He was thrilled to have an audience. It was hard to blame him for wanting to talk. He had been sitting on the side of a mountain for several months just tending to the girls without any human interaction other than the occasional supply drops from Carl. I've always truly enjoyed time by myself, but only in small doses. I would have gone crazy if I had to do it for months. I'm sure the shed on a hot summer day was still better than a prison cell but at least in prison there's always somebody to talk to. There was something I liked about Don. He was a survivor.

One of the subjects Don brought up was his son Dave. Dave was also arrested when Don was but got a shorter sentence for lesser charges. After talking for quite a while, I came to the realization that I knew Dave. After Carl went to California, he continued to supply his clients through Dave, and I had become friends with him. I never knew Dave's last name. Until Don mentioned that Dave was handling business for Carl, I didn't know there was a relationship there. As my dad once told me, "It's a small world...but I wouldn't want to paint it."

As we continued to trim, the day got hotter and hotter. The fan could not keep up, and sweat was pouring down the front of my shirt. My glasses kept steaming up and had to be removed, so I could see the bud. Around four o'clock, King started barking to alert us that someone was coming down the road past the gate. We took a well-needed break and stepped outside the garage to see who it was. It was Carl. As Carl slowly approached the site, we took a moment to stand in the shade by the grill and cool down. As we watched him winding down the hill, we noticed he had his dog Sadie with him. Carl rolled up on the site, and King was going nuts. I think he knew Sadie was in the truck.

The second Carl opened the door, Sadie jumped out and she and King started playing. This was not the first time. These dogs had been playing with each other all summer long. King was a happy dog. It made me think of Don and how happy he was to now have somebody out at the site with him.

Carl walked over to our shady spot and asked how things were going. We told him things were going pretty well and he should see what we've trimmed. We were happy with our progress and honestly couldn't wait to show him what we had accomplished.

When he looked at what we had drying on the wire, he gave us a response we didn't want to hear. "This isn't too bad," he said. "You're going to have to trim tighter than this before you hang it up." He pulled a couple buds off the wire and picked up a pair of scissors. "You have to get real tight to the bud so it will dry faster and be better prepared for clean up." He proceeded to trim a bud that I had already thought was trimmed well. He was eyeing it as though he was wearing a jeweler's loupe. He turned it this way and that way and took tiny snips as he went. "There, that's better."

I couldn't believe it. He took more than five minutes getting every little fleck off the bud. It didn't take a genius to figure out that if we were that meticulous, we would never get the quantity done in the time he had told us it would take. I kept my thoughts to myself. Carl stuck around for a bit while the dogs played. He smoked a couple bowls and left us some hash he had prepared at the house. He grabbed the trim we had created that day and loaded it in the truck. Within an hour of his arrival he was gone.

After he left, Lucas and I went back to work while Don began making tacos for our supper.

"Man, we have been working all day and have less than a quarter pound of pot trimmed," I said to Lucas. "If we trim it like Carl wants, how will we ever be able to make decent money?"

Lucas had the same thought but a better attitude about the prospects. "Maybe once we get the hang of it we can get more done in less time."

"Maybe you're right," I replied.

I said it but I didn't really see how it could get that much faster. I'm pretty sure Lucas didn't believe it either, but he was trying to stay positive.

We continued to trim until supper was ready. We wanted to get as much done as possible before losing the sun. We scarfed down a couple tacos and got back to it. We trimmed and listened to more of Don's war stories. We were okay with most of the stories, but he would always find a way to insult or otherwise berate Carl. I have been upset with Carl almost since we arrived in California, but I still considered him a friend, and both Lucas and I defended him against every slam Don made.

To Lucas and I, Carl was a pot guru. We were voluntary members of his cult of personality. We were fans of pot in a huge way. To us, pot was a different category than drugs. It was pretty harmless and could be considered helpful in many ways. Stress reduction, pain relief, sleep enhancement and glaucoma relief were just a few of the many benefits we saw from this wonderful herb. We also looked at weed as natural and somewhat innocuous. There's a reason when you smoke it it's called catching a buzz. Weed doesn't incapacitate the user like heavy drugs or alcohol. Those who indulged with pot generally appreciated the culture around every aspect of it. First off, it was cool. At least we thought so. Every bowl smoked had a name and a place of origin. Often when two smokers got together, there would be at least two different kinds of pot. Sharing and comparing was one of the things most potheads enjoyed. It was less of a competition and more of a communal enjoyment.

Pot, with very few exceptions, doesn't get people in trouble. The biggest penalty one pays with weed is getting caught with it. Ok, overuse can sap some people of their motivation, but in the grand scheme of things that is a pretty minor side effect. Unless taken to unheard of extremes, there were no stories of it destroying families or transforming neighborhoods into uninhabitable war zones. Potheads generally lacked the motivation to cause such havoc.

Carl represented himself as the bringer of all things green. He was that. The added thing about Carl was his knowledge. When I was first introduced to Carl, he was going to college to get his degree in business management and finance. He did well in college. He was a quick learner. That was evident in the vast amount of weed knowledge he had amassed over the years. If he was on a game show called "Name That Bud", he would have cleaned up. I tested him on several occasions with multiple questions about widely varied strains. He would know whether they were indica or sativa, where it was normally grown, the history of the mix, the type of flavor it produced, the scent associated with it and sometimes some historical data surrounding its naming. With his hippie chick girlfriend and his stockpile of multiple strains at hand, he was beyond being a mere connoisseur; he was an honest to God Bud-Guru. When Carl asked me to join him at Harmony Park, I was not just excited; I was proud that he chose me. When Carl asked me to come out to California, I was honored that he trusted me enough to invite me.

We felt that the stories Don had been telling us about Carl were both untrue and perhaps a little sour grapes that he now worked for somebody on their pot grow and was no longer an owner. The slams against Carl were not sitting well with me, but they were outright pissing Lucas off. We hadn't even been in California for a whole day, and there was already tension building up between Don and Lucas. When Don went to his shed, I got an earful.

"Fuck that dude," Lucas said. "He wouldn't even have a job if it weren't for Carl. It's bullshit that he talks about him this way behind his back."

"Yeah, I agree," I said.

"Why does he think it's ok to rip on Carl to us?" Lucas questioned. "Doesn't he know we're Carl's friends?"

"I don't know, man. It does seem odd that he goes on and on about it. Maybe he's just trying to get a summer's worth of talking off his chest," I offered.

"I don't know, but that shit has got to stop!" Lucas demanded.

When Don came back to the garage, he loaded a bowl and passed it around. The rest of that night Don didn't say anything about Carl. I was relieved. I didn't want to see Lucas lose his shit.

The sun began to fade about 6:45. After trimming all day, Lucas and I were not seeing any hint of the pound and a half or two pounds that Carl had assured us we could trim in a day. We decided to put on our battery operated headlamps and continued to trim. That slowed things down considerably. We put scissors to bud until eleven o'clock and decided to hang it up for the night.

When I looked at the weed hanging from the wires, it was obvious we were both substantially below a half a pound apiece. That quantity coupled with the fact that they still had to be cleaned up after they were dried made me wonder if I had been sold a bill of goods by Carl. I didn't want to believe it, but the thought was there.

Lucas and I treated ourselves to a little trim hash to wind the evening down on a good note. We stepped out to smoke it while looking up at the stars. The day was long and had its share of issues, but I was determined to shake it off and give it another shot in the morning. As I walked toward the tent, the screech owl made its presence known. It reminded me that I was in a strange land doing strange things with strange people (myself included), but I was doing exactly what I had set out to do. I was having one hell of an adventure!

A Beautiful Day in the Neighborhood

The next day arrived and I was happy to greet it. I slept well and didn't start the day with whirling chopper blades. It was early and the dawn was just beginning to make itself known by casting a dull orange hue throughout my tent. I rolled out of bed and got dressed for the day. It was chilly enough to put on the flannel but not cold. I exited the tent to find I was the only soul stirring. I went to the grill and fired it up to start brewing coffee. Before I reached for the percolator, Don stepped out and took over.

"How did you sleep, Chopper?" Don asked.

"I actually slept very well," I replied. "You call me Chopper. Do you have a nickname?"

"Have you seen the Movie Captain Ron?"

"Yeah, that's the one with Kurt Russel, right?"

"Yep," Don said. "Some people call me Captain Don because I can't see very well, and Captain Ron wore the eyepatch. Some just call me Captain."

"Okay, Captain. How did you sleep?" I asked.

"I always sleep pretty well. It's something about the cool air out here at night that knocks me the hell out," he said. "Would you be willing to take me into town today? I have a few things I need to pick up."

I guess it hadn't really even occurred to me that I was the only mode of transportation at the site. Well, there was a small dirt bike, but it wasn't street legal. I didn't really know Don, but I figured it would be one way to get to know him.

"Sure," I said. "Where do we need to go?"

"If it's okay with you, I have a couple places I would like to stop. First, I would like to go to the Holiday grocery store to pick up a few things, and then to the Reservation to pick up some smokes," he said. I'll introduce you to Theo. Also, if you're up for it, we could grab some lunch at the Ono general store, and I can introduce you to those folks."

"Yeah, that sounds good," I replied while pouring myself a cup of coffee. "Hell, I could use some creamer for my coffee as long as we're in town. I don't normally take it black."

I walked my coffee into the garage to get to work, and to my surprise, Lucas was already trimming away. He had been listening to Don and me talking and was quick to head off my next question.

"I'm just going to stay out here and work while you and Don go to town. I really don't want to spend the day in a car with him," he said.

Don was not quite out of earshot from Lucas. "We'll be gone for lunch Lucas, so you can make yourself a sandwich. There are ham slices, cheese, and bread if you get hungry."

"Okay. Otherwise I know Steve has some wine and Spaghetti-O's if worse comes to worse," Lucas said with a smirk on his face.

Don was unaware of the inside joke and didn't care to ask. He just disappeared to the garden with a cup of coffee and tended to the watering.

I told Lucas that I was actually excited to go so that I could call my wife when I was in town. Being out in the boondocks, there was no phone service, and I wanted to let Sue know how I was doing. My last communication with her was the day we left Kelly, Wyoming. Lucas suggested that I take a picture or two to text her before the phone call to show her the camp. I agreed and took a couple pictures of the camp, one of King, and one of me holding a bud before it was trimmed and one after. I knew Sue would get a kick out of it.

After finishing the photo session we got back to work and continued until about eleven o'clock when Don entered the garage and asked if I was ready to go. I put down the bud I was working on, brushed the trimmings from my clothes and joined Don in the car.

"Where do you want to go first, Captain?" I asked.

"Let's get a bite at the Ono General," he replied.

I backed the car around, so I was facing downhill to start the trip. After crossing the creek, we started on the first of the steep grades. The gravel spit out from under the tires as the Maxima was pushed to the limits on the climb. The combination of the incline and loose gravel made it difficult for the car to get significant traction.

"I can't believe how much the car slides trying to attack this pull," I said to Don.

"It's bad when it's dry, but it's impassable when it's wet," he said. "After a rain nothing makes it up the hill until it dries out."

We made our way up to the gate. Don jumped out, swung the gate open and waited for me to get through before closing it and locking it back up.

I retraced Carl's route back through the washed-out roads while avoiding pine cones and keeping my distance from the ledges. After successfully completing the course with the exhausted Maxima, we finally came to the blacktop and picked up speed on our way to Ono.

When we got to the general store, I noticed an odd array of vehicles parked along the road. There were two small tanker straight-trucks and a small open air two man airplane, kind of a motorized glider. We parked at an angle directly in front of the store and stepped in.

The place looked exactly as I expected it to look. Immediately inside the door was a long wooden counter with stools spread along its front side. Down at the end of the counter there were a couple small square tables with four chairs around each. Next to the small dining area there were four shelves spanning about twelve feet with essentials ranging from a few loaves of bread and some canned goods to wood matches and toiletries. On the ground beneath the shelves were a few packs of bottled water, some bags of softener salt and twelve packs of beer and soda. Across from the shelves were two cooling units with glass doors, one for frozen food and the other filled with eggs, bacon, luncheon meat and beer. Like any store that exists out of convenience, the prices were extremely high.

We bellied up to the counter and looked at the menu posted behind it. It was a small variety of café staples. Beside the menu there were a few t-shirts displayed for sale with the words in large print "Ono International Airport", and in smaller print below it "Ono California".

Two stools down from us sat a large man with a full beard and moustache wearing filthy overalls and leaning over his double cheeseburger. Don knew the man and introduced us. His name was Gil and he owned a local farm with various livestock, an almond crop, and of course, weed. The man was fairly soft spoken and reminded me of a stereotypical Midwest farmer. Don and Gil talked at length about their respective crops (Don never mentioning it was actually Carl's crop). Don had the advantage of a creek for watering his grow, but Gil was not so lucky. With the dry summer and the ensuing drought, the creek that ran through Gil's acreage had dried up. They talked about other farmers in the area experiencing the same thing. Every other day Gil was relegated to driving his small tanker truck into Redding to fill up with water. Until hearing their conversation I was not aware of the fact that it requires more than a gallon of water to grow one almond. Not one plant. One almond. Another acquaintance of Don's who was a fellow grower entered the store and sat at the stool between us and Gil. Don introduced us. His name was Rod, and he too was on a run to get some water for his crops.

One thing that struck me about listening to their conversation was how similar they spoke about their marijuana grows. For me, it was a mystical plant. For them it was a crop, plain and simple. They could have been talking about soybeans or corn. They discussed harvesting and the lack of available trimmers. They talked about current market prices and their plans for distribution. They talked about setting up seeds and clones for the following year and their best guesses for what crop would pay the best next year.

The other thing that stood out in the conversation was the shortage of trimmers and the prices they were willing to pay to acquire them. It was twice as much as what I was being paid. I could tell Don wasn't comfortable with that discussion, and he quickly did his best to change the topic. It was obvious Don had a vested interest in having Lucas and I trimming.

We ordered a couple of cheeseburgers, and Don suggested that we get them to go so we wouldn't be away from the grow site for too long. I think it was the uncomfortable conversation that he was attempting to avoid by suggesting we get mobile. When I placed my order, I had to ask about the idea behind the Ono International Airport t-shirts. The man behind the counter said that he was the owner of the store and also owned the small two man motorized glider parked at the side of the road.

"We have a small fleet of one and the best damned pilot in the business," he said while pointing to himself "and we have a great safety record. I've only crashed twice!"

I don't care who you are, you have to appreciate that sense of humor.

When the burgers arrived, we jumped in the car and made our way toward Redding.

"So Captain, what was the deal Gil and Rod were talking about as far as the trimmer shortage?" I asked Don. "Sounds like they are paying considerably more than Carl is."

"Yeah, now that the state has made growing legal, more people are in the game. It is creating a shortage," he said. "But those guys are full of shit that they will pay that kind of money. I think that was meant for your benefit. If you went to trim for them, I think you would find they wouldn't follow through with that much."

"I noticed you got a little unnerved when they brought it up. Are you and Carl partners?" I asked.

"We're not partners, Chopper. I would never partner with Carl. I don't exactly trust him," he replied. "I get a percentage of the harvested crop when the season is done. I have been out on the land since the first seed took root and will be there until the last bud is trimmed. Once it's done, I'm taking my money and getting the hell out of here. Carl thinks I'm going to help him again next year. I don't want you saying anything to him, but that's not going to happen."

I was surprised at his confession. Did he trust me that much? I liked Don, but I was almost uncomfortable with what he had told me. I considered Carl to be a friend, but Don had judged me correctly. He confided in me and his secret would be safe with me.

We pulled into the Holiday and loaded up on a few groceries. The real reason for Don wanting to go to the grocery store was to grab some beer. I was shocked when I went into the store and saw they had a fully stocked liquor store right next to the groceries. That was foreign to me. In Minnesota grocery stores and liquor stores are two different animals. In California they are the same thing. I was also thrown by the fact that booze can be purchased 24/7. In Minnesota the hours are regulated, and it is illegal to purchase on a Sunday. What was this strange land I found myself in?

Before leaving, I texted the pictures I had taken for Sue and called her to give her an update about the adventure so far. All was good back in the land of ten thousand lakes, and she told me to be careful. The phone call was a double edged sword. I loved hearing her voice, but it just made me miss her more.

The next stop was to be the Indian reservation. I asked Don for directions, and he told me we were going to head back to Ono but that we would go a different route that would take us through the town of Igo. Really? Ono and now Igo? Odd abrupt names.

Igo was another small town but not as small as Ono. It was the location of the high school in the area and had a significant number of houses. Well, significant compared to Ono.

We got to Ono, and, instead of continuing straight through toward the grow, we passed the general store and took a right on an extremely skinny two-lane black top. The road had a faint line down the middle with enough room on either side to barely fit the Maxima. As with most thoroughfares in this part of the world it was far from being a straight line. The curves were tight and there were multiple spots where the tire crossing the precipice of the road's edge would result in tragedy. Steep grades and deep ditches threatened safe travel every step of the way. As dangerous as it was, the beauty of the scenery and the charming ranches along the way made it an intense delight. After a dozen miles of rugged terrain, we turned onto a wide gravel road next to a farmhouse, boasting a modern steel shed on its sprawling lawn. Immediately upon passing the farmhouse the road narrowed and became shrouded with trees and shrubs. The path became bumpy and required a reduction in speed. A few hundred yards and we were at the entrance to Theo's place.

The dogs barked and alerted Theo to a customer arriving. Don pointed to the small dilapidated trailer and asked me to park in front of its glass entryway. The trailer was the reservation tobacco store. Across the sparsely vegetated brown lawn sat another age-weary trailer guarded by two large, rough looking dogs. Theo appeared from within his domicile and headed in our direction.

"Hey, Captain. What's up?" he said as he approached.

"Not much Theo. How are things at the Rez?" Don asked.

Many people would answer with "Not much" or "Same old same old" or something along those lines. Not Theo. He answered the question in full. "The old lady's smoking that shit again. She's been gone for a couple days. She blew her whole check on a couple grams of meth and took off with Lucy. I've told her to stop smoking that garbage. We live in the land of bud and she's out smoking battery acid. I'm about at the end of my ability to put up with her bullshit."

Theo stood about six feet tall with an average build and shoulder length black hair. He strolled toward us wearing a flannel shirt, jeans, and leather sandals.

"Who we got here?" he asked with his hand held high offering a thumb clasped handshake.

"I'm Steve man," I replied grabbing his hand.

Theo pulled me close and wrapped his other hand behind my back and gave me a hug.

"What the hell are you doing with this crazy fuck?" he asked while nodding toward Don. "You know he's trouble right?"

"All evidence points to that conclusion," I said.

"Good answer," he said and turned to speak to Don. "I like this guy."

Theo knew without asking that Don was there to buy cigarettes and pulled the keys out of his pocket to unlock the sliding glass door. We all stepped in, and Theo went to the end of the trailer behind the counter and pulled out a carton of Don's brand.

"One or two?" Theo asked Don.

"Just one."

"Do you need smokes?" Theo asked me.

"Do you have Marlboro Menthols?" I asked.

"No, we only carry native brands. Have you ever tried Senecas?"

"No. I'm pretty brand loyal," I said.

Theo opened a pack of Senecas and handed me a single cigarette. "These are about forty percent of the cost of Marlboros, and they taste really good."

I lit it up, smoked it, and agreed to buy the first two of many cartons to follow.

Theo put his hand up to his lips imitating smoking a joint and said, "I assume you smoke the good stuff too right?"

"Does the Pope shit in the woods?" I replied.

Evidently that was a colloquialism only used back home because Theo looked at me with his head tilted like a dog when you change its food.

"It means hell yes!" I clarified.

"Then you have to join me in the house," he said. "Just walk close to me when we get near the dogs so they know you're with me."

I am a fan of dogs, but those were not the type of dog of which I am a fan. Leary of the canines but excited at the prospect of sharing a smoke with Theo, I accepted the invitation.

Theo opened the door to his trailer and ushered us in. When we passed the threshold of the doorway we had to immediately duck as there were buds hanging from wires strewn throughout his living room. The smell of freshly trimmed weed permeated the small space.

Theo pulled out a tray with some varieties and loaded one of them into a three foot long bong fitted with a single hit bowl and passed it to Don. Don took a long pull, pulled back away from the bong and coughed out a huge plume of smoke. He coughed and gagged for a minute or two.

Theo loaded a refill and handed me the monster bong. I would like to say the result was somewhat different for me but it was not. I coughed and gagged.

"That's my Pineapple Kush," Theo said. "It's a serious chunk of heaven."

Not wanting to contradict his obvious pride in his product, I agreed with him. It wasn't a serious piece of heaven. It was harsh and didn't have the taste of a fruity strain. He loaded another strain, and the process repeated. First Don gagged, then I followed suit. That went on through all five strains he had on his tray. None of them tasted any differently from the first and they were all incredibly harsh.

After beating up our lungs for forty-five minutes, Theo asked which one I liked the best. I told him the Pineapple Kush was the best, not because it was, but because that was the only name I remembered. After the first hit, all I wanted to do was get through with the session. I didn't pay a lot of attention to anything other than the pins and needles stinging my lungs.

Theo asked Don what his favorite one was, and Don agreed with my choice. Theo took a baggie and stuffed several buds of the Kush into it and handed it to me.

"That's for the two of you to share," Theo said. "My treat. Enjoy!"

We thanked him, I put the baggie in my pocket, and we all went back out by the Maxima and enjoyed a cigarette together before Don and I hit the road back to camp.

When we were out of sight of Theo's place, Don let out a half a moan as he chuckled and said, "That weed was fucking awful! I was waiting for you to say uncle on that crap, so I could gracefully stop smoking it."

"I was waiting for you," I said. "I didn't want to insult him, but, damn, that was bad."

We had a good laugh about it on the way back to the grow. We weren't laughing at Theo's poor pot but at ourselves for enduring the torture of smoking it.

When we got back to camp, it was late afternoon. Don fired up the grill to make some spaghetti and I went into the garage to get some trimming done. Lucas had been busy while we were gone and his string of drying bud was almost twice the size of mine.

When the spaghetti was done, I quickly ate and got back to work. When the sun retreated, I strapped the headlamp on and did my best to continue to trim while Lucas took it easy, loaded some trim hash for the two of us and kept me company. I wasn't able to catch up to what Lucas had trimmed that day, but I gave it a shot.

Ten o'clock rolled around, and I was beat. I drank a couple beers under the stars and retreated to my bed. It was an interesting day to say the least, but I was glad to shut my eyes.

Oddly Normal

Over the next several days everything had settled into a bit of a routine. We were up at the crack of dawn with about a seventy percent chance of helicopter flyovers. The weather was cool in the morning and became increasingly warmer throughout the day until the cycle started over when the sun dropped over the mountain. The bats and the screech owl remained a constant reminder that we were visitors to their world. We had several nights where the yipping of coyotes could be heard as they circled the camp with our food as the target. It would continue until King's bark replaced their yips and the camp would go back to silence with the coyotes realizing the prize was unattainable. There was the daily balancing act with the rickety throne and showers taken from the hose from the creek. There was mounting tension building between Lucas and Don as Don continued to talk less than flatteringly about Carl. The trimming continued from early morning into the evening, and the prospects of making the kind of money we had been promised were growing slim.

The wires strung up for drying the bud were getting weighed down and there was need for additional wires if we were going to be able to keep the production line going. Don decided to take on the task of adding more wire one morning while Lucas and I were busy at work. He took one wire and ran it the length of the garage before realizing it was too close to the other lines and had to remove it and adjust its location. After relocating the wire, Don came to the conclusion that the newly strung wire was not taut enough, and, again, had to make adjustments. After attaching one end of the next wire to the back of the garage, Don realized the new wire was too short to attach to the other end, and he decided to affix it to run along the short span, from one side of the garage to the other, rather than from end to end. Don opened another package of wire and added four more wires lengthwise and a few more from side to side.

The entire time Don was laboring with his task, Lucas and I were casting smirks back and forth but stayed in total silence. When the job was done Don looked at what he had finally accomplished, and it was obvious he was proud of what he had done.

"What do you think of that?" Don asked, expecting a pat on the back.

Without skipping a beat Lucas replied. "It was like watching a five-year-old tie his shoe."

I didn't want to laugh, but I couldn't help it. I had not heard a peep out of Lucas for over an hour, and his reply took me by surprise.

Later that day we were visited by Carl, Kathy, and a young couple from Redding. They were all scrunched together in the front of the white pickup with Sadie sitting on Kathy's lap and a large pit-bull and camping gear in the back. The last time Carl was out to the camp, he said he would stop by to pick up all the trimmed bud and take it in to be weighed. Lucas and I were excited for Carl to see how much we had accomplished. They arrived late in the afternoon. It was decided that Don would make extra tacos for supper, so we could all eat together.

The new couple, Derrick and Molly, were acquaintances of Kathy's and were going to set up camp to join us in the trimming effort. The pit-bull in the back of the truck was their dog Tank who would also be joining us. Tank and King squared off, and we were unsure how it was going to go. Would King be territorial, or would they become friends? It was a tense few minutes as they looked each other over, sniffed each other, paced around, and eventually decided to be friendly. Sadie was no longer King's focal point. As a matter of fact, Sadie was all but ignored.

As the dogs went off to do their thing, Kathy gave Derrick and Molly a tour, and Carl joined Lucas and I in the garage to look at the buds we had trimmed.

Lucas and I were proud of what we had bagged up and ready for Carl, but it didn't take long for us to be able to relate to how Don must have felt about his accomplishment earlier that day. Carl's first comment was that he thought there would be more ready for him. That took some of the wind out of our sails. It got worse. Carl started going through the bud and removed many of them and put them in the bag for storing the leaves and scraps for making hash.

"What the hell are you doing?" I asked.

"These buds are too small," Carl said. "I can't pay you for popcorn buds."

"What are popcorn buds?" I asked.

"Anything smaller than the width of your thumbnail is a popcorn bud," he said.

We watched as about twenty percent of what we had spent time painstakingly trimming went into, what equated to the garbage bag. We were stunned. We had purchased many bags of pot from Carl over the years and they did not exclude "Popcorn buds."

After an hour of watching our trimmed buds get dwindled down, Carl loaded the bags into the side compartments of his truck and came back to the garage. He then looked around at all the plants hanging on the wire and removed some of them for being too small. He put them in the bag along with the leaves and the popcorn buds he had removed and threw that in another side compartment.

We watched our hard earned, well-trimmed buds get reduced in weight and there was not much we could do about it. We were already unhappy about the quantity we were promised not being attainable and now, what we did trim, was being diminished.

After coming back from the truck Carl loaded a couple pipes and passed them around. Kathy, Derrick, and Molly had returned from the tour and sat down to join us. Before the bowls turned to ash the tacos were ready, and we all ate until we were full.

After eating we sat around in the garage and talked as Derrick set up the tent for him and Molly. All of a sudden an ungodly pungent odor filled the space. It was as though a sewer main had broken open. Out where we were, there were no sewers, so that awful reek was coming from some other source. It was hitting the gag reflex of everyone in the garage. Kathy was the unfortunate one to discover the source of the olfactory nightmare. Sadie had strolled into the garage, and Kathy bent over to pet her. When she did she felt something wet and thick in Sadie's hair. When she withdrew her hand it was covered in feces. Not dog feces. Sadie had found the pile of our discarded bags from the poop chair and tore through them. She must have rolled around in them as her entire coat was thickly covered in the disgusting mess, and she left behind paw prints on the ground leading into the garage.

I was shocked that not a single taco was given flight, but it took a Herculean effort on everybody's part to keep them down. To say that broke up the smoking circle would be putting it mildly. Immediately, Sadie was introduced to the business end of the watering hose, and Kathy and Carl did their best to clean her off. Once the cleaning was done enough to be tolerated on the way back to town, Carl and Kathy took off.

"That was a shitty visit," I said to Lucas.

It was too close to the truth to elicit a response. Both Lucas and I felt deflated and somewhat defeated. The money making adventure we had been hoping to experience had been running into more issues than we had bargained for. We had been at the site for over a week and we had about five pounds of trimmed buds each, making its way to Redding. That was a far cry from the twelve to fourteen pounds we would have predicted when we arrived. We had been putting in full days and making less than half of what we were promised was the standard.

The camp was a somber place the rest of the evening. Neither I nor Lucas felt much like doing any trimming and after an hour of half-hearted effort, we put the scissors down and stopped for the night. Derrick and Molly spent much of that night getting set up and settled in. After the sun disappeared we all sat around inside the garage and had a quiet smoke before retiring to our tents.

When I slid under my sleeping bag I turned on the lamp next to my cot and grabbed the book my daughter had sent with me. I needed a distraction from the anger I was feeling. After reading through two chapters of *Choke*, I set the book down realizing I didn't even remember what I had just read. I couldn't get to sleep.

I got out of bed and went out to look at the stars to calm myself down. Standing in the middle of the spot in front of the garage were Derrick and Molly.

"What's the matter with Lucas?" Molly asked. "He seemed upset when he went to his tent."

"We both are upset," I told Molly. "We came all the way out here from Minnesota and expected to return with some decent money, and it hasn't worked out that way so far."

"Well it looked like you had about ten pounds going in with Carl," she said. "That's a good chunk"

"Yeah, but that's for two people trimming for over a week."

"That sounds about right. How much were you expecting to make?" Molly asked.

"More than twice that much," I replied.

"Derrick and I trim every year and even when we're on a serious roll we can only expect to trim twelve to fourteen ounces in a day."

"That's not what Carl told us," I said. "He told us we would easily be able to trim a pound and a half to two pounds a day."

"Nobody trims that much in a day," she said.

Derrick jumped into the conversation. "Carl's full of shit. He knows that's not possible. Molly has known him pretty much the whole time he's been out here, and she thinks he's an asshole. She says he treats Kathy like shit and uses people for whatever he can get out of them."

"I've known Carl for years. I can't allow myself to believe that," I said.

I was certainly starting to feel that what Derrick was saying was true, but I was unwilling to admit it to myself. I didn't want to think that I had come all the way out to California, through all the trials and tribulations set before me, just to end up being used by someone I considered a friend. The thought was too abhorrent for me to consider. I was wearing blinders, and I was not ready to pull them off.

We stood out under the stars for almost an hour. Even the deep blanket of stars, that had been such a source of amazement, didn't have the desired effect of calming me. I went back to my tent, crawled under the sleeping bag, and did my best to try and get to sleep.

It was a long restless night.

Upheaval

Having barely shut my eyes and tiring of the struggle to get some sleep, I was up before the sun crested into the valley. It was dark, but I smelled coffee wafting in the air. I got dressed for the day and stepped out to see Derrick and Molly standing by the grill making the first pot of the day. I grabbed my mug, threw in some creamer, and filled it to the brim.

As the sun peeked over the mountains and across the valley, the monochromatic greys turned to a kaleidoscope of burnt orange, yellow and dusty green. We drank our coffee in the warming sunlight and I got the chance to learn a little about my new neighbors.

They had been together for the last three years and met each other while trimming at the house across the street from Carl's place in Redding. They had been transient since becoming a couple. They had moved from place to place following opportunities to make a little money. That is exactly what they made, little money. The tent they had set up in our camp was given to them by a friend who had purchased a new one. For the last several months they didn't have a fixed address. Couches of friends had been their only places of slumber until Ricky, Carl's neighbor, made them aware of the opportunity to trim at Carl's grow. It didn't pay as well as others were paying but it came with a spot to pitch their tent and had the added bonus of free meals. They jumped at the chance.

Molly was Native American and had a sweet disposition that made her instantly likeable. She had little in the way of marketable skills but enjoyed the variety of gigs she was able to land. She was in the process of changing her prospects and going to school. She met Kathy while attending. Derrick was an aspiring cartoonist and though he had submitted his work on several occasions he had yet to be published. Tank was a recent addition to the threesome and seemed quite happy with his new family.

When my cup reached the last cooled swallows, I refilled it and we went to work. A half hour later, Lucas joined the party and we were stringing up bud at a rapid rate. The hanging plants were becoming so populated, they required masking tape attached to the wire, adorned with the name of the trimmer, to keep them organized. It became a competition and every time a new rack of buds was placed on the wire we would take a small piece and pack it in the bowl to send around.

We were all laughing and enjoying each other's company. It was a stark contrast to the mood the previous evening. It was going very smoothly until Derrick said something about how big of a cheapskate Carl was. I ignored the comment and continued to trim, but Lucas did not allow it to go unanswered.

"If you don't want to work for Carl then what are you doing out here?" Lucas asked.

"I didn't say I don't want to work for Carl," Derrick replied. "He just pays quite a bit less than we could be making at Ricky's place."

"Well you decided to take this gig, and I'm sick of everybody always bitching about Carl," Lucas said. "Can we just trim without crapping on the guy who is paying us to be here?"

I was still wearing my blinders and was not really in the mood to hear the constant buzz of criticism. It brought my mood down, and I didn't want to get back in the funk I was in the night before.

As if on cue Don came in the garage and announced that lunch was ready. It could not have been timed better.

While we were enjoying our bratwursts, the weather began to change. Slowly at first. A few clouds and a cool breeze was a welcomed contrast to the heat that had been building all morning. Little did we know, it was an indication of things to come.

We finished lunch and went back to work. I turned on the music on the laptop and we trimmed to the sounds of Tom Waits. Derrick was unfamiliar with Waits, and I told him I would give him a few samples of his body of work. The tent was filled with the sounds of *Fumblin with the Blues, Clap Hands, Pasties and a G-String, Dead and Lovely, Chocolate Jesus, Romeo is Bleeding* and about thirty others that were part of my extensive collection.

In the midst of one of Waits' raspy vocals there was a scream from Molly and the tent broke into chaos. A large black snake had slithered under the edge of the garage and over Molly's open-toed sandals. She jumped up, and the box that was resting on her lap catching the trim became airborne and the tent started raining little green flecks. The snake was about four feet long and looked like it was just as shocked as we were. It slid from Molly's feet over to the table where I was sitting. When it couldn't find a spot to exit the garage in that direction, it seemed to bank off the leg of the table and turn again in Molly's direction. Her olive skin turned pale as she scrambled to get out of its way. She lunged out of the main entrance of our workspace, and the snake followed her out into the open. We watched as the serpent disappeared up the side of the mountain. Molly gave one last scream, and her entire body began to shake in a fluid motion that traveled from her toes to her shoulders and culminated with her hands shaking in front of her. She kicked and shuddered one last time as though the snake was still underfoot.

It was then that the skies decided to open up and dump a year's worth of pent-up rain. The winds instantly picked up. The drought ridden landscape made up for lost time as rivers of water began flooding through the camp. Don's shed, only thirty yards from the garage, almost faded completely from our vision as the sheets of rain hammered over the once dry area between the two structures. The garage shuddered from the velocity of the wind. We were concerned it was going to rip up from its stakes and blow away.

I couldn't remember if I had left the window unzipped on my tent and stepped out into the torrent only to see my tent leaning at a steep angle trying to hold on from the push of the wind. With the tent at that angle I knew it really didn't matter if the window was closed, the top of the tent was built to allow circulation and only had a tarp over the top of a screened covering. The contents were going to be soaked regardless of the window's status.

As quickly as the downpour began it relented. The entire storm lasted less than twenty minutes. We stepped out to survey the damage and with surprisingly few exceptions all remained relatively unscathed. Lucas's tent suffered no ill effects. Derrick and Molly's tent had collapsed but was intact. My tent somehow avoided becoming soaked. One of the rivets where my top tarp attached to the front of the tent had ripped open and left about an eight inch tear. That was the extent of the damage and we were all relieved.

We went back in the tent and all contributed a little trim hash to the communal bowl. We laughed thinking about how the snake probably sensed the impending rain and looked for shelter only to find some local wildlife trimming pot in its selected sanctuary.

The water quickly soaked into the parched ground and the sun broke back through the clouds. It was sunny once again. Lucas, Derrick, and Molly went back to work trimming and I retrieved my tent repair kit and got to work sewing the torn tarp. I was filled with the pride that only over-preparation can bring. My years as a Boy Scout and anal-retentive traveler had paid off.

The rest of the day was pretty routine: Pork chops for supper and weed trimmed or smoked throughout the evening.

That was the way things went for the next few days. Routine. Get up, swill coffee, trim, lunch, trim, supper, trim, sleep repeat.

All was going smoothly, and Derrick had learned to keep quiet about Carl in front of Lucas. Smooth sailing. Don and Lucas' relationship remained tense, but it was at a tolerable level. The whole operation was as smooth as a Guinness flowing into a chilled mug.

If we had been left to our own devices, we would have been fine but that *Kumbaya* feeling ended the day Carl showed up to get another load of completed bud. This time he chose to make the trip by himself and arrived early.

He rolled up on the camp and all but ignored the trimming crew as he went to the garden farthest from my tent and asked Don to join him. They walked around the garden for fifteen minutes while we continued to trim. On previous occasions when Carl came out to the camp he always made a point to immediately ask how we were doing. The lack of a greeting was noteworthy to me and Lucas.

After the garden walk, Don came down to the garage to collect the paper bags of completed trim and brought them over to Carl's truck while Carl went to the other garden. Don seemed agitated, and when he knew we were looking in his direction, he gave an obvious eye roll.

Lucas and I stood up and went toward the garden Carl was in the process of investigating.

"What's going on Carl?" Lucas asked.

"Just checking in on the girls, Duder," Carl answered.

"Is there a problem?" Lucas asked. "Don seems kinda pissed off."

"He'll get over it," Carl said. "I told him he needs to make sure you guys have everything you need at all times, so we can get more production. The last batch was way less than I was expecting, and less than needs to be done, if we're going to finish harvest in time."

Blaming Don for the lack of trimmed bud was his way of not having to directly tell us that we needed to step it up. As a true master manipulator, he knew this would also stop us from voicing any complaints of our own. He was right. In fact, my tact was to defend Don.

"He's been feeding us lunch and supper every day, making coffee in the morning and keeping the Gatorade stocked at all times," I stated. "Other than hearing a few of his war stories, he pretty much stays out of our hair. What was the total weight so far?"

"Don should be out in the garage the whole day," Carl said, while not answering my question about the weight. "He should be cleaning your scissors when they get sticky, so you don't have to. He should be staying in the camp, not running to town with you, Steve. Don told me you two were gone for half a day getting supplies and smokes. He knows I will bring supplies. The only reason he wasted half a day was to get booze."

Again, knowing his audience as he did, he distracted us from asking about the weight. I again felt compelled to defend Don.

"I told Don I needed coffee creamer and smokes. That was my fault," I said.

"Well Duder, it took money out of everybody's pockets. Don knows better. I could have brought you some creamer."

In retrospect, it was very telling that he didn't offer to bring cigs or booze. Carl wanted things done his way and his way only. I didn't understand his moral compunction about getting alcohol or smokes. I didn't bother to argue the point, that if I waited for him to bring me creamer, or anything else for that matter, I would have to wait until the next time he visited, then give him the order and wait until the time after that before I could sweeten my coffee. I was getting angry and eventually asked for the elusive answer about the trim weight once again.

"So what was the total weight? I would like to know where I'm at."

Begrudgingly he replied. "The total was eight pounds six ounces. Lucas had four pounds and eight ounces and you had three pounds and fourteen ounces. I left a few popcorn buds in the bags and rounded up to the nearest ounce."

He actually said it like he was being magnanimous. I felt gut-punched. I know Lucas felt the same way. Neither of us said a word.

"Can you guys go ask Don to come up here?" Carl asked.

We were being dismissed. I didn't think Carl had any more to talk to Don about but he wanted our conversation over. We obliged. I was hot. I knew myself well enough not to stay in the garden and provoke a more violent end to the reply he had given. My choices were to argue my objection and risk him setting me off, or relent and perhaps broach the subject after he talked to Don. It would give me some time to defuse. I chose to remain as calm as I could and send Don to another possible slot at the whipping post.

I went back to the garage.

"Dear leader wants another word with you," I said to Don as I sat back down to work, in an attempt to distract myself.

"What's going on man?" Derrick said.

"Don't ask. I don't want to talk about it right now," I snapped back.

My hands were shaking as I tried to steady them for the task at hand. My thoughts were racing, and it made it difficult to concentrate. The voice in my head wouldn't shut up. How could that possibly have been less than ten pounds? I have been trimming now for two solid weeks and my total weight gives me a take-home weight of less than four ounces. If this continues I will go home with less weed than I owe the benefactors who staked my trip. If I don't come home with what I owe them they are going to be pissed! Sue is going to be pissed! How many more hours in a day can I possibly be expected to trim? Should I pull up stakes and find a farmer who pays better? Should I start trimming for Carl's neighbor Ricky? Should I just point the Maxima toward Minnesota and forget the whole charade?

I needed some alone time to shut off, or at least reduce the volume of the voices. I stood up and announced that I would be right back. I walked over to the garden that Carl and Don were not occupying, unlatched the fence and stepped in. Maybe the girls could calm me down.

I walked to the farthest plant in the garden which also happened to be the biggest plant in the garden. The Ross plant. It was called Ross because it had no tag to identify what strain it actually was. The person who supplied the clone it came from had the last name of Ross. Carl could not remember what strain it was, so he named it Ross. I had not taken my rubber gloves off when I left the garage, and I had an idea that I thought may calm me down. I reached a gloved hand into the cage that surrounded Ross and put a grip on a huge bud. I squeezed it. I squeezed it and moved my fingers around getting deep to the core of that gargantuan bud. I wasn't squeezing it to let off physical tension. I was squeezing it to transfer as much of the trim hash onto my gloves as possible.

It was a verboten action that would draw the ire of any reefer trimming purist. It was my personal little "screw you" to Carl. It had the desired effect. I was beginning to calm down. I stripped the hash infused glove off my hand, turned it inside out to preserve the sticky goo and placed it in my shirt pocket. If one sticky glove calmed me down, I figured two might be just what the doctor ordered. I repeated my trimming offence on another Ross bud. I had to admit my dirty little act of defiance was bringing me immense satisfaction. Carl would loathe the idea that I was squishing his precious bud and that brought me enough joy that the anger began to subside.

I had calmed myself down enough to rejoin the fray. With my two sticky gloves and a reformed disposition, I walked back to the garage and sat down. I had reduced my anger enough to speak with Carl in a calmer frame of mind. That was when I heard the sound that recaptured some of my anger. It was the sound of Carl's truck being started, put into gear and driving away.

No good bye. No chance to talk. Gone!

The voices returned. The chatter was almost deafening. I knew the only cure at my disposal clung to my gloves. I started cleaning them off and got a fair quantity rolled into a ball and stepped out of the garage. I asked Lucas to take a walk with me, and he complied. If I was feeling that way, I had to assume Lucas was as well. I didn't want to share my ill-gotten cure with anybody but Lucas. This was our bandage. We smoked as we walked, and to my surprise Lucas was far less upset than I was.

Lucas has a great way of being able to give benefit to doubt. He is not one to ignore issues; he was just able to see that there might be a way to change things to achieve a more desirous outcome. His thoughts tended to lean more toward solutions rather than hostility. Maybe we could work later into the night. Maybe we could trim some for Ricky to make up the deficit. Maybe we could find a more efficient way to trim in order to increase production. I admired his calm but I was not able to follow suit. My source of calm was bubbling, melting, and emitting smoke from the bowl we shared.

We went back to the job and trimmed with a renewed vigor, trying to outpace our previous trimming attempts. It wasn't working, but we were indeed trying. The truth was, we had been trimming efficiently the whole time. We kept our heads down and produced at a steady rate until it dawned on us that we had trimmed past the time we normally had lunch. We were so involved in doing the job that it didn't dawn on us that we hadn't seen Don at all since Carl left.

I walked over to Don's shed. The door was open but I knocked on the wall to announce my presence.

"Yeah?" Don said.

I poked my head through the door to see Don lying back on his bed staring up at the ceiling with both arms bent and his hands behind his head. I'm sure he was contemplating his whole situation and whether or not it was all worth it. That was a position the voices in my head would have certainly been in agreement with.

"Are you okay, Captain?" I asked.

"No, Chopper, I'm not," he said. "I don't really want to talk about it right now. I suppose you guys are getting hungry."

"Don't worry about lunch. I think there are some left over brats we can reheat."

"No," Don said. "I don't want to catch any shit from Carl claiming that I didn't keep you guys fed. Go back out and keep trimming. I'll be out in a few minutes."

True to his word Don came out and prepared some sandwiches and heated up some soup for lunch. Derrick and Molly stopped working and had their lunch. Lucas and I stayed working and took occasional nibbles. We were intent on squeezing as much trim time into the day as we could manage.

I selected some funk from my playlist. My intent was to trim to the beat and hopefully raise the mood a little. It didn't work. Carl had completely removed any joy from what should have been a joyous labor of love. We trimmed straight through the afternoon and barely broke for supper. We trimmed through the evening and when the sun retreated we donned our headlamps and continued. We encouraged each other to forge on until close to midnight. We were alone and the site was quiet. Derrick and Molly quit working when it got too dark to work by sunlight but stayed in the garage and kept the bowl warm until about ten o'clock when they sauntered off to their tent. Don had disappeared after supper and never reappeared.

When Lucas and I finally gave up for the night, I went into my tent and sat by the table reflecting on the multitude of events that culminated in the situation I found myself in. I was not only feeling trapped, I was feeling shame for having placed so much faith in a man who was now turning out to be profoundly disappointing.

How could I have misread the man so egregiously? How much was I to blame for not having read the warning signs before implementing plans to make the journey? Was it simply greed that brought me here? Was it the hunger for an adventure that caused me to discount all the doubts of others and those I held myself? I started searching in true Lucas-like form for the silver lining. There had to be some value brought forth through all the turmoil and triumph over adversity our undertaking had wrought.

The adventure itself. That was silver lining number one. From meth heads in Sheridan and Moose in Kelly, to bats and the celestial views of the Northern California sky, I had certainly had one hell of an adventure. Not all of them could be considered good but they could all be classified as spectacular. They were not the stuff of a daily grind existence by any means. My mood lightened slightly.

Absence truly did make the heart grow fonder. I was missing my wife terribly. I wasn't sure if I wanted to chock that up as a silver lining, but I was grasping at straws. I already knew how much I loved Sue, but after suffering through a day with such an agonizing mental component, I couldn't think of anything I would have loved more than to see her. As much as missing Sue may not have felt good, the deep realization of how profoundly that love ran had to be scored as silver lining number two.

Lucas. Lucas was silver lining number three. If I had never accepted the proposal of coming out to California, Lucas and I would have remained shoestring acquaintances. In the span of less than a month, he went from being somebody who I barely knew to being what I would consider to be a true brother. We complimented each other well with our differing outlooks and styles. Lucas was a quiet and honorable man who was willing to take on the adventures by my side and seemed to let adversity make him stronger rather than cause him to flinch. His sense of humor was such a deviation from mine that his well-timed and infrequent jokes cracked me up without fail. We had proven to each other at every step along the way that I had his back and he had mine. Of that there was no doubt. I gained a brother. Silver lining number three.

With my mental gymnastics calming to a basic floor routine I finally had a frame of mind suitable to catch some shut eye.

I slept well for the few hours I slept. I woke to the sound of two helicopters hovering low. That was a departure from the norm. Until that morning it was always a single interloper. Now it was a pair. The amount of time they hovered was also an anomaly. On previous occasions they slowly flew by. That morning they loomed directly overhead for several minutes. They were putting in some seriously early hours. The sun was barely shining as they menaced our site.

I emerged from the tent as they were still above the camp. Derrick was standing in the most visible area, between Don's shed and the garage, flipping the helicopters the bird. It was a classless and stupid move if you ask me but I took a "to each his own" attitude toward his salute. I didn't feel that they were going to land and arrest him for showing his disdain. I think they already knew all the growers in the area had the same feeling as Derrick.

I made my way to the coffee pot as the choppers made their way over the mountain. Don was standing by the grill slowly shaking his head at Derrick for his juvenile antics.

"You know it's not a great idea to poke the bear, right?" he said to Derrick as he was approaching the grill.

"I'm sick of those fuckers," Derrick replied. "We're just trying to make a few bucks. They should just leave us alone."

"Do you think flipping them off will stop them from making future visits?" asked Don.

There was no good answer, and Derrick didn't offer a reply.

Don had obviously worked through the demons that had possessed him the day before. His mood had changed. It wasn't a great mood but a far cry from the morose state he had been in.

We all went into the garage and to no one's surprise, there sat Lucas already trimming away. We made it through the whole morning and almost to lunchtime without anybody touching on the subject of Carl's visit the day before. It seemed like it was the third rail. Nobody wanted to touch it for fear it would spark something catastrophic.

It couldn't last forever. Derrick touched the rail.

"So how much did Carl say you earned?"

I answered that it was a total of eight pounds six ounces.

"Bullshit!" Derrick said. "That was easily ten pounds worth."

"It's none of your God-Damned business!" Lucas shot back. "Worry about your own weight not ours!"

"Carl is screwing you guys," Derrick continued. "I wouldn't put up with that. He better not try to screw me like that."

"Shut the hell up," said Lucas. "I don't want to hear it."

Derrick wouldn't relent. He didn't direct his comments at Lucas or me anymore. He just grumbled under his breath about how it better not happen to him. The random comments served to heighten the tension. I could see Lucas's blood was starting to go from a simmer to a boil.

Don decided to step out of the garage. I think he wanted to say something but didn't want to make himself go back to the dark place he inhabited the day before. Additionally, he didn't want to cause Lucas to boil over. I felt similarly. I stepped out and joined Don by the grill.

"I'm going to start lunch a little early. I think everybody could use a break."

"I agree," I said.

Derrick and Molly vacated the garage and left Lucas to his trimming. They joined us by the grill, and Derrick decided touching the rail wasn't good enough. He doused himself in water and grabbed on.

"Carl is planning to fuck us all. I'm not just going to trim and let him get away without paying me what I'm due."

Don couldn't hold back any longer. "You think you're getting screwed? I have been out here all summer! Every pound is part of my pay! If any one of you gets screwed, that means I'm getting screwed!"

The conversation got uglier and uglier. I refrained from saying much because I knew Lucas could hear the whole thing. I agreed with much of what was being said, but I didn't feel the need to ramp anything up. It went from ugly, to loud and ugly. I was expecting to have Lucas come out and perhaps even throw down with Derrick. I wouldn't have blamed him. Lucas had already told Derrick he didn't want to hear any more of it, and now it was being amplified. Derrick knew there could be no doubt that Lucas was hearing every word.

Of all the scenarios I had imagined could happen, I was surprised at the one that did.

"Screw you guys!" Lucas said as he appeared with a few of his belongings which he had just grabbed from his tent. "I'm outta here!"

With that Lucas began walking down the hill. I was dumbstruck. Was he really leaving? At first I didn't think it would continue. I watched as he crossed the creek and started climbing up the other side. King had followed him and was walking by Lucas's side. He can't be serious. I should have known better. In the short time I had gotten to know Lucas, backing down had not seemed to be in his nature.

Don commented that he would be back. I told Don I would be surprised if he did. I was shocked, but I figured if Lucas returned, it wouldn't be anytime soon.

"He better come back," Don said. "He's got King with him!"

We all waited to see if he would return. Derrick made an off handed comment about Lucas, and I set him straight that it was now me that didn't want to hear it!

About forty-five minutes went by with no indication that Lucas was going to return. Don decided at that point he needed to go attempt to retrieve King. He jumped on the dirt bike and made his way up the hill and through the gate. Thirty minutes later Don and King returned but there was no sign of Lucas.

"He's not coming back," Don said. "He's pissed!"

I learned later that Lucas made his way to the road outside the reserve. He hitchhiked into Ono with the intent of calling Carl to come get him when he had cell service. Those plans didn't work out as he had hoped. He dropped his cell phone, and it was run over by the people who pulled over to pick him up. When he was dropped off in Ono, he called Carl from a payphone and was picked up later that day.

In the space of one morning everything changed for me. Not for the better. The man I considered a brother was gone. As I feared, Lucas did not return to trim for the duration of our stay in California.

Indentured Servant

With Lucas's departure came a sinking feeling that the long days made better by our friendship would become unbearable. I knew the stresses of the whole adventure weighed on Lucas, but I had no clue it would culminate in his leaving the site. I was angry about the fact that I had evidently not entered into his considerations prior to making that monumental move. I was angry at myself for being so immobile from the shock of his leaving that it never entered my mind to jump in the Maxima and take pursuit. If I couldn't have convinced him to return, I could have at least given him a ride to Carl's place.

I had no idea what was going to happen with Lucas. Would he go back to Minnesota and chock the episode up as a learning experience and not much else? Would he find a place to stay in the area temporarily and still continue to trim? Would I see him for the remaining weeks of the trimming yet to be done?

My questions were answered the next day. Late in the morning the familiar barks of King and Tank alerted us to the approach of Carl's truck. As the truck drew near the site, I could see Lucas was with him. I was hoping that he had reconsidered, and we could continue on the journey we had started in the same manner, together. That was not to be.

Carl parked and Lucas walked up to his tent. I followed.

"What's going on, man?" I asked him.

"I'm going to be staying at Carl's from now on," he replied. "Sorry I took off like that, but I wasn't going to listen to any more of their bitching."

"You threw me for a loop," I said. "I was more than a little shocked, and I half expected you to turn around. I should have come after you or given you a ride."

"Don't worry about it, man," he said.

That's when I was told about his misadventures on his trip to Redding the day before. As he talked, he began loading most of the contents from his tent into the truck.

"What are you going to do about trimming?" I asked.

"Carl brought a large cooler out here. We're going to fill it with bud to bring back to the house to trim."

Sure enough, Carl was already clipping buds from the garden and placing them in the cooler. Lucas and I walked over to join him. We talked about the new arrangement, and I was told I could come into town on occasion and bring some buds with to trim. The invite from Carl seemed more of a conciliatory patch rather than a sincere invite. I could feel a change in the way he was speaking to me. Our relationship had soured since I arrived in California. The line between us being friends and us merely being a means to each other's ends was being indelibly drawn.

The blinders had come off.

The visit angered me. The way Carl spoke to me. The pomposity reflected in his general manner offended me. He was no longer the guru or connoisseur I had once admired. I had ignored those feelings as much as I could for the last weeks. I made excuses for his cheap, self-serving tactics at every opportunity. The feeling I had been developing about him since arriving no longer needed to be kept at bay. It was a strain for me not to let loose in a fit of rage and tell him how I felt. I had to stay cool. He was after all the means to an end.

"So what was the weight of the last batch?" I asked Carl.

"Two pounds ten ounces," he replied.

I didn't respond. I was convinced that there had been at least three and a quarter pounds of my labor accompanying him on the last trip. Without saying a single word I turned and walked to my tent. I stepped in, pulled up the chair next to my table and stared into space.

He had me. I was a captive of the situation I had voluntarily entered. I had invested my time, other people's money, and more than a modicum of preparation into the venture. In order for me to get to the basement level of expectations, I needed to return home with a minimum of three pounds. I was two and a half weeks into the nightmare and had earned about seven ounces. There was enough product in the field to get me to my goal, but it was obvious it would not be completed within the four weeks we had been assured would be the limit of our stay.

I had been lied to. I had been manipulated. I had been conned.

In the midst of my anger and the numbing contemplation of my situation, Carl stepped in front of the doorway of my tent.

"Why don't you join us in the garage for a little smoke before we leave, Duder?"

I couldn't believe my ears. I knew he was aware of my level of anger, but he felt safe asking me to join him. He knew he had me. Calling me Duder on previous occasions was bad enough. At that point it just felt dirty and disrespectful. It took every ounce of restraint for me to leave the machete in its sleeve. Never in my life had I considered homicide as an option. For the first time, I not only considered the option, I briefly contemplated it.

Hard rocky ground in the remote mountains of rural California could hide a lot of transgressions. In my past I had several occasions where physical violence erupted after other alternatives had been exhausted. I had never been one to use violence as a first response but I never backed away from it when other options were unavailable. I knew if I lashed out at Carl, it would end badly. Lucas was still wearing the blinders, so he would not be a cheerleader for Carl to receive a beating. All of us needed the income associated with the grow, and Carl was the only one with the distribution connections.

In the split second between him calling me "Duder" and my response, I had a whirlwind of thoughts. I was mired in hostility and facing narrowing options. It left me with the gut-wrenching realization that I was left with a clear choice that made me nauseated. I either had to end him or swallow a big bowl of shit by joining him for a smoke. I was in too deep.

Event horizon. Point of no return.

It took all my strength and a large dose of humility to reply "I'll be out in a minute."

Joining him for a smoke was offensive to me at a deeply personal level. I always considered a shared smoke to be something that was enjoyed between friends. Lucas was still the brother I knew, and I was glad to share a bowl with him. Don was growing on me, and I was glad to share one with him. Derrick had his issues, but I was glad to partake with him. Molly was sweet, and it was an easy call to share a bowl with her. Sharing one with Carl was not just unappealing but utterly abhorrent. He was a man who was once one of the people I most wanted to smoke with. That had changed. He was taking all the pleasure out of the experience and replacing it with a deep-seated, profound hatred.

I stepped into the garage and stood opposite Carl so I wouldn't have to pass or receive the pipe from him. Carl took the bowl and handed it to me. His etiquette felt like an affront. I took it in hand and Bogarted two hits in a row before passing the pipe to Derrick. Bogarting (taking more than one hit before passing it) is bad etiquette. Carl cast me a knowing glance as the bowl was passed around. When it made it back to me for the second time I rudely took two more hits and passed it to Derrick. On the third round I once again took the opportunity to Bogart the final two hits that remained. It was a pretty innocuous move on my part, but it gave me a small semblance of satisfaction.

Carl made conversation as though it was just another day in Shangri-La. I could not trust myself. I took the only option I could think of and walked out of the garage and once again took refuge with the girls. I walked amongst them and took an inventory. We still had a variety of strains left to trim. Sour Diesel, Purple Train Wreck, Purple Kush, Headband, the big Ross plant and Cinderella 99 were all waiting for their turn. Half of the available Purple Train Wreck was gone. It was sitting in the cooler about to be driven to Redding.

Lucas walked into the garden where I was standing. For the first time since leaving home our conversation felt awkward. I honestly had no real anger lingering toward Lucas and still thought of him as a brother, but the circumstances made things feel a bit off.

"We're taking off," he said. "I'm sorry things worked out this way. I couldn't take any more of Derrick and Don. You should really come in and trim some at Carl's sometime soon."

"Yeah, I will," I said.

"By the way, I met Carl's neighbor Ricky. He said he has plenty to trim," Lucas offered. "He pays an ounce and a half per pound. Maybe we could trim over at his place some night."

"I'll plan on it," I said.

"Good luck out here man," he said. "See you soon."

"Thanks, and good luck to you too."

With that Lucas joined Carl in the truck. They wound their way up to the gate and out of the camp.

I decided I was not ready to engage with the others quite yet and opted instead to go for a walk. I needed to blow off some steam, expend some pent up energy and rage, and center myself. I needed time alone to contemplate how I could salvage this shipwreck. Not having Lucas with me was tragic but not remotely the biggest problem I was confronting. I had to make the financial shortfall a priority. I simply could not allow myself to return to Minnesota without enough resources to cover my expenses and a bit of the almighty dollar left over to compensate me for the effort.

I walked over to my tent, grabbed the machete and told Don I was going to go for a walk to clear my head. Don did not know what Carl reported to me as the weight from the last batch, and I didn't want to divulge that quite yet. Don informed me that lunch would be ready a little late today, so I had about an hour before I needed to be back. I thanked him and started walking down toward the creek.

As I started my walk I heard Derrick calling after me.

"Hey, Steve!" he said.

I turned around to see Don running interference for me. He stepped over to Derrick, put his hand on Derrick's chest and shook his head.

My intention was to go to the creek, but I never made it that far. When I was almost to the bottom of our mountain I saw a clearing off to my left that I had never noticed until that moment. I walked in that direction and both dogs caught up to me and decided to keep me company. Their presence was welcomed.

Sometimes when the voices in my head got riled up, they tended to trample over each other and stop any clear thoughts from emerging. I took advantage of the dog's attendance and bounced my ideas their way.

"Well guys," I said to the canine duo, "I have really landed in a tough spot. I don't know what to do. I can't leave empty handed, and I can't make enough to walk away with any profit. At least I can't do it working for Carl."

I swear the dogs understood. They were intent on listening to what I had to say. They would walk in front of me or fall behind but they always had their eyes darting in my direction as if to say "Go, ahead. We're listening."

So I continued. "Carl is not the man I thought he was. Cheap, petty, and now I can add vindictive to the list. I know he intentionally lorded his position and my predicament over me. Derrick had told me that Molly said he was an asshole. I think that was a serious understatement!"

Tank barked in agreement.

"So what do I do now?" I said as if in response to Tank's bark. "I can trim for Ricky, but that can't make enough of a difference to help me in the time I have left. Speaking of the time I have left, I don't have enough money to stay for the duration of the harvest, not if I still want to have enough travel money to get home. I can't think of one legitimate idea that could save this fiasco from hobbling me financially."

Both dogs barked. I know they didn't truly understand and I was not losing my faculties but they timed the barks perfectly. It made me ponder the words I had just uttered. Actually one word in particular. Legitimate.

It dawned on me in that moment that I was not going to be able to make anything work if I restrained my thoughts inside the boundary of what I would consider legitimate. I had to pull a Belichick. I had to do whatever it took to win. I had to cheat. A plan was formulating, and I would put it in motion that night.

I thanked the boys and turned back toward the camp. Don was firing up the grill.

"Welcome back, Chopper. Do you want a burger, a brat, or both?" Don asked.

"Two burgers and a brat," I replied.

"Well, I guess you cleared your head enough to eat something."

"Yeah, I'm feeling a little better."

I went into the garage and put scissors to bud while waiting for lunch. I was not in a great mood, but I had managed to come up with a plan to solve, or at least mitigate, one of my problems.

Lunch was finished cooking, and Don called us out to grab a plate. I fixed my brat with some ketchup and mustard and put the hamburger patties next to it. I walked over toward the garden and called Tank and King over. I thanked them properly for giving me council earlier. A burger each seemed nominal, but they appreciated the reward.

I went back to the garage, turned on some tunes, and got back to work. Derrick and Molly knew I had been upset earlier, but didn't ask for any details. Don came in after putting the lunch supplies away and sat down. We took a break from trimming, loaded a bowl, and passed it around. Don was the first to ask.

"What happened earlier to make you need to clear your head?"

"Carl happened," I said. "This concerns you, too. I asked him how much the last weight was, and he said I had only trimmed two pounds, ten ounces."

"You have GOT to be kidding me," Don replied. "That was between three and three and a half pounds!"

"I wish I was kidding, but I'm dead serious."

That's when the serious bitching session began, without the constraints of having Lucas in earshot. It was almost as if it was a competition.

Derrick started it off with the simple fact that Carl paid less than anyone else.

Molly brought it to the next level by talking about how shitty Carl treated Kathy and how cheap he was.

I trumped that with my tale of woe. I explained how he lied to me about how many trimmers there would be. I told them how he lied about how much money could be made. I pointed out that I had arranged to get money for the trip by promising weed when I returned. Weed I had no way of trimming. I also explained how I wouldn't have money for the return trip because I was lied to in regards to how long I would need to stay.

Don won the competition hands down. He let loose a torrent of foul language and even fouler stories. The day Lucas left the camp it was in part because Don became so vocal about Carl. What I didn't realize then? Don was holding back. Not today!

Carl had asked Don to come out and work the site with the promise of all expenses being covered. Don was broke, and Carl knew it. He told Don he would cover all meals and give him fifty dollars a week to cover other expenses. He told Don he was going to get a self-contained R.V. to park at the site. He said he would run supplies out to Don twice per week to make sure he had enough ice and drinking water. He promised Don that they would split all the profits from the grow. He made other assurances too numerous for me to remember.

Don agreed to everything, sold most of his possessions, and put his notice in to leave his apartment. Upon his arrival everything changed.

The fifty dollars a week became twenty-five. It was enough money for Don to get cigarettes but not enough to buy beer.

There was no R.V. at the site. Instead, Don was expected to help Carl build a shed. In the construction of the shed, the living quarters took a backseat to the need for storage. Don's comfort was not Carl's priority or even really a concern at all.

The two supply drops per week continued until Don was set up and the girls were in their cages. After that the supplies arrived a week apart and sometimes stretched beyond that. Don told us of times that ice had run out and food had spoiled. He was reduced to dry goods and the need to ration water and cigarettes. When Carl would come out after a long period between drops, he would have excuses and say it wouldn't happen again. It did. It happened over and over again.

After about two months of late drops, 100 degree nights in the shed, and being alone with nobody but King to keep him company, Don was getting frustrated. The frustration went into overdrive when Carl came out for a drop and told Don he would no longer bring cigarettes out for him. Don was told if he wanted cigarettes he would have to get them himself. Needless to say, Don didn't have transportation other than the dirt bike. For the rest of the summer he either had to risk being ticketed for driving a bike that wasn't street legal or hitchhike into Theo's place thirty miles away.

Carl conveniently forgot his promise to Don that they would split all the proceeds from the grow. The day that I visited Don in his shed to find out why he was so upset and he didn't want to talk about it, was the day he had received the new deal from Carl. Carl decided that Don would only get a split from the actual trimmed buds. They would not be splitting anything that came from the excess trim. No hash, no butter and no tincture profits would be part of the agreement.

Last, but by no means least, every time Carl came back with the report of the total weight, it was far less than the estimated total when it departed. Every popcorn bud that was removed from our trim was placed in the bag for making butter, hash and tincture. That was product that would no longer profit Don.

The more we talked, the less we trimmed, but it was a needed release. Derrick and Molly had little to say, but Don and I kept the narrative lively and continuous.

It was cathartic, but the trimming needed to get done. Don went up to the garden to water the girls, and we got back to work. We kept at it until Don had supper ready.

A good meal of barbequed chicken, baked (technically grilled) potatoes, and corn-on-the-cob was had by all. Don cleared everything away once the last piece of chicken disappeared and asked me a question I wish I had said no to.

"Chopper, you still have those beers in your cooler?"

"I sure do. I'll go grab 'em."

I went into my tent and grabbed the cooler. There were several kinds of beer and three bottles of wine in the chest, and I also grabbed the scotch. I had thought about having a couple belts of scotch to smooth out the day, but once Don inquired about the beer, I decided to open the flood gates. The sun was beginning to fade, and I wanted to say good bye to it, and the misery of the day which accompanied it. I was going to get drunk. Maybe I would be the only one to go to that level, but I didn't care. They could join me or watch me.

Molly wanted to have some wine, so I started there. I poured her a glass. I didn't bother pouring myself any. I started swigging directly from the bottle. Don and Derrick opened some Negra Modelo beer. We all had the same goal. None of the first drinks went down slowly. Once again the members of the garage social club seemed to be involved in a competition. This time we were not competing to see who hated Carl more; we were competing to see who could forget him first.

By the time Don finished his first beer, I had drained the first bottle of wine, opened the second, poured a glass for Molly and was halfway on my way to polishing off bottle number two. Before Don got to the end of his second beer, I was done with wine and switched to a Negra Modelo myself. I asked if anyone wanted a cigar. Derrick and Don both said yes. I went to my tent, removed my portable humidor and brought it into the makeshift California night club. They each picked one of the varieties of cigars I had available. They were allowed to choose anything I had except the Maduro's. They both chose an Acid. I cut off the ends for them and they puffed them to life. I had reserved three nice Maduro's for myself for just such occasions. I got one prepared and joined in. I took a pull off my scotch and followed it with a big draw from the heady Maduro.

As the drinking continued, the mood changed. Derrick became a bit silly. Molly got quiet. I got a bit louder. Don became an asshole and a bit crazy just like Carl had warned. Don started looking for ways to argue. It didn't matter the subject, Don was both an authority and the voice of opposition. He began slowly at first. He didn't like what Molly was wearing. It made her look fat. It made her look like a man. It wasn't ladylike. The more he drank the worse it got.

"Why are you such a fucking loser?" Don asked Derrick. "Living on the side of this mountain with your girlfriend is something a loser does."

Derrick tried to ignore the comment, but Don repeated it. Louder.

That was when Molly decided it was time to leave. She told Derrick she would be in the tent. As she was leaving, Don made a comment about her having a fat ass. She ignored him, and to my surprise Derrick said nothing.

Then Don made a mistake. He turned toward me and asked why I was such a loser.

I was a happy drunk most times. When Don tried to interrupt my happiness, I became something else entirely.

I got in Don's face and squared off in a stance that meant one thing. His next words would determine if I would back away, or provoke me into doing something he didn't want. I volleyed his question back at him.

"Why are YOU such a fucking loser?" I asked. "Hell, the three of us are here for only a few weeks. You've been here all summer working for Carl!"

No response. I repeated it. Louder!

Don was not sure what to do. He knew I was not in the mood for his shit. He was unsure just how far I was willing to go to shut him up. I wasn't sure either.

When Don finished his beer he reached for another, and I stopped him.

"I think we've all had enough for one night," I said. "The rest can be for another time."

He staggered a bit and backed away from the cooler. I closed the lid and brought it back to the tent. When I came back out, Derrick was in the garage alone. Don had retired to his shed.

Derrick and I loaded a small bowl, and we smoked it under the stars. When it was done Derrick walked up to join Molly in the tent. I stayed in the garage. I was drunk but not drunk enough to forget that I had a plan to try to make things right. They were plans that nobody else could know about. Well, King and Tank knew.

It was time to get to work.

Paradigm Shift

My thoughts upon awakening were a bit blurry. The scotch, wine, and beer had worked the magic of temporarily allowing me to erase my angst from the day before, but now brought on the curse of numb thoughts accompanied by acid reflux and a headache. The whirling chopper blades from the low flying alarm clock added to my misery.

As with most days following a good tear, I was in recall mode. What happened last night? Did I square off with Don? Yes I did. Had the warning of Don's drinking persona actually been the solitary truthful utterance from Carl thus far? Yes it was. Did I make the first steps toward righting the ship of my financial foundering? Indeed I had.

I slipped slowly out from beneath my sleeping bag, and got dressed for the day. It was cool enough that the flannel was now hidden by my sweat jacket. Before leaving my tent, I wanted to make sure my plans were in motion, and not a piece of false memory. I reached into the bag reserved for my dirty clothes, and retrieved a hefty bag with a rubber band around it. It assured me there was no false memory. I actually did it. I had transformed my plans from concept to reality. King and Tank would be proud.

I walked out into the sunlight, and made a b-line to the coffee. All three of my fellow camp mates were standing by the grill waiting for the java to be ready for consumption. My alarm was theirs as well. Everybody was slow but cordial. It was like the blade of Don's wrath last night had remained sheathed. No animosity, no resentments, no harsh recriminations, just impatient anticipation for the first cup of the day.

"How did you sleep, Chopper?" Don asked.

"I slept well, I think," I replied. "I didn't wake up so well."

"I don't think anyone woke up bright-eyed and bushy-tailed this morning," He said. "I saw you were putting in some late hours last night."

Oh shit. Did Don see me last night after I had assumed he was dead to the world? What did he see? I was rattled, but didn't want to assume anything.

"How did you know I put in overtime last night? I thought you were in a coma."

"I stepped out to take a leak, and saw your head lamp shining. You might want to recheck the buds you trimmed. As messed up as you were I doubt you trimmed them very well."

"I'll do that. Thanks." I said.

When the coffee was done the mugs were filled, and another pot was made ready for round two.

The day went much as all the others. It was back to business after recovering from our drunken respite. Don informed me that he was down to his last two packs of cigarettes, and asked if I would mind giving him a ride to Theo's later that day or early the next morning. It was perfect timing. The plan I had discussed with King and Tank had three parts. Theo was an integral part of that plan. I needed to have a conversation with him, but that conversation needed to be private. I thought perhaps I could get some space between Don and Theo to broach the subject. If not I would try to at least get some clarification on something Theo had said the day of our first encounter.

"Yeah, I can plan to drive us over this afternoon," I said. "as long as we have a ready-made excuse to leave before he introduces us to more of his samples!"

"I swear if he brings out the bong, I'm going to feign a heart attack."

"Agreed," I said. "I'm going to hold you to that."

I went back to work with a list of blues tunes pouring out of the laptop. Derrick and I started to bond a bit. He had a juvenile sense of humor, and was no replacement for Lucas, but that was an unfair bar for me to expect him to clear. Most of my jokes landed with a thud. Derrick was not the sharpest tool in the shed. I missed the chemistry Lucas and I shared, but I made due with what was at hand. Occasionally, Derrick would miss the joke, but Molly would give a quiet chuckle. At least I was not completely without an audience.

We had a simple lunch of cold sandwiches and chips. Don didn't want to have a mess to clean up, as he was anxious to get to Theo's. When the last of the fixings were put away, Don asked if we could go. Truth be told, I too was anxious to visit Theo, so I agreed.

I apologized to Derrick and Molly for leaving them in silence, but the laptop was getting low on its charge. I thought I would kill two birds with one stone, and charge it while making the trip to Theo's. I plugged it into the cigarette lighter, and Don and I left the camp.

After navigating the treacherous route, we arrived at Theo's. Theo wasn't there. There was a handwritten note attached with tape to the sliding glass door that said he would be back at 12:45. It was 1:30. We decided to wait while we listened to Theo's dogs bark themselves hoarse with disapproval.

As long as we were just waiting, I thought I would confront Don about his behavior from the night before. I had barely started broaching the subject when he cut me off.

"A six pack is my limit," he said. "Once I hit number seven, something happens, and I can be a total jerk. Molly didn't seem real happy with me this morning when we first saw each other.

She didn't say anything, but I assume I said something I shouldn't have."

"You don't remember?"

"No," he said with obvious remorse in his voice. "I'm sure it wasn't good."

"It wasn't," I said. "You said she had a fat ass. You said her clothes made her look like a man. You also called Derrick a loser."

"That explains it," he acknowledged. "But he is kind of a loser."

It was a halfhearted attempt to make a joke. I laughed. I was fine with letting him off the hook...but not completely.

"You called me a loser too."

"Oh shit Chopper, I'm sorry."

"It's okay," I said. "I put it right back in your face. Next time, six is the cut off."

"That's fair."

We talked a little longer, but finally decided we couldn't waste the whole afternoon waiting. We jumped in the Maxima, fired it up, and as we were backing up to leave, Theo pulled in the driveway. It was 2:30.

He pulled up next to the office trailer, stepped out of his car, and popped open the trunk. He pulled out a large green bag, and stepped over to unlock the glass door.

"Sorry I'm late, guys. I hope you weren't waiting long."

"We've been here for a bit," Don said looking at the spot a watch would be if he had one. "That's okay, it gave me and Chopper some time to shoot-the-shit."

Theo slid the door open and motioned us inside. He walked the short distance to the counter and dropped the bag on it. It landed with a dull thud.

"You gotta check this out," he said as he unzipped the bag.

We didn't need to look to know what it was. The fragrance emitting from the bag was divine and denoted potency. The instant the contents were unencumbered, it overtook all odors that previously existed in the tiny room. Even the smell of stale cigarettes had vanished.

"Twelve pounds of killer herb!" Theo announced. "That's four pounds of Blue Cheese, four pounds of Afghan Kush, and four pounds of AK-47 on consignment. Are you ready to sample it with me?"

Don did not feign a heart attack. Theo had just answered one of the questions I had for him, in the best way possible. He had said on the last visit that he took pot on consignment from several local growers. I didn't need to get him alone to ask him my questions. He opened up the floor to allow me to ask my questions without Don having any idea why I was asking them. It appeared that I was simply curious.

"So, how much does a pound of something like that go for out here?" I asked.

"It depends."

"On what?"

"How many pounds are purchased, and who I'm selling it to," he replied.

"What do you mean?" I asked.

"If I was selling to a tourist (people who are not in the business), I get $1,500 to $1,900 per pound. If they buy multiple pounds, I'll knock it down a little. If I'm selling to a brother, I'd let it go for $1,400 per pound. If they want three or more pounds, I could bring it down to $1,300. For Chopper or Captain, it would be $1,200."

Bullseye! He just gave me the answer to the question I most needed answered. The only other question I had would be kept to myself until I had his ear, and Don was not around.

Theo brought out a water pipe from the back room, and asked which strain I wanted to try first. It was a toss-up between the

AK-47 and the Blue Cheese. I deferred to Don. He chose the cheese.

We smoked for a good hour, and Theo sent us home with our tobacco supplies, and a small sample of each reefer strain to share with the other trimmers. When I got in the Maxima, I had to put serious thought into every move. Normally smoking was not a big hindrance to my road performance. That trip was a different story. Both Don and I were peering through the slits that used to function as eyelids. We were seriously stoned, and I had to take extra care on the drive back.

We made it back to the site just in time for Don to start supper. It wasn't a shock that the chili Don made that night was extra tasty. Anything would have tasted great that night.

After supper it was back to trimming. We shared our samples with Derrick and Molly, and we all worked with very little conversation.

When the sun went down the temperature dropped quickly. The sweat jacket I had removed before lunch was back on. That wasn't enough. I added a sweatshirt underneath. It was just enough to break the chill. With my headlamp in place, I continued to trim. Derrick strapped on a headlamp as well. Normally when the sun stopped shining, Derrick stopped trimming. I wanted him to go to his tent so I could implement my plan. He seemed determined to stay with me until I was done. I couldn't let that happen. It became a cold marathon. The rubber gloves gave no protection against the cold, and it made the trimming difficult.

I was determined to outlast Derrick, but he kept trimming. It was after 11 o'clock, when he finally said it was too cold, and decided to call it a night. I continued to trim for another 20 minutes, until I was pretty sure nobody was awake.

I opened the paper bag where all the bud I had trimmed that day was sitting in wait for the trip into town with Carl. I remembered the bud I was looking for, and after searching for a few moments, I found it. It was a large, thick, heavy bud of the Purple Train Wreck. I slipped it into my jacket pocket, turned off the headlamp and went to my tent.

I went into my dirty clothes bag, and removed the hefty sack adorned with the rubber band. I removed the band, and unrolled the bag. I removed the Ziploc bag within, and pulled the bud out of my pocket. Soon my well-selected bud was in the bag with the Purple Train Wreck bud I had put there the night before.

It went against every fiber of my being to be reduced to stealing bud to make up my shortfall. I was doing something I didn't know I was capable of. I hated doing it, but when I considered who it was I was stealing from my pangs of guilt lessened.

Carl forced me to shift the paradigm from legitimate, to the realm of necessary evil. My conscience wasn't clean, but I would sleep just fine...if it wasn't for the cold.

Game On

Doubled socks, doubled sweatpants, a t-shirt and a sweatshirt allowed me to sleep comfortably for the night. I awoke refreshed and had a feeling I had been missing over the previous weeks. I felt confident. I was not completely sure my plan would work but I did have confidence that if I was able to pull it off I could be made whole again.

Step one was underway. If I slowly accrued enough stolen green booty I could return home without suffering the consequences of Carl's deceptions. I couldn't take a large quantity and expect that Carl wouldn't notice. A sizeable bud removed from my trimmings each night would not present any red flags. I would need to pick up more Ziploc baggies so I could label the strains as they were being compiled. I would also need to find a secondary stash spot to store the stolen bud when my dirty clothes were not a deterrent from investigation. When I laundered my clothes I couldn't bring the bud with me and I couldn't leave it in the open. I would need an alternative location that would be immune to any curious eyes. I didn't expect that anyone would be looking but I couldn't take the risk if my assumptions were wrong.

Step two was looking hopeful. With Theo assuring me that I would have a workable price on his consigned inventory, I had the chance to make my meager profits grow. I had more questions for Theo but the initial information I had received was a step in the right direction. Step two was a long range plan that would involve considerable risk. It would hinge on me gaining enough profit through the other phases of the plan and my legitimately earned compensation. Every $1,200 I accumulated could be used to purchase a pound from Theo. If I could earn enough to return to California, purchase five or six pounds, and bring them back to Minnesota to sell, I would make well over twelve grand. That would be less than what I was originally promised, but far more than the pittance I was making.

If any step of the plan faltered, I would be back to the distasteful prospect of admitting that Carl had beaten me. That couldn't happen. I couldn't allow it.

Step three would be the most difficult. It would require subtlety, cunning, a fair amount of guts, a heaping portion of false humility, and the skills of an accomplished thespian. I would need to con the con man. Steps one and two would be stopped in their tracks if Carl sniffed them out.

I had to lead Carl to a place where he saw me as someone who had learned his lesson and was ready to be a team player. Team Carl. I needed Carl to think I had a change of heart. I needed him to trust me to be the one who would have his back. At least until I found a good spot to thrust the dagger in. In other words, I had to be just like Carl. The thought both nauseated and excited me. I was excited to take on the role. It would be the role of a lifetime. If I pulled it off, I would get the award. I could not afford to tank at the box office.

In a way Carl's own mistrust would make him vulnerable to my objective. Carl didn't like Don and was more than happy to see him suffer. Carl didn't care about Derrick or Molly and, other than added trimming help, they didn't really factor into any of his long term plans. He wouldn't allow himself to trust them.

If I could convince Carl that I sincerely wanted to be back in his good graces, I could gain his trust. I needed to be so trusted that he would cheer for my success or at least help finance getting me home. But how? What would convince him that I had his best interests at heart without damaging the others at the camp?

The answer? I needed to create a question with no clear answer. I had to set it up so Carl would have some suspicion, but make sure I left ample room for doubt. The idea came to me out of the blue. An unmarked bag.

The idea was simple. When Carl came to retrieve the next batch of trimmed bud I would pull him aside and give him an extra grocery bag with just a few trimmed buds inside. I would tell him I found it tucked behind the cooler. With Carl's suspicious nature I knew he would assume that somebody was doing what I had in fact been doing. He would think somebody was putting together a collection of bud to keep for themselves.

There was beauty in the plan. The recovered bag could have been a bag that had been started, lost and forgotten. I would be sure to make it clear that it wasn't hidden, just out of view. That would achieve two things. First it would give Carl the feeling that he needed to have somebody in the camp keeping a watchful eye out for any thievery. Secondly, by bringing the rogue bag to his attention, I would prove myself to be that person.

At the end of the night, I would have to have a few extra buds readied for the charade. I needed one for my stash and a few for the diversionary decoy.

I worked that day like a man possessed. I needed as much production as possible. I needed my own production to be so high Carl would see I was making a serious effort to earn the money legitimately. I took ten minutes for lunch and twenty for supper. The rest of the day I ripped through the buds at a rapid pace. I worked until the camp had shut down and everybody had gone to sleep.

At the end of the day I had everything in place. I added a bud to my dirty clothes stash and four sizeable buds to the extra grocery bag. I placed the grocery bag behind the food storage cooler in the garage and went to bed.

It was another cold night and required extra clothing. October visited us with huge swings in the temperature. The afternoons would get up to eighty degrees or warmer, and the nights would drop below sixty. The financial concerns were in competition with the concerns over the changing weather. The changes over the last three and a half weeks had been pretty dramatic. I was sure there would be at least another two and a half weeks before the harvest would be done. How cold would it get?

I went to sleep that night knowing that the stage was set to put my plan into action. I was nervous. I was resolved. I was excited. I was cold.

I spent the next day listening for King and Tank to announce Carl's arrival. It never came. I thought the timing was right for Carl to visit the camp. I was disappointed that it didn't happen but I practiced patience and increased my production. Any extra income I could make by trimming would add to my eventual bottom line and prove to Carl I was falling in line.

Another cold night followed and another day without a visit from Carl came and went. I was getting frustrated and worried. The longer the grocery bag remained behind the cooler the more the chances increased that it would be discovered before I had a chance to use the prop in my performance.

It was midafternoon the following day that the dogs finally announced Carl's return to camp. I was surprised and a little disappointed to see that Lucas was not with him. As he made his way down the hill I gathered the seven grocery bags. Six bags containing the trimmed bud from Derrick, Molly and I and one small bag from behind the cooler. When he parked I approached.

"Hey Carl," I started "We have some pretty sizeable bags for the trip this time. All three of us have one of PTW (Purple Train Wreck) and one of Headband."

"ok."

"This small bag," I said as I held it up "must have gotten misplaced. I found it tucked around the back of the cooler."

"Whose bag is it?" Carl asked.

"I don't think it's anyone's," I replied "it was just sitting behind the cooler. I found it this morning. There's no label on it but I think it's PTW."

"Okay, thanks," he said. "Lucas asked me to see if you wanted to come into town to trim some afternoon."

"Yeah that'd be nice. Maybe I'll come in tomorrow afternoon. I want to finish trimming the rest of the Headband first. That should be done tonight."

"Sounds good, Duder. I'll let him know."

Carl went up to the garden to make the call on the next variety to be trimmed and load the cooler for Lucas to work on back in Redding. After inspecting the girls he came back to the garage and sat down to share a smoke with us. He announced that we were going to start working on The Ross plant. He passed the bowl around and when he knew we were all good and relaxed, he asked the question I was hoping to hear.

"Steve found a small bag behind the cooler with some buds. It looks like it may have been misplaced or forgotten, does anybody know about it?"

Nobody answered. Carl didn't ask again. We finished our smoke and Carl left us a small baggie with some hash to smoke later. He went up to the garden and asked me to join him with the shears. There was no more mention of the mystery bag. We cut some branches down to load the cooler, and Carl left the camp.

I was hoping for more of a discussion about the unclaimed bag but was left unsatisfied. Did I underestimate his suspicious nature? Did he accept my explanation that it was just an oversight? The only indication that my plan had any traction at all was his asking me to help him in the garden. That may simply have been out of necessity.

When they day was done and the chill had gripped the camp, I stretched out on my cot shivering and wondering.

Eyes on the Prize

Almost all of the heat from my portable heater was escaping from the tent. I didn't dare put it under my cot for fear of fire...but it was tempting. I increased my sleeping wardrobe to three pairs of socks. I only had two pairs of sweatpants, so that stayed the same as the night before. Three sweatshirts and two sleeping bags were making it tolerable. The prospect of the temperature decreasing even more was becoming a major concern. Carl had said on a recent visit that the Cinderella 99 was reaching maturity too slow. He said it may not be ready until after the first week of November, and it was the strain that comprised almost a third of the total weight. Considering Halloween was only a couple days away, the pressing question was, how much colder was it going to get before we'd be able to call the harvest complete and pull up stakes?

I managed to get some sleep, but not much. I was awoken by the helicopters approaching from a couple mountains away. By the time they flew over our camp I already had the pot on the grill waiting for the warmth of the first cup. The sun was cresting over the mountain and bringing with it some warmth. I was thankful for that. I was also excited to head into town.

I hadn't seen Lucas for over a week and I was looking forward to catching up. I had already moved my ill-gotten booty under the outside corner of my tent, so I could bring my clothes in to be washed at Carl's place. I was also looking forward to an actual toilet and a shower. A real shower with hot water. My showers for the last month were taken with the hose used for watering the garden. After the morning watering the hose would lie in the sun and build up some heat, but it was only enough lukewarm water to last for a quick five minute shower. There was every possibility that Carl would deny me the basic comforts out of spite. I was hoping he would see me as an ally and allow it, but that seemed to be a bit of a long shot. I knew it was possible that I would have to find a laundromat and perhaps a truck stop with showers to clean away the last month's grime. Whatever it took, I would come back degreased.

I trimmed away the morning hours. When Don fired up the grill to make hamburgers for lunch, I loaded my laundry and toiletries into the car. When my burger was ready, I wolfed it down quickly. I was anxious to get my trip started. My planned schedule would bring me back too late for supper. I told Don not to expect me.

"Give my love to Carl," Don said. "And Lucas."

"You know I will," I said.

With the pleasantries out of the way, I was gone. I took the Maxima up the hill and pointed it toward Redding. That would not be my first stop. When I hit Ono, I took a left and headed north to have my talk with Theo.

When I pulled into the driveway at Theo's and pulled into the spot next to the store, I was flanked by two trucks and a car that was held together by rust and luck. I stepped through the glass door and was hit by plumes of dank smoke. On the other side of the smoky barrier were four men all clad in flannel and sharing a single mouth full of teeth between them. I was waiting for the banjo music to start playing in the background.

"Hey Chopper, you're just in time. Guys, this is Chopper," Theo said. "He's good shit."

Theo introduced me to them. I don't recall their names. I don't recall a lot after the first thirty minutes inside the store.

"Hey guys, cut a line for Chopper," Theo said. "You up for a line of coke, Chopper?"

I hadn't noticed through the pot smoke that they were doing lines of cocaine on a mirror on the counter. It had been a while since I had last indulged with coke, but considering I needed to get close to Theo, I decided a small bump would be fine. It was, in essence, another piece of etiquette. I stepped up to the mirror and took the rolled up dollar bill from Theo's hand and made the tiny snow drift disappear. It was a small line but it hit me like a freight train. After I took the line I was informed it was a snowball. Coke mixed with heroin.

Not informing me before I accepted their offer was the antithesis of etiquette. I have never shied away from any drug in my past. At one point or another, I had tried everything from the natural varieties of marijuana, alcohol, mushrooms, peyote, opium, and heroin to the lab concoctions of LSD, Methamphetamine, speed and pain killers. What I didn't appreciate was the fact that I was not forewarned. I was not happy about the deception or more hopefully, the oversight.

The sensation the mixture delivered was unlike anything I had tried before. There was the euphoric rush from the coke but the debilitating floating feeling from the heroin. It did not make the cut for my top ten list of preferred drug combinations. Judging by the impact of my high and the small quantity I consumed it was pretty pure stuff.

"Welcome to the cloud Brother," Theo said. "Are you here to grab some cigarettes already?"

"No, I'm pretty flush with smokes," I said, while trying to gain a modicum of control over my speech. "I wanted to talk to you about the big green bag you had the other day."

"Okay, these boys are getting ready to leave. Let's walk and talk."

Everybody stepped outside the store, and all but one lit up a cigarette. They all said their good byes to each other and Theo. Theo and I and took off. We started walking toward the trail at the back end of his property. My head was reeling and my feet did not feel like they were in contact with the ground. My addled brain began reciting the lyrics from the song in the movie *Santa Claus Is Coming to Town;*

Put one foot in front of the other
And soon you'll be walking 'cross the floor
Put one foot in front of the other
And soon you'll be walking out the door

Concentration was difficult to come by but I managed to achieve a "walking and chewing bubble gum at the same time" level of competence. How long we walked I couldn't say. Time didn't work the way it had prior to my stepping up to the counter. What mattered most was my ability to confirm two things. I managed to lock down the price of the consigned goods and its future availability.

The walk must have been fairly long. When we got back to the front of the store, a semblance of normalcy had returned. As I was preparing to leave, Theo asked me to hold up for a minute. He wanted to give me something.

"I don't know what it is about you, Chopper, but I feel like we've become brothers in a short time," Theo said. "I want to give you something to bring you some good vibes."

I was in no position to refuse good vibes. I was willing to accept any help I could get. Theo went in the store and came out with a dreamcatcher. He said he noticed me eyeing it the first day we met. He was right. I had. When I was in high school my nickname was Lucan. It referred to a T.V. series about a boy that was raised by wolves (long story). The dream catcher was beautiful and had a Native American in the middle of a group of animals including two wolves. I had considered buying it before leaving California or picking it up on my return trip. Theo was giving it to me as a token of friendship. I took it as a good omen.

"Take this with you, man," he said. "It will keep bad things from happening to you."

"Thanks, Brother. I truly appreciate that."

The lingering numbness from the snowball had not gone completely away. I was not in the best shape for getting my goals accomplished for the day but my clothes and my body needed to be washed. I had told Carl to tell Lucas I would be in town, and I was looking forward to that as well. I had the long and winding road to try and snap myself back into reality.

The trip was over quickly and I found myself standing at the doorway to Carl's house. Before I could knock, Carl opened the door. It caught me by surprise. The upstairs office where Carl and Lucas spent most of their time had a window facing the street. Carl saw me pull up and park.

"What's wrong with you?" Carl asked. "You look like you've seen a ghost."

"I was not expecting the door to open just by my sheer will." I said.

"C'mon in, Duder."

"Before I do, I brought my clothes." I said. "do you mind if I use your washer and dryer?"

"No that's fine. Do you need a hand?"

"No. I'm good. I'll be right back."

Who the hell was this man talking to me? Cordial Carl? That didn't seem possible. I looked around for the alien pods.

I went to the car and grabbed my clothes and my shower kit. Had my ruse taken effect? I thought it landed flat and was forgotten. Maybe it sunk in deeper with him then he had let on. He was after all a world class con man. I didn't want to get my hopes up.

"I'll help you get your clothes in the wash, then we can go up and have a smoke with Lucas."

"Actually, I brought a clean set of clothes." I said. "Can I take a quick shower and start the laundry when I get out? That way I can wash these disgusting clothes as well."

"Yeah, that's fine."

The shower had the desired effect of not only cleaning my body but clearing my head. The cleared head only lasted until my clothes were in the wash; then it was smoke time. At least that was a style of fuzzy headedness I was used to.

It was an odd feeling. It felt like old times. Carl was nice. It was great having a smoke with Lucas. I couldn't let my guard down, but it was difficult not to hold on to the hopes that the soured relationship between Carl and I had just been a bad dream.

"So, Duder, where did you say you found that extra bag?"

There it was! It did sink deeper than he let on. I had to answer his question as though I had not given it a single thought since he left the camp the day before.

"It was sitting behind the food cooler in the garage."

"When you gave me that bag you said it was tucked behind the cooler. Was it in the open, or would tucked be the right description?"

"I don't know why I used the word tucked," I said trying to minimize my discovery "It was about a foot in from the end, just sitting there."

"Was it folded? Was it pushed under the cooler at all?"

"It was folded but it was just sitting behind there. Like I said, tucked may have been the wrong word."

He had the look of a man in deep contemplation. He knocked out the ashes of the first bowl and loaded a second.

"Kathy is making stuffed green peppers for supper tonight," Carl said "I assume you're going to join us."

"Yeah, I was hoping to stay for a bit and maybe get some trimming in while enjoying some heat. The nights are getting pretty cool out there."

"I was thinking maybe Steve and I would trim some over at Ricky's place after supper," Lucas said to Carl. "I think Allison is working tonight."

Carl looked over at me and laughed.

"Lucas doesn't like Allison very much," he said. "He thinks she's kind of a bitch."

"Not kind of," Lucas replied. "She's a total bitch, and I'm not the only one who thinks so. Hell, even Ricky agrees."

We finished our smoke and the three of us had a decent talk. Old times. I missed it. I was not deluded. I knew it felt that way because I presented new value to Carl. I knew without the newly added value I would not be showered and most likely be headed for the laundromat...without supper.

After supper, I thanked Kathy for the meal and stepped out to have a cigarette. I went to the Maxima and grabbed my portable smokeless ashtray and cigs. When I returned to the deck to have the cigarette, Carl was waiting for me.

"Steve, I need to talk to you about something."

"Shoot man," I said. "What's up?"

"I think that bag you gave me might be more than just an oversight," Carl started. "I think somebody might be trying to add to their earnings."

"Why don't you think it was just an oversight?'

"The buds in the bag were big, prime buds," he said. "It was like they were selected."

"I don't know man," I said. "Who would do that? Don wouldn't use a bag in the garage if it was him. I don't know Derrick or Molly very well, but they don't seem like the type to do that."

"Lucas told me they were saying some shit about me behind my back," Carl said. "Maybe they're doing it together. Who knows?"

I couldn't believe how deep the hook had been set. I knew it must have been wearing on him since he left the camp.

"It could be nothing," Carl continued, "but it would be great if you could keep your eyes peeled for me."

"Of course." I lied.

I saw my opening for the final push on my plan. I took advantage.

"I don't know if I can stay for the final trimming, Carl."

"What do you mean?" Carl asked.

"I have enough money left to make it to the end of harvest if it doesn't last much longer," I replied "but I don't have enough to get home. If I leave in the next week, I could get home but even that would be pushing it."

"Don't worry about it, Duder. I'll make sure you can get home," Carl said. "I assume you wouldn't mind bringing some more weight home with you since you're going to have to haul yours anyway."

"Well, I don't know. How much weight are we talking?"

"Lucas may be taking a bus home, so it would be his weight and a few pounds of mine."

I really didn't have a problem with a few extra pounds. I should have close to two pounds of my own on the return trip. If I got caught, it would mean a prison term either way.

"Yeah, I guess I could do that," I said.

The plan was complete. Not the minutiae, but the broad strokes. I would have the legitimate weed I had earned. I would have my pilfered buds. I had assurances of consignment weed when

I returned. I had my travel money to get home. I wasn't able to spike the ball in the end zone, but I was marching down the field.

Lucas and I went across the street, and I was introduced to Ricky...and Allison. She got the night off from work. Lucas wasn't too thrilled. I actually liked meeting Allison. Maybe it was because I was expecting a horror show of a human. I thought she had a good sense of humor. It was a rough sense of humor. She was brash, but I wouldn't have classified her as Lucas had.

There were three bonuses working for Ricky. He paid better. He fed everybody beers while they trimmed. He wasn't nearly as anal as Carl when it came to how tightly the buds needed to be trimmed. That meant more bud could be trimmed in less time.

I stayed long enough to trim about six ounces and downed as many beers. I enjoyed spending the evening with Lucas, and after collecting my clean clothes, I headed back to the camp. When I arrived, the only conscious human was Don. He was out having a cigarette with King and Tank when I rolled up.

"How was his royal highness?" Don asked.

"No change," I replied. "He was a dick. Oh, and Lucas sends his love," I said with a smile.

We enjoyed the stars and a few smokes before retiring to our respective beds.

It was a cold night and I added the appropriate layers to keep me from freezing. It was a long and incredibly challenging day. I slept deep with the satisfaction that I had indeed conned the con man!

The Balancing Act

Halloween had always been one of my favorite holidays. Not that year. Trick or treating was not a common activity in the rural back hills of Northern California pot country. In fact I had forgotten that Halloween was upon us until Don suggested, as a holiday treat, we make some pot butter cookies for the night's desert. None of us had ever made pot butter. We thought *how hard could it be*? We improvised. As it turned out it wasn't that difficult but it was a mess. We melted some butter in a pot, threw in some recently acquired trimmings and let it bubble for about twenty minutes. The messy part was trying to strain the pot out of the butter. I used a clean pair of socks. It wasn't exactly a MacGyver move considering butter doesn't easily drain through cotton. I squeezed the hot sock until most of it went through to the Tupperware beneath. My hands were coated in the slippery mess and the socks were discarded.

Don went to work whipping up some dough and put the cookies on a baking sheet inside the grill. They ended up a bit burnt but we ate them nonetheless. We had no idea how potent the concoction would be until we actually sampled them. A half hour after we each consumed a sizeable cookie we had our answer. They were extremely potent! There is a downside to edibles. Once they have been eaten there is no turning back. We got higher and higher for hours. We had gotten too high to trim. The rest of that day was spent listening to music and wishing we could turn back the hands of time and only eat half a cookie. It was fun but unproductive. The numb headspace that evening was a welcome substitution for the usual Halloween celebration. It distracted us from the cold.

The end of October and the early days of November were mostly unremarkable. The days were filled with trimming and guesswork. How much was left to trim? When would the Cindy 99 be ready to get into production? When would the end of harvest finally arrive?

All in all, the adventure had its ups and downs, and was loaded with experiences I would not have changed at all. I was thankful for most of it. However, by the time November rolled around, I just wanted to be done. The cold was starting to take a toll, and my lack of legitimate pay wasn't helping my attitude. The resentment and frustration were substantial. I missed seeing my wife, and I was beginning to wonder if I would make it home for Thanksgiving.

I balanced my time between working at the camp, moonlighting a few times at Ricky's, and hauling the trimmed bud into Redding. I had earned Carl's trust to the point that he no longer came out to retrieve the bud. That had become one of my assigned tasks. Another new task was bringing untrimmed bud in for Lucas to work on.

I would trim for a few days then take the trimmed bud in to Carl and step across the street to have a few beers and trim a few buds for Ricky.

About seven or eight days into November we had the harvest completed with the exception of the Cindy and the remaining buds drying on the wires. Carl came out to inspect the remaining plants to make the call as to their maturity. They were not ready.

That was bad news for everybody. There would be no more production at the camp until Cindy was ready. I volunteered to drive to Redding every day to trim at Ricky's place. Derrick and Molly made the trip in and back with me until Ricky ran out of bud to trim. I had earned seven ounces from Ricky before the well dried up.

The next few days were spent at the camp finding things to do to pass the time. We took walks, ate our meals and swapped stories.

Two weeks into November, Carl finally made the call that we could attack the Cinderella 99. He was not happy with its level of maturity but knew he would be without trimmers if he waited any longer. We all tore into the remaining crop with a vengeance. We were nearing Thanksgiving and everybody wanted to be done.

A new problem emerged. For several days while trimming what remained the weather changed. The swing from the warmth in the afternoon to the cold at night stopped. It was cold all day and included an almost constant light drizzle. There was no more relief from the cold. The moisture coupled with the cold made trimming miserable. It also caused the bud to take more time to dry which slowed the process down. It was miserable and the cold became all consuming.

The nights became unbearably frigid. Fighting to get sleep had become a serious challenge. I spent my nights sleeping while sitting in my chair with the heater on full blast...until I ran out of propane and the money needed to replenish it. The end could not arrive soon enough.

Three weeks into November we finally trimmed the last of the harvest. My four week stay had turned into almost seven. I was exhausted. I was relieved. I was nervous. I still had to get home with a carload of illegal product.

The last full day in camp started early. We spent the first part of the day bagging up the last of the trimmed buds. I took them into town, so Carl could get the final tally and have my earned bud ready when I came back the next day.

The last night in camp had a celebratory feel. My cooler stash was down to one bottle of wine, a six pack of beer and a quarter of my bottle of scotch. After supper that night we all concentrated on emptying the cooler. I was happy to be at the end of the harvest but I was going to miss my odd camp family.

It was a cool night, but happily, it had warmed up just enough to give me the sleep I would need to make the dangerous trek home.

I awoke the next morning looking directly up at two scorpions on the top screen of my tent. I had not seen scorpions the whole while I was in California, and now they were greeting me on my last day. What kind of an omen was that? I didn't want to think about it.

I spent most of that morning tearing down camp. The trickiest part was stashing my ill-gotten bud in a place I would feel secure would not be detected by Carl if his trust happened to fade at the last minute. I opened my trunk and pulled back the liner from the passenger side. I pulled the bud out from my dirty laundry bag when I knew there were no eyes on me. I wrapped the hefty bag with duct tape and used several pieces of duct tape to secure it to the metal inner wall of the back quarter panel. I then snapped the liner back in place.

I estimated that I had added one full pound of stolen bud to my totals.

The tent would not be coming home with me. The tent was one of the three gifts I gave to Derrick and Molly. It was much nicer than the two man tent they had been calling home for the last several weeks. I also left them my now empty cooler.

The other gift I gave to Molly was a walking stick I had made from a piece of driftwood I had found on McGowan's Farm (a local Mankato legend). I had spent weeks sanding it smooth and added several layers of lacquer. It was truly one of my prized possessions, but it seemed fitting that Molly should have it.

I told Molly that the native peoples considered the area where I found the stick as sacred. I told her about the bloody history of the Mankato area regarding the Sioux uprising and the consequent largest mass hanging of Indians in U.S. history ordered by Abraham Lincoln. She was fascinated and said she truly appreciated the gift.

I packed the rest of my gear in the Maxima and said good-bye to Don, Derrick, and Molly before heading toward Redding. I was finally saying good-bye to my mountain home.

When I arrived at Carl's, I had a space I had left open to put my buds, Lucas's buds and the few pounds from Carl. Few pounds my ass! I expected Carl was understating how much he intended to load in my car. I had anticipated it. Hell, I counted on it. What I had not anticipated was the total he actually had in mind. Carl's few pounds became forty-two pounds of pot, over a pound of hash and a cooler stuffed with twenty pounds of butter.

I knew arguing would be futile. I was broke. I wanted to get home. Carl held all the cards.

I had to move everything that had been packed into the trunk into the passenger seat of the Maxima. The paranoia I once had about Lucas' dreads was now replaced by camping gear visible through every window of the car. It was a red flag that would be visible from a distance.

And my legitimate pay for my trimming? One pound, twelve ounces. Seven weeks for that pittance of a bounty figured to four ounces per week. Carl's assurances before I agreed to go on this escapade were that I would make a minimum of ten per week.

My plan was successful enough to have brought my total to just over three pounds. I had achieved the minimum I had to have to stop the bloodletting Carl had invited me to.

The temperature was dropping quickly as we loaded the cannabis menagerie into the trunk. Carl invited me in to have a quick smoke before hitting the road. I declined. I had not smoked anything that day. I wanted my wits about me for the perilous mission I was facing. I didn't want to spend another minute with Carl, and I wanted get through the mountains before darkness descended upon me.

I pointed the Maxima east and began my long journey home.

Danger Zone

As I put Redding in my rearview mirror, I was struggling to keep my cavalcade of conflicting emotions in check. It was not an easy task to accomplish. I was relieved to be done with the harvest but terrified of the miles, fraught with danger, that lie ahead. I was angry at Carl's taking advantage of my situation, but hopeful because I had managed to amass the minimal bounty I required to set things right. I was excited to be on my way home to see the family I had missed so much but worried about the gauntlet of law enforcement that could take that prize away indefinitely.

I plugged my phone into my car stereo and played some familiar music in an attempt to distract me enough to gain a sense of calm. It didn't work. I lit a cigarette and tried to think of what had been going right so far. Harvest was done, I had my pay, I was on my way back to the woman I loved, and I was within twenty-four hours of being able to finally exhale. The plan was to drive straight through without stopping. Carl had given me enough money to allow me to stop for one night at a hotel if I needed to. I didn't want to. I couldn't imagine it would be possible to get any sleep when home was within reach. If I had good weather and no issues, I could be home by lunchtime the next day.

As I took the last turn to get on the road toward Lassen National Park and make my way over the Sierra's, the weather turned. It turned quickly. It went from bright and sunny to grey and snowy. I flashed back to the two scorpions casting an ominous shadow on the beginning of my day. I am not normally one to give credence to omens, but in that moment I considered turning around. If I did, what then? No choice. I pushed on.

As I hit the first steep grade, the grade my daughter and I had narrowly survived, the roads began to get slick. The weight of the contents of the Maxima kept the car grounded enough to ascend to the top. My speed was reduced as I navigated the snaking highway through the upper ranges and through its forests. The last thing I wanted was to slip off the road and be a sitting duck for any law enforcement that might happen by.

It was then that I smelled something that added to my terror. I could smell weed. I knew Carl's product was vacuum sealed and not the cause of the escaping vapors. It was my duct taped contraband. It was a smell that I had always loved until that moment. It smelled like incarceration.

I turned up the volume on the stereo in a desperate attempt to once again bring my heartrate down to a tolerable level. Again, my music was not potent enough to allow my anxiety to subside. I opted for the one thing I told myself I would not do. I reached into my pocket, retrieved my one-hitter, and loaded some Headband. I smoked two hits. Enough to calm me down but not enough to destroy my concentration. The song *Into the Mystic* by Van Morrison came on. A song that made me think of my wife. I lost myself in the thought of being a day away from holding her in my arms and I began to calm. It sustained me as I wound my way through the mountains and found my way to the grade leading back down to the valley and the town of Susanville.

As I descended from the Sierra's, the snow started to relent. I was about to enter the law enforcement gauntlet I had feared, but at least I wasn't going to have to contend with the additional hazard of snow. On my previous trips the area where I saw the most highway patrol and sheriffs' vehicles was the stretch from Susanville to Fernley Nevada, thirty miles on the other side of Reno. Coming out of California after harvest time with a car loaded with camping gear scared the hell out of me. My only choice was to remain as calm as I could and forge onward. Fuck the scorpions.

To my pleasant surprise, I only saw two bubble topped vehicles on that entire stretch of road, and they were thankfully going in the opposite direction. I eyed them in the mirror as I passed, and they continued on, oblivious to the conviction they had passed up. Maybe the trip wouldn't be so bad.

As I passed through Fernley, the sun started to withdraw from my sight in the rearview. I would need to get fuel soon. I looked forward to getting the chance to stretch my legs and get a cup of coffee to help me replace some of the energy that had been sapped by the Headband. I found a station a few miles down the road and pulled in. When I got back on the road, I had a renewed sense of optimism. I assumed the worst part of the trip was behind me. I was smiling and enjoying the music on the stereo. With the setting of the sun my overflowing camping gear was no longer the big red flag it had been in the sunlight. The Minnesota license plates were still problematic, but they were not easily seen from a distance. I was a happy camper...or ex-camper.

It had been only 250 miles since I filled my last cup of coffee, but it was making a bathroom break a necessity. I pulled off at the next filling station, got rid of my last cup, and refilled my mug. As long as I was stopped, I topped off the tank as well. Five miles after hitting the road again, the first flakes began to fall. I hoped it was going to be a dusting. My hopes were not realized. The first flakes were followed by a steady progression of more and more flakes until I was, once again, driving through significant snowfall.

I was able to maintain close to the speed limit until I hit the Nevada, Utah border. Visibility diminished as the snow on the road began to build. It was no longer just a snowfall. I was in a blizzard. The wind was blowing the large snowflakes sideways. I turned off the music to give full attention to the task at hand. The music was replaced by the sound of the snow pelting against the window. It sounded like sand being dropped over tin foil. The road was beginning to disappear. The only hope for making headway was to follow the ruts of the previous travelers. If they went in the ditch I would be joining them.

No cars passed me, and I passed no one. Occasionally a semi-truck would slowly approach, ease into the undefined lane to my left and leave me in a swirl of snow. Thirty seconds after being passed, I lost sight of their taillights or any other indication there had been another vehicle on the road. Any indication except, of course, the grooves they left behind. My hands gripped tight to the steering wheel, and my eyes were in a constant state of peering through the void, hoping to see the lights of the truck stop I knew sat on the west side of Salt Lake City. I didn't dare pull in to a rest area for fear I would find myself stuck. Forward momentum was my only sane option.

It felt like an eternity, but I finally saw the lights of the truck stop and pulled in to get some gas and take some deep breaths. I considered the idea of staying at one of the hotels next to the truck stop. That would put me twelve hundred miles from home with almost no money. The thought of pushing my home arrival off and perhaps not having enough money to get there at all was a motivator. I pointed the car east and ventured on.

When I made the outskirts of SLC, the roads were in better shape, and the lights of the city made travel tolerable. Until that night, I had never thought to myself *I'm really glad to be in Salt Lake City*, but that moment became the exception.

I made my way through the city and began the long climb up the grade to Park City. The snowplows were out in fleets, and the roads were better than I had expected them to be. I was truly glad for that little piece of kindness. Up and over the mountain and down through the winding descent, I had passable roads. My heart rate was high but far lower than it was while crossing the Salt Flats.

I knew my luck wouldn't hold for long. It didn't. After leaving the more populated areas in the valley, I went back into "follow the tracks" mode while driving through the curving canyons leading to Wyoming. It was early morning, about three or four o'clock, and my hopes for a noontime homecoming had evaporated. The slow rate of speed had me adjusting my potential arrival time. Midnight may be possible, though not probable. I would not make it home to Sue today. I just had to make it home. Slow, methodical, and cautious resolve was all that mattered at that point.

I was relieved when I saw the first exit signs for Evanston, Wyoming, but I was also nervous knowing that the next obstacle was the Three Sisters. As soon as Evanston vanished behind me, I started climbing the first of the sisters. The road was so slick and snow packed that I was forced to hover my speed around forty-five miles per hour. It would have been slower, but there had been a plow that had recently opened up the right lane. I made it over the first sister...two to go.

The sun was starting to rise in front of me as I neared the top of sister number two. I found myself easing up on the plow that had been clearing my lane. He was traveling very slowly. As much as I didn't find any appeal in the idea of attempting to pass him, I couldn't bear maintaining the snail's pace he was going. I approached his back end and made an attempt to pass. It was glare ice underneath the heavy snow in the left lane. The car began to slide and I quickly tucked back in behind him. I stayed steady on the wheel while I worked up the courage to give it another try.

As I started to make the attempt, the driver of the plow decided to give me a break and moved to the right just enough to give me some added room. I checked my mirrors and there was no approaching traffic. We had crested the top of the sister and the road flattened out a bit. I started to make my move.

The minute I pulled out it became glaringly obvious that acceleration was going to be difficult and dangerous. It was going to take some time to actually complete the pass. It was taking longer than I was comfortable with, but at that point I was committed and continued to make the effort. I slowly accelerated only to feel the tires lose purchase on the pavement below. I was forced to reduce my acceleration even more. I kept a slow steady pace. It was taking me an uncomfortable amount of time but eventually I found myself making progress around the towering snowplow. I knew that if the car slid it could result in a tragedy too awful to consider.

I made it just about even with the door of the snow plow when my terror was sent into sheer panic mode. I saw headlights approaching from behind and they were closing in far too fast! We had just begun the descent of sister number two when the semi-truck in my rearview saw the folly in his rapid speed. He was going to hit me if he didn't stop. I knew he had seen me. I saw the telltale signs of a truck on the verge of a jackknife. As someone who had logged over a million and a half miles behind the wheel of an eighteen wheeler, I instantly recognized the peril he was facing. The back of his trailer began pulling toward the median. He was attempting to stop but if he continued to hit the brakes he would bring the trailer around to his side and hit me and the snowplow on his way to following us into the ditch. It was a no-win situation. He took the only option that was available to him. The snowplow had pulled as tight to the right hand side of the road as possible which left a little room between my car and the center median. He kept slow and steady pressure on the brakes and angled to the left of my car. He maintained that trajectory until his front tire began to pull into the median. To avoid leaving the road entirely he had to correct his direction by turning slightly to the right. When he did, he clipped the rear quarter panel of the Maxima.

The push from the mammoth vehicle sent the car into a spin. I was completely out of control. My eyes were looking through the windshield but my view altered from the open road ahead, to the median, to the grill of the semi, to the plow truck. I spun completely around two and a half rotations without hitting either of the deadly trucks. I ended my dance with death as I left the road, sliding backwards in an explosion of fresh snow. The semi-truck came to rest with his front tire slightly in the median ten yards short of my location. The snowplow pulled over to the right shoulder of the highway.

My heart threatened to beat out of my chest. I barely caught my breath when the next horrific thought began to sink in. I was stuck in the snow with what amounted to bails of illegal weed. I had to get out, and it had to be fast. It wasn't a steep median, but it was steep enough that when I attempted to climb out, I reached almost to the road and began to slip backward again. I repeated the effort with the same result. And again. And again.

I put the car in park and stepped out to see if there were any other options open to me. Behind my back bumper the median gained in its angle. I couldn't try to rock the car to gain momentum, or I risked getting myself even deeper into the median.

While I was sweating my predicament, the semi managed to pull back onto the highway and drove forward to park in front of the plow. The driver walked over to me to see if I was alright.

"Jesus Christ, man," he said. "Are you ok?"

"Yeah, I'm fine. I'm shaken, but I'm ok."

The snowplow driver joined us.

"Do you want me to call in for a tow truck?" He asked. "I could call dispatch."

"I was almost able to get the car out," I stated. "Do you think the two of you could help by giving it a push while I attempt to gun it out of here?"

They both agreed, and on the second attempt the car found enough of the gravel on the shoulder to lurch up and onto the road. I pulled my car up to the front of the procession of vehicles parked at the side of the road. As I parked I was trying to think of some way I could justify asking my fellow road warriors not to call the authorities. My mind was blank. I couldn't really say "Hey, I have a bunch of drugs in my car. Can we just pretend none of this happened?"

I stepped out of my car to go talk to the semi driver. When I stepped up to his door, he opened it and said the best words I could have possibly imagined.

"Man, if I get one more ticket on my record I'm going to lose my job," he said. "Can we just exchange information and deal with this one-on-one?"

"Well, I don't know," I said trying to look like the idea was not exactly what I hoped for "I'm an ex-hand (Hand is trucker-speak for truck driver), so I guess we can do that."

He pulled out a pad and a pen and we exchanged information. As we were wrapping everything up the snowplow driver stepped up.

"I just called in the accident. The highway patrol is busy but they said to pull over there and wait for them to show up" he said as he pointed to the next exit down the road.

With that bombshell dropped, he went back to his plow.

"I don't care what he says," the truck driver said. "I'm not stopping."

"I have no problem with that," I said. "I'll go back and tell him we've already exchanged information and I'll see if he can call off the patrol."

When I started to make my way back to the plow, the semi pulled back out on the road and started rolling.

I stepped up to the plow truck, and the driver rolled down his window.

"We just exchanged information," I said "I don't think we need to bother the highway patrol. Like you said, they're busy today."

The driver saw the semi passing the exit.

"That son of a bitch isn't stopping!" He exclaimed.

"Yeah, I told him I'd be ok without filling out an accident report," I said "I'm fine, and, with the exception of a small dent on the back quarter panel of the car, there's no damage. He doesn't want a bad mark on his record, and I just want to get down the road."

He was not happy about it, but he did finally pick up his radio and called his dispatch to cancel the accident report. He explained that nobody was hurt, and that we had exchanged insurance information. The dispatcher agreed to make the call to cancel the call with the authorities. I thanked the man and went back to the Maxima.

As I pulled back out to the road I couldn't help but think I had hit a homerun with a full count. Strike one getting hit by the semi. Strike two getting spun into the median. Homerun, here I am rolling toward home.

The snow had stopped falling, and the sun made a welcomed appearance. I was shaking. The gravity of the situation I just avoided hit me hard. I had a hard time driving. I was filled with thoughts of being handcuffed to a hospital bed or sporting a toe tag in the morgue. I wanted to pull over and call Sue. Hearing her voice would have been just what the doctor I had just avoided would have ordered. I wanted to pull over but I also wanted to put more distance between me and any possible law enforcement that could be looking for the car that didn't want to wait to fill out an accident report. It may have been paranoia, but paranoia had served me well in the past. It's the paranoid types who prepare for the worst because they expect the worst. I continued down the road another hundred miles. I did discover an injury that I was too shaken to notice at the time of the collision. Either the impact of the truck hitting the Maxima or the impact of the Maxima hitting the ditch had broken one of my molars. A piece of the battered tooth worked itself loose and fell onto my tongue as I was lighting a cigarette while looking for a place to pull over.

When I finally did pull over, I loaded up on coffee for the road, grabbed a breakfast sandwich and gassed up the car. I pulled out of the fuel island and found a parking spot to make my call to Sue.

"Hi Baby!" She said. "Where are you?"

That voice! That hauntingly beautiful voice! God I loved that voice! It was the tonic I needed. It was salve for my tired, road-weary ass. I gave her a summary of the shitty trip I had had so far and explained that the arrival time I had predicted and wished I could have accomplished wasn't going to happen. She was not thrilled with the delay, but was happy I was ok. I explained that I was super tired, but I was still going to try to make it home without pulling over...if I could. I told her I was just outside of Rawlins, Wyoming and explained that I had another eight hundred and fifty miles to go. I told her even with the best of luck, which I certainly hadn't come to expect, that would put me home around three or four o'clock in the morning. She encouraged me to pull over and get a room if I got too tired and I assured her I would. We talked for a few more minutes, and when I hung up, I had a renewed desire to put miles behind me.

Before leaving the gas station, I called Carl to give him a progress report. That voice! That miserable shitty voice! God I hated that voice! I told Carl what had happened on the trip so far, and he feigned concern for me. He was concerned for the contents of my trunk.

I was going to stay as far off the beaten track as possible. The paranoia of seeing highway patrol monitoring the interstate was not appealing to me. I turned north out of Rawlins and took some backroads that lead through the heart of Wyoming which according to my map (yes a paper atlas) would bring me through to the western edge of South Dakota, and put me back on the interstate just north of Deadwood. The miles went slower on the two-lane, but the paranoia was being kept at bay. A fair trade.

I followed highway 187 for what felt like days. That briefly hooked up with Interstate 25, but soon I was back on two-lane. When I turned onto highway 18, I was dragging ass. I didn't think I could drive any longer. The motivation was there, but the fear of falling asleep at the wheel was becoming a real possibility. I had to get some sleep. I vowed to get a room at the next hotel I saw. When I entered the sleepy little town of Lusk, Wyoming I came across the Best Western Pioneer hotel. It was a bit of a dive, but to me it looked like paradise. It had beds.

I pulled in and put my money down for a room. I couldn't afford to risk that somebody would see the camping gear and break into the car while I slept. I wasn't worried about the gear. I was worried they might find the treasure in the trunk. I backed in to the spot in front of my assigned room, popped the trunk and brought the three large hefty bags full of weed and the cooler full of butter into my room. I was in my room at eleven o'clock. I set my alarm for four thirty. I was asleep on top of the covers of the bed by five after eleven.

I could have sworn my eyes had been closed for no more than ten minutes when the alarm went off. I dragged myself out of bed, brewed the two cups of coffee provided in the room, and set to the task of packing the car and filling my mug for the drive.

I jumped in the Maxima and headed north. When I went through the only traffic light that Lusk possessed, I saw a police car waiting at his red light to my right. As I passed by, the cruiser pulled out behind me. I half expected the disco lights on the top of the car to start flashing. They didn't, but he stayed on my tail. I pulled out of town. The road became a series of tight curves and changing speed zones. He was watching my every move. Warren Buffet once famously wrote "If a cop follows you for 500 miles, you're going to get a ticket." I believe that was what I was dealing with that morning. He followed me through curves, over hills, around reduced speed zones and did not give up for close to a half hour. I knew it was well over twenty-five minutes because shortly after he started tailing me, my stereo started playing Tchaikovsky's 1812 overture (one of the favorites on my phone), and he was still behind me for a few songs after the last orchestrated cannon shot had fired. The overture is an eighteen minute song. When he turned around, and my butt cheeks unclenched, the sun was rising on a new day.

I pulled through the town of Deadwood, and though I was still five hundred miles from home, I felt like I was back in the neighborhood. I knew, barring any added problems, I would be pulling into Mankato late that afternoon. If my trip thus far was any indication of the luck I would experience the rest of the way home, I might have been in trouble, but it was surprisingly smooth and involved zero tragedies.

I cruised into Mankato about five o'clock that evening. I called Roz who was the man Carl asked me to deliver his goods to. I got directions to his place and made my delivery. To my shock Roz asked me to wait for a gift from Carl. Roz pulled out a digital scale and weighed me out fourteen grams of hash.

"Carl said to give this to you," Roz told me. "He said something about you getting hit by a truck? Anyway he wanted you to have this."

I thanked Roz and pointed the car toward home.

When I pulled in the driveway, my wife was waiting by the door. I jumped out of the car without grabbing any of my gear. I just wanted to hold Sue in my arms. It was a long, tight, beautiful hug. It took great effort to stop. I didn't want to let go. I was home.

The Race to Return

California was behind me. California was ahead of me. My time spent enjoying my return to Mankato was limited. The first night I spent at home was bliss. I was with my wife, who I adored. Seeing her beautiful smile and haunting brown eyes brought me to a place of appreciation and made clear what I had taken for granted. I could have been reduced to only seeing her through Plexiglas. It hit me in a profound way.

Putting my head on my pillow in the bed I had not disturbed for seven weeks was another little slice of heaven. The comfort of my mattress coupled with the feeling of being back home put me into a slumber that nothing could have disturbed.

I awoke the next morning without the sound of choppers overhead. I don't know if I actually slept with a smile on my face, but it was there when I woke up. I was refreshed. I was relieved. I was ready to get to work.

I had not divulged the full scale of my plan to Sue when I was out in California. I didn't want her to become disheartened with the slow progress I was making out west. I didn't want her to fear the part of the plan which involved the return trip. I had to broach the subject and trust she would be on board.

Sue was not working at the time but was putting in full-time hours as a student. The student loans helped with the bills but we were struggling to get by. There was a stack of bills that had piled up since my departure and needed to get paid immediately. That presented a number of problems.

My total weight on my return from California was three pounds and three ounces of pot, fourteen grams of hash, and a sizeable ball of trim hash. I owed one pound and two ounces to the people who staked my California excursion. That left two pounds, one ounce to secure the return trip. Without the stack of bills, it would have been insufficient. With over $1,500 in overdue bills and new bills on the way, I was sunk.

I had told Theo to reserve me a minimum of four pounds, and I would be back to pick them up within the month. He told me there would be plenty to fill my order, so quantity wasn't a concern. Coming up with the finances and doing it in short order was indeed an issue. I've never been one to shy away from a challenge. I had to make sure that the roadblocks I was facing would not be the exception. I had to find a way.

I relayed the situation to Sue. I told her of the plan I had concocted to make the income we sorely needed. I explained that I had been short-sighted, and the amount of pot I returned with left us short. We would need a new plan. I had committed to Theo and still intended to make that purchase happen, but how?

The plan that hit me was a repeat of sorts. I would need to presell enough pounds with enough built-in profit to allow myself to purchase the needed weight. I was able to finance my previous trip by promising pot at a reduced rate. I would have to do that again. For each pound I sold, I would require $2,600. That price would add $900 to their typical bottom line. Pounds were normally purchased at $3,500. They would gain $900 but they would risk losing it all if I was arrested. It was a risk to them. Compared to my risk however, it was minimal.

I spent the morning separating and weighing out all of the pre-ordered pot. When it was ready to be distributed to those who were owed, I made some phone calls. Big Mark was the first to come pick up the pot he had been patiently waiting for over the last eight weeks. I sat him down, and we smoked a little of each of the varieties I had brought back. I gave him the quantities he had ordered. I had taken the percentage of every strain that I was paid, and gave him multiple bags of green bud totaling what he was owed. He was thrilled with the quality and the variety he received. He was like a kid in a candy store. The first we sampled was the Headband. We followed it with Purple Kush, Cinderella 99, Blue Cheese, Purple Train Wreck, Jack Herer, Blueberry Kush, and of course, the Big Ross. Every strain came with a story from me and a smile from Mark. When we reached the last of the samples, I told him about my plans to do a run back out to California. It was the easiest sale I had ever made. Big Mark was in for two pounds. I wasn't satisfied. Any good salesman worth his salt will tell you not to walk away if there is anything left on the table. I told Mark if he bought one more pound, I would give it to him for $2,200. As he was mulling it over, I loaded some trim hash and told him how it was acquired. I told him about scraping the sticky scissors and rolling balls off the rubber gloves. When the hash turned to ash he agreed to three pounds.

I attempted to make the same magic happen with the other clients who came to pick up their long-awaited weed. I had no takers.

The next thing I had to consider was how I would squeeze as much profit out of my personal take as possible. There were two ways I could accomplish it. Both took time. First, I would have to sell what I had in smaller quantities. The price of a full pound varied between $3,200 and $3,500. An ounce sold for $300, making the value of the pound increase in value to $5,400. A quarter ounce sold for $120 which would shoot the value of that pound up to $8,600. That method would take time. Selling that much in small quantities also came with increased exposure which was added risk I wasn't thrilled about. Also, half of my clientele had just received a delivery from me and would not need to replenish for a while. That led to option number two. Offer something very few people had access to...edibles.

When Carl brought me to Harmony Park to sell tincture, he showed me how the sausage was made. Carl was able to ask ten dollars for a single teaspoon of the elixir. With the fourteen grams of hash I had been given, as a gift for almost meeting my maker at the front end of a semi, I could make over a quart of tincture. That would make an extra thousand dollars. I took it farther. I researched what it would take to make hard candies from the tincture. Twelve teaspoons would make forty hard candies. Each hard candy would sell for four dollars which would almost double that thousand. I also learned the proper way to make pot butter. Our experimental attempt at the camp in California was way off!

Neither plan afforded me the ability to get the required funds in the short time available. I set them both in motion nonetheless. I spent the next couple days creating tincture, candies, and pot butter caramels. I put the word out that there were edibles available, and to my surprise I had more interest than I thought possible. Within a week I was $2,000 closer to the goal. I made more candy; I gained more headway. It was going well, but the mounting bills combined with the time it was taking to sell were keeping me short of the money I needed. It was time to look for a straight-out investor. I needed somebody who had enough money to float me a loan. I knew plenty of people with money but very few who would invest in something as high risk and illegal as what I was proposing. The one name that came to mind was Sam. Sam was best known by the nickname Slim. His nickname was akin to calling a bald man curly. Sam was over six feet tall and tipped the scales at over 450 pounds.

Slim ran a weekly poker game out of his house and even invested in a few slot machines for his regulars. He was a cautious and decent poker player who played the odds and read the poker tells on the faces and in the mannerisms of those he opposed. He had earned himself some significant money over the years putting time in at a local plant from which he had since retired. With his nest egg secured and his weekly take from the slots and poker games, I knew he would have to be the focus of my hunt.

After the following Sunday night poker game, I asked him to talk. I told him what I wanted was a loan. Slim was a shrewd business man, and he smelled the money. He didn't want to give a loan. He wanted to invest in a partnership. He started asking all the pertinent questions. What was the price of the weed in California? How much could I get for it when I returned? How often would I make a run?

I told him the basics and was pretty forthright in my replies. The idea of making multiple runs had occurred to me but wasn't something I had seriously considered. While sitting with Slim the wheels started spinning and the idea became more plausible. If I had an investor I could get more weight and turn more profit. One thought went through my mind; *did I really want a partner*? No! I had partners in the legitimate business world, and it always ended badly.

Slim was very interested and I have to say, he made me consider the idea very seriously. I knew it would be something that I would have to speak with Sue about. I was not sure how she would take the idea of me risking multiple trips. She was okay with me doing one return trip to try and make ourselves whole, but multiple trips? Going to California on multiple runs with a two thousand mile turn around? Away from home and risking the possibility that I would not make it home from one of them? I had to talk with her before anything could be decided.

I told Slim I was open to the thought but we'd have to hammer out specifics. I needed to know how much he would expect to profit from my taking such a risk.

"You know yours is not the only risk," Slim pointed out. "If I invest and you don't make it back after the first run, I lose all that money."

He had a point. He also had the leverage to raise his payoff.

"What kind of arrangements do you have in mind?" I asked.

"I give you the money, and you handle the rest."

"That's not what I meant," I replied. "How much do you expect to be paid?"

"I think forty percent sounds fair," he said.

"I think you need to get your hearing checked if you think that sounds fair."

"Why?" He asked. "What sounds fair to you?"

"I'm not even sure if I want to do it at all," I countered. "I could maybe see my way to cutting you in for twenty percent."

"That's not worth it for the risk. I could lose it all on one trip."

"So could I Slim," I said. "Your risk is only financial whereas mine is my very freedom. On top of that, I would be the one responsible for all the work of selling, plus I would have to cover all my expenses on the drive out and back. Forty percent is a hard no."

"I guess I could maybe do it for thirty percent," Slim said.

"If I did it for thirty percent, and that's a big if, it would have to be thirty percent of pound prices. If I get better than pound prices I keep the difference," I said.

"I think we have a deal," Slim said.

"Not yet we don't," I said. "I still have to see if the boss will let me. Sue may not be on board with it at all."

I stepped away from that meeting with a lot to digest and more than I was comfortable discussing with Sue. She's going to see it as another get-rich-quick scheme. I couldn't blame her. It was.

The next morning I sat down with my cup of coffee while Sue was busy studying. I wondered how I could start the conversation. How could I convince her it would be a good idea when even I wasn't convinced? The most powerful argument I had for myself was simply *I could try it, and if things didn't work out, I could stop.* The only problem with that line of thinking was, if it didn't work out, steel bars would be the reason I had to stop. Failure in that endeavor could result in my freedom, my family and indeed any hopes for a desirable future being torn from my grasp. No more get rich schemes would be possible beyond amassing prison yard cigarettes.

I decided to lay all the cards out on the table. The worst thing she could have said was no. Perhaps the best thing she could have said was no. I found myself being my own devil's advocate. I would explain to Sue what I had in mind and instantly counter it with the arguments against the idea. The more I talked, the more the plan sounded foolhardy in its initial vision. Every hole I found in my planning, I plugged with an idea that could make it work. Sue listened to my self-directed monologue and watched as I tied myself in knots, then found a way to untie them. The further I went down the rabbit-hole, the more my ideas molded into plans. It was shifting from a discussion on whether I should move forward with the idea, to more of a strategy session.

The obstacle of Slim's greed made it necessary that I find ways to earn enough outside of the deal we struck to grow larger profits.

The obstacle of sticking out like a sore thumb with out-of-state plates morphed into the concept of traveling routes where those plates would blend in with other traveling motorists. Vacation destinations, convention areas and major Interstate thoroughfares would determine my path. That part of the conversation led to ideas on how and where to stash the weed, which led to what steps I could take to make me look less like a red flag, which led to the plan of action if I actually found myself being pulled over.

"Well it looks like you've thought this through pretty thoroughly," Sue said.

"No Babe," I said. "I actually haven't. In fact, I wasn't really sure until now that I would really want to go through with it. I think I want to give it a try."

With our financial predicament looming large in her mind, Sue reluctantly agreed. Her biggest concern was my possible incarceration. I obviously shared her concern. The thing that we both feared most would have to be mitigated through careful planning. I could not afford to do any of the preparation in a half-assed manner. I had to have a clear plan and never deviate from it. My life would depend on it.

I contacted Slim and agreed to the terms we had discussed. I asked for $12,000 to be ready the following weekend. It was Wednesday. I planned to be on my way back to California on Monday. It was time to prepare.

Due Diligence

I have always been told that everything is fine in moderation. Moderation, however, was not what was needed in this situation. As was the case when preparing to go to California to trim weed, I was committed to being overly prepared. One slip could be the slip I regretted for my remaining days. Everybody who ever sat in an eight by ten cell had regrets. I didn't want mine to be that I didn't prepare. If I was locked up through unavoidable circumstances along the way, I would regret being caught. I was not willing to face the regret of landing in prison for something I had simply not prepared for.

Step one was the need for two distinct looks. Theo was reserving me four pounds, but I would be buying much more than that. I had to prepare to deal with others I had not met yet. I had been told I looked like a biker, which would serve me well while working with any of Theo's friends. I was not very tall but I was big. I stood only five feet, seven inches tall, but my weight was normally around two hundred and seventy pounds. The weight was not fat. It was the combination of a broad frame and fairly significant muscle. I was bald with a long moustache and a tuft of hair on my chin.

I was once in a bar in Mankato when a biker friend of mine asked if I knew why people didn't fuck with me.

"No," I said. "Why?"

"It's your neck," he said.

"My neck?" I asked.

"Yeah, you ain't got one," he replied.

So part of step one was covered. The second look had to be that of a businessman. My plan was to take a grooming kit along for the trip. From the time I left home until my return from California would be a full week. I would grow the tuft on my chin into a small beard and tightly trim the moustache to meld with the beard. It would give me a more professional look. Throw on a suit and I looked like the stereotypical salesman on his way home from a convention.

The convention itself was the next step in the plan. I would plan on taking the route which would bring me through Reno, Nevada when returning from California. Reno always had a convention taking place, and many of them happened over the weekend. They made a Monday passage look like a return trip for a businessman. I don't recall what that first convention was. Over the years I "attended" everything from acting conventions to wild sheep conventions and everything in between. In Reno, conventions were never difficult to find. Once I located the convention that would coincide with my travel dates, I would download their itinerary and put them in my see-through plastic sheeting in my book. I would grab the logo for the convention and print off a color copy. On that color copy I would put a row number, a booth number and my promotional company's name. I laminated the final product and put it on a lanyard. It made me look official.

The next step was to book a room. I always used the La Quinta Inn. It was a mid-budget stay which would make perfect sense for the frugal salesman on a budget. I would go online and go through the steps to reserve the room, print off the dates and room information then cancel the reservation. That gave me the booking dates that lined up with my travel.

The last step I took in order to look the part was packing the car full of promotional materials. The promotional company that I had briefly worked at had given me samples of everything. When I say everything, I mean everything! Pens, hats, lanyards, glasses, cups, mugs, can coolers, t-shirts, jackets, awards, notepads, stuffed toys, luggage, picnic gear, books and anything else you could possibly attach a logo to. My back seat would also be filled with catalogs and ordering forms from multiple marketing companies. Even the bag I would put the pot in was a large zippered promotional bag bigger than twice the size of a hefty garbage bag.

The last thing I needed to do to complete the ruse was to know the area. I knew there were two La Quinta's in Reno, and I knew where they were located. I would make it a habit of driving by the one I booked the room in every time I passed through on my way to California. I would travel from the hotel to the location of the convention, so I knew the roads and would be able to talk intelligently about the area if needed. If there was construction, I needed to know that. If there were any notable landmarks, I needed to know that. The conventions were always held in one of two places. I would need to know if it was held in a convention center or a casino. I never went into the buildings but between the online diagrams, the displayed photos on the website, and a quick lap around the buildings I was able to get the general idea.

I called Theo, and without saying too much over an open line, I told him I would be coming out to see him the following week. I also let him know that my original estimate had grown considerably. He assured me that would not be a problem, and he said he would introduce me to somebody who could help complete the order.

When I had all my ducks in a row and was ready for the road, I hit a snag. The Maxima died. It was a sudden death. We had just finished getting the muffler officially replaced when the front end gave out and the front passenger side tie rod broke. While I was certainly thankful it didn't happen on the way back from California, I was not happy with having to secure a new vehicle.

My friend Jim, who I had played poker with many times, owned a car dealership. I contacted him and asked him if he had anything that would fit my needs. I filled him in on the need for reliability and the ability to blend in. I didn't want anything that would make me stand out. I was pretty candid about the purpose of the vehicle. He found me the perfect car. A green Toyota Camry with low miles and a six cylinder engine which would tackle the mountains well. It would cost me $5,000.

With the $12,000 from Slim, the $7,200 from Big Mark and my own stake of close to eight grand I had over $27,000 at my disposal. I bought the car. As a bonus Jim threw in a huge sub-woofer he had taken out of one of his trade-ins. I laid down another twelve hundred to have a decent stereo installed. I had planned to buy a stereo for the Maxima, so I had hands-free phone capabilities. The last thing I wanted was to be pulled over because I was talking on my phone in a state that required hands-free. I had planned on getting one that would cost me $700, but with the new sub-woofer I decided an upgrade was warranted. I couldn't let the sub-woofer go to waste. I would be rocking on my way out to Cali!

The cost of the car reduced the size of the purchase I would be able to make, but it would still put me in the black. If I watched my expenses, I could buy eighteen pounds from Theo and his friend. I had enough to cover the ten pounds for me and Slim, three pounds for Big Mike and five for myself. That would be enough to hold off any need for a return trip for at least six months. I was ready to hit the road and hit it in style.

Because of the time it took to replace the Maxima and get the new stereo installed in the Camry, my trip was delayed a week. I needed to select a new convention and prepare new materials to coincide with the new travel dates. I again did the due diligence and prepared for the new date. I called Theo and informed him of the delay. The following Monday I was ready to point the Camry west.

Wanderlust King

I woke up early that Monday morning. I went through the checklist to make sure I had not overlooked anything. I had already packed the Camry the night before. I was excited to get on the road and had a renewed sense of hope that I was at the threshold of profitability. I was looking forward to seeing Theo and going back to the land of milk and honey, or more appropriately the land of weed and wine. As I was packing the final provisions in my suitcase, I started laughing. The tune to the old *Beverly Hillbillies* song was going through my head...only I had revised a few of the lyrics.

Come and listen to a story 'bout a man named Steve
Poor ex-trucker felt an urgent need to leave
Then one day he was trimming up some weed,
And up through the ground come a plant made from a seed
(Pot that is, Mary Jane, Cali Green)
Well the first thing you know old Steve's a millionaire
Kin folk said Steve take a trip back there
Said California is the place you oughta be
So he loaded up the Camry and he headed west with glee
(Happy that is, fields of pot, stellar deals)

I didn't feel I could relay that one to Sue. She would have thought I was losing my mind. Maybe I had, a little. I was kind of giddy. It was a new adventure, and I felt I was ready for it. I said good-bye to Sue and grabbed a cup for the road.

I jumped behind the wheel and fired Candy up. Yes, I named the Camry Candy. I selected the perfect song and put it on hold, so I could crank it when I actually left the city limits. I stopped to top off the tank and grab a breakfast sandwich for the road. I got to the edge of town, accelerated to sixty-five and took the stereo off pause. *Wanderlust King* by *Gogol Bordello* punished my ears but shot me full of excited adrenaline. I was enjoying the moment to its fullest. California here I come!

I opted to take the route I would be traveling home. Instead of my past route which took me through South Dakota, I guided Candy south through Sioux City, Iowa then south and west around Omaha to join Interstate 80. I would stay on that solitary road for almost fifteen hundred miles until reaching Reno where I would get on highway 395 north to California. From the moment I left Sioux City until I entered California, I would not see a two-lane. I would be cruising at seventy miles per hour for the whole stretch...or so I thought.

On my approach to Cheyenne, Wyoming the snow began to fall. I had been on the road for over ten hours and had said farewell to the sun a little over an hour before. The Interstate outside of Cheyenne was a slow steady incline. The roads seemed fine but soon I found myself catching up to some traffic that had passed me earlier. Assuming they knew something I didn't, I eased my foot onto the brake. The car slid slightly. The road was covered in black ice. I was glad I had been given the indication from my fellow travelers, or I might have had a much more tragic awakening to the slickness of the road. I slowed Candy down to forty-five miles per hour and kept pace with the other traffic.

When descending Sherman's Pass, the pass that brings you down to the town of Laramie, Wyoming, the traffic slowed to thirty-five. The road was getting worse and becoming snow packed. I had a bit of a PTSD moment. I began flashing back to the fun

I had on the other side of Wyoming while returning from the trimming trip. I stayed steady and, other than a reduction in speed, I had no issues. I passed the miles slowly but enjoyed the new satellite radio package I had purchased. It was two hundred miles before the roads dried up, and I was able to resume a seventy mile per hour pace.

I drove straight through the night. I had established the pattern of driving four hundred and fifty miles, and then I would stop for gas and a coffee refill and drive another four fifty. It gave me the break I needed when the miles began to wear on me. It also broke the trip into bite size pieces. On my fifth stop for gas I would be in California.

I pulled into the Reno area in the late afternoon and followed the route from the La Quinta Inn to the location of the faux convention. I noted my landmarks and noted that there were no issues with construction or any other obstructions. I stopped and got fuel, washed the car near the hotel and continued on.

I arrived in Susanville, California at six o'clock on Tuesday night. I had left home at seven in the morning the day before and with the two hour time difference I considered my arrival time a success. I booked a room at The High Country Suites on the outskirts of Susanville. There was a reason for the choice I made for my hotel stay. Across the parking lot was a pizza place called The Pizza Factory. It was the sister of the Pizza Factory twenty miles before Susanville that Lucas and I had stopped at on the way into California on our trimming adventure. It was good damned pizza.

I brought my luggage into the room and ordered a small Mediterranean pizza. I was living life large. I could eat my well-deserved pizza, get a good night's sleep, get up in the morning, stop at the Starbucks across the highway to get a Depth Charge (Regular cup of coffee with a shot of espresso) and be rolling through the beautiful scenery of Lassen National Park in the morning. It would be hard to top but there was an extra cherry put on top that night. *The Big Lebowski* was on the movie channel in my room. The Dude (NOT Duder) abides...life was good!

As planned, I made my way over the mountains of Lassen with my Depth Charge in hand. When I reached the other side I remembered the Vineyard Lucas and I had attempted to visit before. I decided to try once again to have my California wine experience. I had plenty of time to kill before my meet with Theo on Thursday afternoon.

I pulled into Anselmo Vineyards at lunchtime. It was everything I had hoped for. I sat up at the tiny bar next to the dining area and ordered a cheese plate and a flight of their wines. It was six samples of some of the best wine I had tasted in ages. I planned on buying a bottle or two to accompany me out to Theo's, but I wasn't sure which I wanted. I needed another flight. I enjoyed my second flite and ordered a full glass of their Majorette. I loved it. I enjoyed one more glass, bought three bottles and walked to the car. Correction, stumbled to the car. I wasn't aware of just how much alcohol content was in the varietals I had consumed. I had never let that stop me before and wasn't going to at that point. I fired up the car and headed to Redding. Forty minutes later I was pulling into the Oxford Suites on Hilltop Drive. That would be my home for the next five days.

As if the wine coursing through my veins was not enough libations for the day, I dropped my luggage in my room and found my way to the bar by the lobby of the hotel. I asked the bartender for a suggestion of a decent local beer. She knew her trade well and asked me my preferences. She suggested a *Lost Coast Great White* which was a Belgian style wheat beer with a hint of citrus and coriander. She said it would complement the two fingers of scotch I had already requested. I remember the taste of the combination was exactly what I was looking for. I don't remember much else.

When my eyes opened, I found myself half-dressed and lying on top of the bed covers. It was a rude awakening and slow. I used the coffee maker on my counter to try and regain some sense of normalcy. What was it about California that brought out the drinker in me? The last time I felt this way, I was waking up in my tent after Don had passed his drinking limit, and I had passed mine.

I made my way down to the lobby to grab some free breakfast to tamp down the queasy feeling in my stomach from my day of overindulgence. I forced myself to eat some scrambled eggs, a couple sausages, a pancake and glass of orange juice before returning to my room for a shower and another cup of coffee.

When I started to feel human again, I readied myself for the run to Theo's. I stared at the three bottles of wine sitting by my luggage. The idea of drinking had no appeal. I did, however, buy the wine for that reason. At least that's what I told myself. I grabbed a bottle for the trip. Theo said he was going to introduce me to one of his growers, so maybe two would be a better plan. I grabbed the second bottle. Hell, I could always bring one back if we didn't drink it. The third bottle made the cut.

I jumped in the Camry and set out to Theo's, but before leaving town I stopped at the local Walmart to purchase a pair of scissors, a vacuum sealer, some vacuum sealer bags and some bleach. I didn't want the hotel room to be inundated with the pungent aroma of the local crops.

I took the backroads through Igo and Ono and made my way to Theo's. I was not surprised to see a note on the glass door to the store stating he would return at 12:00. It was 1:00. I pulled one of the camping chairs out from the back seat of my vehicle. I had three chairs that were samples from my former employer's promotional company. I was prepared to wait. I kept the back car door open and turned on the stereo to drown out the sound of

Theo's barking dogs. I didn't wait long before Theo entered the grounds as a passenger in a green Subaru Outback. The man behind the wheel could not have looked more like a backwoods mountain man. He had long grayish white hair, a long beard, and moustache. I assumed this was the grower Theo wanted me to meet.

"Hey, Chopper," Theo said as he emerged from the Aussie auto. "Glad you made it out! Did you have a good trip? No problems?"

"A little choppy weather," I replied. "Other than that it went pretty smoothly."

The mountain man stepped out from the driver's side of the car and approached.

"Chopper, this is Mack. Mack, meet Chopper."

"Glad to meet you, Mack," I said as I put my hand out.

Mack shook my hand and immediately asked about my name.

"My name isn't Chopper," I said. "It's Steve. It's a long story."

"Would you rather I call you Steve or Chopper?" Mack asked.

"Either one is fine. My name is Steve. My nickname out here in Cali has become Chopper."

"All right, Steve," Mack said. "Glad to meet you as well."

"New car?" Theo asked.

"Yeah the Maxima died shortly before coming out here. I just picked this one up last week."

"Glad it didn't happen on the road," Theo said. "That would have been a mess. It looks like you two coordinated. Your car is almost the same color as Mack's."

On the basis of first impressions, I liked Mack. He may have looked backwoods, but he was sharp. He had a nice smile, a good sense of humor, and the ability to quickly put me at ease. Before we even broached the subject of weed, we had a good conversation. Mack asked about the weather back in Minnesota. When I told him on the day I left it was below zero, he shuddered.

"I think people from Minnesota must have lost their damned minds living in a place that gets that cold!"

"Why do you think I'm out here?" I replied. "I had to get out of the crazy weather and come visit a different style of crazy. California crazy is my favorite kind of crazy. I assume you don't hold Theo here as the model of stability!?"

"No." Mack said. "He sure isn't that!"

Theo took the comment in stride and invited us into the store to conduct business. Before going in Mack went to the back of his Outback and popped the back hatch open. He removed what looked like an army rucksack. It was a big olive green canvas bag with a strap. We all went into the store and congregated up at the counter.

"So how did your trip back to Minnesota go?" Theo asked.

"It was crazy," I replied.

I told Theo about the snow while driving through Lassen, the blizzard I chased through eastern Nevada and into Wyoming, the brush with death on sister number two, and the cop following me in western Wyoming.

"And you're back for more?" Theo said. "I guess Mack was right. You Minnesota people really are crazy."

"Yah, sure, you betcha," I said, doing my best *Fargo* impersonation.

We discussed the trip and the trials I went through in securing the money to come back. We had a good conversation and again held off talking business for a while. I asked them both if they were up for some wine. Theo didn't drink wine but opened up the cooler in the small room behind the counter and brought out some beer. It wasn't just any beer, it was Lost Coast Great White. For me it was the hair of the dog that bit me. Mack didn't drink at all. According to Mack pouring alcohol down his throat would give rise to a brand of California crazy that nobody would want a part of.

When the topic of business came up Theo reached under the counter and pulled up five one pound bags of high quality weed. All varieties had a pungent smell and all but one was deep green with purple or dark blue hairs poking out from the buds. I recognized them right away. I didn't recognize the exact strains but I knew they were various Kush strains. The exception was a bag with a lighter green color and dusty looking hairs. I had trimmed plenty of that one at Ricky's. It was the Blue Cheese. I was thrilled with all the selections.

"All of these were grown by Mack with the exception of the cheese," Theo said. "You said you were going to need more, so that's why I asked Mack to join us. How many more are you looking for?"

"I'm going to need eighteen pounds total and, of course, with that quantity, I was hoping to get a reduction on the price per pound."

"Oh shit," Mack piped in. "I only brought eight in with me. I don't know if I have enough trimmed bud to cover your order."

"Do you have more you can get?" I asked.

"Not trimmed," Mack replied. "I might have another two back at the house. My wife does the trimming by herself. I could have her get to working on getting more done. How long are you in town?"

"I'm leaving early Monday morning, so I would need to vacuum seal and bleach the bags Sunday night."

"I can't guarantee I can cover it but I'll have Dana get to work on it right away," Mack volunteered. "Are you staying in Redding?"

"Yeah, I'm staying at The Oxford Suites on Hilltop."

"I can try to get the full order ready by Sunday night and bring you what I have. As far as a price break, I can't go under a $1,050 per pound"

"That works for me," I said. "Thanks for pushing to get it ready. Give my thanks to Dana!"

"Will do," Mack said with a smile. "Now let's make this relationship official."

With that Mack pulled out a tightly packed blunt (Cigar leaf rolled around weed). It was bigger than most blunts I had smoked in the past. It was the size of a large cigar.

"You do the honors, Steve," Mack said as he handed me the blunt.

I set my self to lighting that bad boy. I puffed and puffed until I finally sprung that monster to life. I offered it back to Mack, and he deferred to Theo. Theo took the blunt and handed me another Great White. The blunt took so long to smoke that I had finished two more Great Whites before it was gone. The store was a haze of billowing smoke and all eyes had become red slits.

Mack suggested we step out from the smoke cloud and have a cigarette outside the store. When we exited the trailer I grabbed the remaining two promotional camp chairs and we all kicked back and relaxed in the sun. Mack was intrigued by stories of the frozen lakes, mountainous snowbanks, and bitter cold weather of Minnesota. We talked for over an hour and Theo kept refreshing me with beers. I don't think I finished a single one before he gave me another. I didn't want warm beer, and I didn't want to waste any, so I chugged the ends of one beer before starting the next. I thought we were winding down when Mack pulled out another blunt and handed it to me to light. I didn't want to be rude. I sparked it up, and we passed it around. More weed and more beers made me less anxious to head back to the hotel.

It was a great afternoon getting to know Mack. He was truly on my "coolest people on the planet" list. The time had rolled on to the late afternoon, and Mack said he had to get going so he could put Dana to work.

I thanked Mack for everything, said good-bye to Theo, and loaded the thirteen pounds into Candy's trunk. Mack borrowed me his rucksack. I was in no condition to drive but that never stopped me before. It wasn't going to stop me then. I jumped into the car and made my way back to the hotel.

How I made it back to the hotel, I'll never know. I brought the bags, the newly purchased vacuum sealer, and the wine into my room. I set to the task of vacuum sealing the various varieties. I opened a bottle of the Majorette to drink while I worked. Once the entire haul of weed was sealed I filled the bath tub half full of water and poured half of the gallon of bleach in. I threw the thirteen bags in. I thoroughly washed my hands so the weed residue from the process of sealing didn't transfer to the newly bleached bags. I scrubbed the bags and toweled them dry. When the procedure was complete I placed the finished product into my promotional bag and threw away the empty bottle of Majorette.

I was hungry, and I had noticed an interesting looking place located next to the hotel called Logan's Roadhouse. I decided to walk over and check it out. The menu was on the pricey side, but I wanted to order one of everything. Mack's blunts made it even more appealing than it normally would have been. I ordered the country style buttermilk chicken dinner at the suggestion of the waitress. It was Thursday night, so martinis were the special. I felt special, so I ordered one to sip while I waited for my meal. The food was delicious as was the martini. After dinner I had a Sierra Nevada beer and payed the hefty bill.

When I got back to the room, I collapsed on the bed. It had been a long day and the full belly combined with the over indulgence of booze pulled me into a deep and instant sleep.

My pounding head alerted me to a new day. It wasn't a hangover headache. Well I guess it could be considered as one. I awoke in much the same position I had fallen asleep. My head was pounding because my neck was in a weird position. Eight hours of bad posture took a toll. A familiar theme was emerging. What was it about California that makes me act like a drunken sailor on shore leave?

That entire day was about enjoying my surroundings. After a couple cups of coffee and my free breakfast I made plans to call Sue, visit the exercise room, take a swim, enjoy the hot tub and top it off with a movie rental. It was Friday and I had the weekend to look forward to. Mack had committed to joining me on Sunday, so Sunday night would be reserved for making final preparations for the road.

I called Sue and gave her an update on the trip. I told her I planned to be back Tuesday night after my early Monday departure. Her voice always had a calming effect on me. That call was no exception. I was stressing out about the trip home. Memories of my last run home from California loomed large in my mind.

I threw on a pair of shorts and ventured down to the exercise room. The alcohol poured out of my sweat glands as I worked out.

I took a quick rinsing shower and went out to the pool. I was the only one swimming. The fact that it was winter and I was swimming was heaven to me. I thought perhaps the other travelers considered it a bit strange.

When I had my fill of swimming, I was hit with the urge to grab a bottle of wine and hit the hot tub. What is it about California? I resisted that urge. I replaced the idea of a glass of wine with a cup of coffee. I sat in the hot tub enjoying the jets and warm water while I read a book and sipped my coffee. It wasn't long before a young couple joined me. As I said before, I like to talk. I struck up a conversation with the couple. Tony was a tall man with shoulder length brown hair, a full well-groomed beard, a sleeve of tattoos and an earring. He worked for the state of California as a professional firefighter. Bree was his wife of four years. She was close to Tony's height with short cropped blonde hair and had her own sleeve of tattoos. Bree was a bartender in Red Bluff, California where the couple hailed from. Very nice people. They had come to Redding to visit friends.

We hit it off and enjoyed a long conversation. After a bit Bree announced it was time for a nice afternoon beer. She got out of the hot tub to head to the bar and grab herself and Tony a beer.

"Why don't you grab one for Steve," Tony said. "What are you drinking?"

Without hesitation I answered "I'll take a Great White. Thanks."

Bree returned with three plastic cups of beer. The hotel did not allow glass in the pool area. The conversation continued and I told them about the great vineyard I had visited. Bree was a big fan of wine and asked all about the vineyard and the varietals they produced. She had heard of Anselmo Vineyards but had never been there. I offered to share a bottle of the Majorette with them. Wine was not Tony's thing but Bree was excited to accept. I excused myself and went to the room to grab a couple plastic cups full of wine. Bree loved the Majorette. When we had finished the first round, I went in to grab a refill for Bree and me. I took the last bottle and wrapped it in a towel. When I got back out to the hot tub, I gave the bottle to Bree and said it was my gift to the couple for the excellent conversation.

"Are you sure?" Bree asked.

"Yes, of course."

"Tony, we should see if Steve's free to join us for supper."

"That's a great idea," Tony said. "How about it Steve, are you up to having a nice meal at the restaurant next door?"

"Logan's Roadhouse?" I asked.

"Yeah, we've eaten there several times. We love their food," Tony said.

"I'd love to join you. I ate there last night," I said. "You're right about the food. I had their buttermilk chicken, and it was fantastic."

We made the plan to meet at Logan's at six-thirty that evening. We all went back to our respective rooms and I showered and made myself ready. I had a half hour to kill before our plans to meet so I went down to the bar in the lobby and ran into Tony who had the same idea. I ordered a Sierra Nevada and Tony ordered the same and a shot of scotch.

"As long as Tony's grabbing a little scotch," I said to the bartender "I'll have a shot as well."

"Are you a fan of scotch?" Tony asked. "Logan's has a pretty good selection."

"I am unable to refuse good single malt," I replied.

We enjoyed our beer and scotch and talked about our favorite blends. When we were done Tony said he was going to the room to get Bree and he would meet me over at the Roadhouse. I went back to my room, used the facilities, and freshened myself up for supper. When I was almost out the door my cell phone rang. It was Lucas. I answered it.

"Hey man, what's up?" I asked.

"Just thought I would call and let you know what's going on with Chelsey and me," Lucas said. "We're planning to sell all our stuff and move with Amy out to California."

Chelsey is the woman Lucas had been with for the last several years and Amy was their daughter. I didn't want to tell Lucas that he had coincidently called me while I was actually in California. I had not told Lucas I was coming out because I didn't want Carl to know I was even in the area.

"What made you decide to move out to California?" I said while almost saying *move out here*.

"Carl offered me Don's old job." He said. "Only difference is I won't have to stay at the shed out on the property. The three of us are moving in with Carl and Kathy."

"Wow, that's crazy man. Congratulations," I said "I hate to say it, but I'm just stepping out the door. Can I maybe call you back tomorrow?

"Sure. Talk to you tomorrow."

Holy shit; did I really just hear what I thought I heard? I couldn't believe it. I couldn't quite wrap my head around it. The news was dizzying. It would be one thing to come out to work for Carl. That was crazy enough. Uprooting the whole family and actually living with Carl sounded insane.

I ventured across the parking lot and stepped into Logan's. To my surprise Tony and Bree were sitting at a table with two other couples. Tony waved me over and used his foot to push out the chair next to him. At my place was a beer and next to that was a glass with three fingers of scotch. Tony said it was his gift to me after my gift of Majorette to Bree. I was introduced to the two couples.

"These two are the Dave's and these two are the Tammy's," Tony said with a smile. "Yes they are both named Dave and Tammy. Only her name is spelled T-A-M- I," He said while pointing to one of the women.

"That's too funny," I said.

The couples were the friends Tony and Bree were visiting. This is where I started to get a bit confused. Dave number one could have been Tony's clone. He was about the same height as Tony, had the same long hair, and was riddled with tattoos. Dave number one worked with Tony as a firefighter. His wife, Tami with the short spelling worked at a bar in Redding where Bree used to work before Tami started. Dave number two was a short stalky man with a crew cut and not a tattoo in sight. He worked as a security guard at a business in Redding. His girlfriend Tammy, with a y, worked with Tony and Dave number one as a firefighter. She was about five feet ten inches tall and built like a pro wrestler. Her muscular arms were covered in tattoos as was her neck and lower legs. Her straight, fire-red hair hung halfway down her back.

They were a fun crew and we spent hours talking over beers, mixed drinks and, of course, a goodly amount of scotch. At the end of the visit to Logan's, Dave and Tammy with a y, joined Tony, Bree, and me at the hot tub to wind down the evening. My final drink for the night was from the bottle of Majorette that Bree brought down from her room.

When Dave number two and Tammy with a y left I went back to my room. It was too late and I was too drunk to think about renting the movie I had promised myself. It had been another long day and my pillow welcomed me. I went down for the count.

First thought when I came back to life the next day? What is it about California? I pulled my battered and beaten body out of the room and pointed myself in the direction of the free breakfast. I was moving slowly. I could still feel the remnants of last night's brain cell slaughter.

When I walked into the breakfast area there was Tony, Bree, Dave number two, and Tammy with a y. The visitors Tony and Bree had been here to visit crashed on the extra bed in their room. They were smart enough not to have risked driving home. I grabbed a plate and sat down on the chair they offered me.

"Are you still on for tonight?" Tony asked me.

I was confused. I did not recall anything that had been discussed about any affair happening that night.

"On for tonight?" I asked. "What's going on tonight?"

Tony laughed and said that we had talked last night about an underground hold 'em game that was held less than two blocks from the hotel. It was a game held in the back room of a local business owned by one of Bree's former employers. Tony reminded me that I had told him I would join him, and Dave number one, the other Dave, tonight. It was starting to come back to me. I had indeed agreed.

"What time are we going over?" I asked.

"We had talked about meeting at the bar here in the lobby about six thirty to get primed for the game," Tony said. "Do you still want me to grab you a six pack of Great White and split a bottle of scotch for the game? If you want cocktails, you have to bring your own bottle. I told you I would be stopping at the liquor store this afternoon to pick up our supplies."

"Yeah, sure," I said somewhat stunned. "How much cash do you need?"

Tony laughed again.

"You already gave me thirty bucks last night to cover it."

"I'm sorry, man," I said. "I got a little carried away last night."

"Everybody did," Tammy said. "It took me a minute this morning to remember where the hell I was."

I finished my breakfast and repeated some of the routine from the day before. A workout, a swim, and some relaxing time in the hot tub were followed by a new addition to the schedule...a nap.

I met Tony at the bar at six thirty, as promised. Dave was with him. My intentions were to do a slow sipping kind of evening. I didn't really even want to partake at all. Tony had already ordered me a scotch and a Sierra Nevada. As if that wasn't a rocky start all by itself, two minutes after I sat down the bartender served three shots of Jagermeister that Dave had already ordered. *Here we go* I thought.

After round one made it down my throat, I was ready to get back in the groove. The rest of the evening was a blast. The underground game was interesting. The front entrance brought us through a small diner. At the back of the diner was a long hall with bathrooms on the left about halfway down. At the far end of the hall was a door. Through the door was the game room. There were four large tables adorned with felt and drink holders like an actual casino. When we checked in for the game, we checked in our drinks. They would be served throughout the night when requested. It was like I was in a mini Vegas.

My stacks of chips were on a roller coaster ride. They went up and down and up and down. At one point I was up over $500. Later in the evening I had my Jacks full of Kings beat by Kings full of Jacks, which dropped me two hundred in the hole. There was a pair of jacks and a pair of nines on the board. I had a King and a Jack in my hand. I had Jacks full of nines. The turn card was a king. I had my Jacks full of kings. Unfortunately, the man who beat me had pocket kings. It was a tough beat.

I managed to bring myself back to one hundred dollars profit by the end of the night. After paying for my booze, my tips to the man who served the drinks, and the ten dollar entry fee to play in the room, I had pretty much broken even.

I had plenty to drink that night but managed to keep myself more in check than any night since entering California. After walking back to the hotel with Tony and Dave, I agreed to meet Tony and Bree for breakfast in the morning.

I woke up a little numb, but, again, in better shape than the other mornings. What is it about California? I met Tony and Bree for breakfast and we exchanged phone numbers. They told me they would call next time they planned on coming up to Redding in case the timing worked out to get together again. It was a hell of an adventure meeting them and I appreciated their company. We said our good-byes and went our separate ways.

I again repeated my daily ritual and was feeling pretty good when Mack showed up late that afternoon. Dana was not able to trim quite enough to cover my order, but she came close. Mack had four full pounds and a little shy of seven ounces. He gave me the seven ounces for free. That was unexpected and thoroughly appreciated.

Mack and I went out to my car, pulled out the promotional camp chairs and enjoyed the last of the sun with a little weed and a couple cigarettes. I really got to like Mack. He was like nobody I had ever met. I got to hear his story.

Mack had been heavily involved in dealing Meth in the Redding, Red Bluff and Chino areas. He was pretty much the main guy in the area to get hooked up with that drug. He was making very good money. He was even able to buy his mother a small house in Chino. He was married to Dana at the time and she enjoyed the money but kept trying to get him to give it up. She was almost ready to leave him. He ended up getting busted and served several years in prison. Dana stayed with him through his prison term and Mack promised her he would never touch the stuff again. When he was released from prison he kept his word to her and never touched it again. He loved pot, and started growing some personal stash. Without telling Dana, he was also growing a small garden further down on his property. He wasn't sure how she would take it, so he kept it a secret.

One day when Dana was on her way to her nursing job, her car broke down. Dana was depressed because they didn't have enough money to fix the car or replace it. That's when Mack let her know about the garden. They sold some weed, bought a new car (well, new to them), and have been growing and selling ever since. Dana eventually quit her job to be Mack's full-time trimmer and partner.

When the sun set, we said good-bye, and I went to work preparing for the long trip the next day. I vacuum sealed and bleached the bags. I gathered everything together so I could get up and drive out early in the morning.

I had my first sober night of sleep since my arrival. I got up refreshed and loaded the car. I checked out of the hotel, drove to the gas station, filled the tank and grabbed a cup of coffee. By seven in the morning I was pointed east and Candy took me out of Redding.

I was trying to enjoy the scenery while traveling through Lassen. I couldn't. The stress was pushing down on me. I was scared and couldn't let my guard down. Once I made it past Fernley, Nevada I was able to lighten up a bit but not completely. The stress was taking away any enjoyment of the beautiful route that had unfolded before me. I don't think I relaxed a single moment during the whole drive home.

I drove straight through and made it home early Tuesday evening. I was glad to be home, but I was a wreck. Four solid days of drinking followed by over thirty hours behind the wheel had taken a toll on me. I enjoyed my wife's company before collapsing in my bed. I slept for eleven hours. I woke up with a feeling I didn't expect. I was refreshed from the nice long sleep. I was relieved to be home. I expected that.

What I wasn't expecting was the dominant feeling I had. I was worried.

The Candyman Can

I made it home safely and was in a better position than I had expected. I was able to secure seventeen pounds at a savings of fifty dollars per pound, giving me an extra $750. I was given an extra seven ounces from my new mountain man friend. That was at least an extra $2,100. I had given Theo and Mack the heads up that I planned on making another trip in four or five months, and they assured me I would have plenty of bud to choose from. Things were going my way, and instead of feeling happy, I was overcome with trepidation.

I called Big Mark and we enjoyed a sampling session, and I made delivery of the three pounds he had ordered. He was thrilled with the quality of the weed. I informed him that it was my intention to make another trip later in the year.

The next few weeks were a blur. I spent time dividing up the varieties I had brought back home into smaller quantities. I had my handy sealable kitchen container loaded with half ounce, quarter ounce, and eighth ounce bags. I weighed out a half a pound into full ounce bags and put them in a duffle bag. The rest I resealed and kept in the promotional bag they came home in.

I created butter to make some treats, and, although it's a much easier process with hash, I made tincture from the raw bud. I did some research and found more candy recipes online. Some I went by the instructions, but some I expanded on or altered slightly.

When I was done making candy, I had a veritable candy store opened and ready for business. I had tincture divvied into the small dram bottles that originally contained the flavorings used to create my hard candies and suckers. I had grape, cherry, butterscotch, root beer and strawberry suckers. I had grape, cherry, butterscotch, root beer, spearmint, strawberry and cool mint hard candies. I had grape, cherry, butterscotch, root beer and strawberry gummies. I had caramels. I had cookies. I had black licorice. I even made homemade Snickers.

I got the word out, and things started selling as fast as I could make them. Some would buy a bag of pot and see what they had left for cash-on-hand and spend the rest on candy. Some had no interest in candy. Others wanted the candy above all else. I even had a few occasions where I was commissioned to create full pans of Snickers. I was happy to provide it.

Snickers were in high demand and became somewhat legendary. They were often used as a challenge. People would say to their friends "I bet you can't eat a whole snickers and come back for more." Making them, however, was a process. It was a layer of chocolate, a layer of nougat, a layer of peanuts, and a layer of caramel topped with another layer of chocolate. My cost to make a pan was around seventy-five dollars. I charged two hundred.

I charged four dollars for a hard candy, seven dollars for a sucker, seven dollars for a cookie, seven dollars for a square of black licorice, seven dollars for a square of caramel, ten dollars for a small bottle of tincture, five dollars for a gummy, and twenty dollars for a large Snickers bar. I would cut a Snickers bar in half if requested. I was the one stop shop for all the reefer aficionados. I had the challenge of trying to service as many people as possible without getting so much traffic that I would put myself on the law enforcement radar. Back in the 80s, I was selling small quantities and the traffic drew attention leading to my unfortunate incarceration for possession with intent to distribute. Those charges were expunged from my record, and I didn't want to tempt them to come back.

I decided to limit purchases to no more than one visit per person, per week. It accomplished two things. It diminished the traffic to my front door, and it meant when I got a visit I would sell a higher quantity. It worked out well. My candy and pot sales were exceeding expectations, and I was paying Slim off at a pretty rapid rate. So why wasn't I enjoying it? It was the beginning of what I was working for, and it was going better than I thought was possible.

I assumed I would have to wait for big Mark to need replenishments before I would be in need of opening any of the resealed bags. As fast as the pot was flying off the shelves, I found myself needing to open them again and again to replenish the ounces, halves, quarters and eighths. What I assumed would take me four or five months, was now looking more like a return trip would be needed in less than three. I was making decent enough money, but as fast as my stock was diminishing, I thought it would be significantly more. Between having to give Slim his share and trying to keep up with the monthly bills I was unable to really put anything away.

During that period I also had to say good-bye to Lucas as he, once again, was on his way to Carl's. That time Lucas was bringing his girlfriend and daughter with for the California experience. I was excited for them to make the trip to California. I was scared for them to be moving in with Carl. No good could come from that. I considered myself lucky to have had the blinders slip from my eyes early enough, that I was able to write Carl's bullshit off as a bad experience, while I was still in California on the first trip. I feared what Lucas had in store for him.

Lucas's girlfriend Chelsey was somebody who was very easy to like. I didn't get the chance to get to know her real well, but what I knew of her I liked. Lucas's daughter Amy was as cute as it's legal to be and inquisitive beyond her years. She reminded me a lot of my older daughter in that she was comfortable talking to adults at an early age and strived to know more about everything.

The one thing that made me feel better about their decision to move out west was that Chelsey worked in management for a national chain store, and she was able to get a transfer to Redding. They wouldn't starve when Carl inevitably showed his true colors. It wasn't a question of if it would happen; it was just a matter of when. I would miss having Lucas in Mankato, but part of me was happy that perhaps, down the road, I would be able to visit him in California. I wouldn't visit him if he was still with Carl but like I said, that was not destined to be long-term. It couldn't be.

As I saw the sealed bags dwindle down to dust, I knew I had to arrange another pick up with Theo and Mack. Unfortunately, I was short of money. I couldn't afford to cover a significant purchase, so first I would have to speak with Slim. Before hitting him up I called Big Mark and asked if he was ready to pick up another few pounds. His sales were not going as quickly as mine had. In the time it took me to move over thirteen pounds, he had only been able to move less than two. The candy was the difference.

Big Mark was in for a pound and a half for a total of $3,900. I had six grand of my own. I would have to talk to Slim to get another infusion of cash. I asked for $13,000, and without hesitation he agreed to it. I called Theo and told him I would be ready for another round of approximately the same quantity as before in two weeks' time. He told me not to worry. He would start making some calls to make sure I was covered.

With Lucas staying at Carl's, I didn't make him aware that I would be heading west. It was hard to do. I would have loved to visit him while I was out there, but I couldn't bring myself to ever put myself in a position to be in the same room with someone I had come to loathe as much as Carl.

I finished selling almost everything I had in stock and readied myself to head out west again. It was spring, and the weather was beginning to warm up. I would be taking the same route. I figured the trip would be nothing but good weather the whole way.

When the day to leave arrived, I was excited to once again be rolling west to see Theo and Mack and get a dose of California crazy. The trip was quick and easy. There was no bad weather. There were no issues of any kind. It was like the universe was telling me I was good to go.

When I rolled into Susanville, I booked a room at the High Country Suites and enjoyed my Mediterranean pizza in my room before getting a good night's sleep. I took my trip to Starbucks and sipped my Depth Charge on the way to Anselmo Vineyards. I had to get a few bottles of the Majorette. That time I intended to bring at least two bottles home. As luck would have it, I made it to the Vineyard at lunchtime again. I ate a light lunch consisting of a small salad, a half sandwich and three glasses of wine. I bought four bottles of my favorite and rolled on to the Oxford Suites in Redding.

After checking in, I went down to the bar and ordered a scotch and a Sierra Nevada. I looked at it as my celebratory return to California. I had many conversations with a variety of people throughout the afternoon and lost track of how much beer and scotch was consumed. It was significant. What is it about California?

I, of course, continued the drinking at Logan's Roadhouse when I ventured over for supper. It may sound a bit crazy, but I was no longer questioning my consumption. It was California. Screw it. It was my time to enjoy whatever the hell I felt like. It was almost a rebellious feeling, but who was the rebellion against? I was there on my own volition. Nobody had forced me to be running weed. I actually loved the freedom I was experiencing so why the rebellion?

It made no sense. I swallowed the feeling along with a bunch of high quality scotch.

I went back to my room, threw on some shorts, opened a bottle of Majorette, poured a plastic cup full of the elixir, and walked out to the pool area. It was pretty packed for a Wednesday night. I stepped into the hot tub and joined the other seven or eight adults. It was a party atmosphere. There were a lot of plastic cups. I was amongst my kind.

"Were you at the hold em game a few months ago?" One of the men asked.

I didn't recognize who he was until that moment. The man asking me about the game shared the table I was on when I was playing cards with Tony.

"Wow, you have a good memory," I said. "That was a hell of a night."

"Hard to forget a bad beat like you had that night," he said.

"Yeah that was a tough river for me."

"That guy was insane to stay with you until the river," he said. "If it makes you feel any better, he didn't take your money home that night. The rest of us at the table beat up on him pretty bad the rest of the night. He was a total fish. He just got lucky...or you got unlucky."

"Yeah I was just happy to get a little back before I left that night," I said. "He took the wind out of my sails. My heart wasn't in it after that hand. He put me on tilt."

"I don't blame you," he said. "I'm here for the next week, and I'm planning on going to the game on Saturday if you're interested in joining me."

"Sure," I said. "Why not?"

The man's name was Gordy. He was a hotel auditor. I didn't know what that was until he explained it to me. He worked for an independent company that got hired to do undercover stays at various hotels. When he stayed in the hotels, he conducted audits on everything from customer service and cleanliness of the rooms and grounds to the number of towels and type and quality of amenities offered. I was asked not to say anything to others about his reason for staying at the hotel. I assured him his secret was safe with me. Gordy was about six feet tall and weighed about three hundred and fifty pounds. He was an extremely hefty man, but he didn't seem self-conscious at all. He was a pretty happy dude with a bit of a sharp edge to his humor. He noticed my George Carlin tattoo and commented on how Carlin was one of his favorite comedians. I was certainly glad to have made Gordy's acquaintance. He was a fun guy.

As Gordy and I talked, the hot tub became less populated until we were the only two enjoying the bubble jets. I went and filled the last glass of the night from my bottle of Majorette and went back out to chat with Gordy until they closed the pool area down for the night.

I retired to my room and fell asleep on my bed while watching TV. It was a deep and long sleep.

"I know what you're thinking. Did I fire six shots or only five?" were the first words I heard that morning. I had left the TV on and woke up to *Dirty Harry*. I knew the words by heart, and I had to ask myself, do I feel lucky? The answer was a resounding yes! I was sitting in bed watching the end of one of my favorite movies, and, spoiler alert, he only fired five shots. The bad guy in the end felt lucky then felt nothing at all. I was waking up with the knowledge I would see Theo and Mack that day. The expediency of my sales was beyond expectation. I was lined up to have a Saturday night game with Gordy. I completed my last run with no interference from Johnny Law. I awoke with a groggy feeling but no real hangover...*what is it about California?* I had a wife I adored and a family that made me happy and proud. I felt lucky. So what was it that had been gnawing at me? Something was bothering me and I was not able to pin it down.

I pulled off the covers, freshened up, and went to grab my morning freebies. I recognized a few people from my conversations at the bar and my time in the hot tub. Gordy was not there. I took my plate and walked out to the pool area and enjoyed my meal in the sun near the pool. It was a beautiful sunny day without a cloud in the sky. Chemtrails, yes, clouds no. I finished my meal, returned my plate and decided to skip my visit to the exercise room and instead threw on my shorts and enjoyed the pool area for the entire morning. I finished one of the two books I had brought with me. It was a wonderful morning. The kind of day I was having so far could not have been scripted any better.

I went back to the hotel, took a quick shower and threw on my jeans, a t-shirt, and my hiking boots. I thought as a treat I would bring some food out to Theo's for lunch. Either I would eat it waiting for Theo and Mack, or they could join me. Either way it felt like a good idea. To have a little something to drink with lunch, I grabbed a bottle of Majorette. I loaded a cooler with ice and went to the same Holiday grocery store I had brought Don to when we were trimming. I remembered they had a pretty kick-ass deli. I selected a variety of sub sandwiches and noticed that they had a sushi station. I loaded up on several varieties of sushi trays. I loved the idea of having some sushi by the pool for lunch the next day. I went out to the parking lot, loaded the cooler with the lunch supplies, and woke Candy up for the ride to Theo's.

When I pulled into Theo's I saw the familiar green Outback. It wasn't parked in front of the store. Instead, it was parked across the lot next to a small, old, gutted-out shell of an RV. Theo appeared next to Mack's Outback and waved me over. I drove over and parked Candy next to Mack's vehicle. From the entrance there were no people visible, but when I pulled next to the RV things changed. It was Mack, Theo, a woman I had never met, and off in the distance were two teenage boys.

That was my introduction to Mack's wife Dana and their two boys Ned and Cody. Ned and Cody were busy entertaining themselves near the creek that ran through Theo's property. The introduction from Theo was yelled to them and their response was to wave at me. There were several chairs sitting around a small campfire and Mack and Dana were sitting next to each other. Dana was hard at work trimming some pretty buds.

"Steve this is the trimmer you put to work last time you were out here," Mack said. "Meet my wife Dana."

"Nice to meet you, Dana," I said offering my hand. "I hope I wasn't too much of a pain in the butt on the last trip."

Dana smiled, set down the bud and her scissors and shook my hand. "No trouble at all. If it wasn't for you, we wouldn't have enjoyed going out to eat that week. The money came in handy."

Dana was the epitome of the word mom. She was pleasant almost to a fault. She sported a great smile and was the perfect match for her mountain man husband. I could easily see what Mack saw in her. The beauty of Dana was her soft-spoken demeanor coupled with an innate *something* that made those around her feel they were being paid special attention to. As I eventually found out, she was soft-spoken but could curse like a drunken sailor when the mood moved her. She was something special.

Theo offered Dana a new beer to replace the one in front of her. She accepted and Theo asked if I wanted one as well. I gladly accepted. I announced that I had lunch in the cooler. Dana immediately asked what I had. I gave her the list.

"I'll take a turkey combo, if that's ok," Dana said. "Did you say you had sushi?"

"Yeah, would you like some?"

"Oh, God no!" She exclaimed. "I can't understand why anybody would eat that stuff, but the boys love sushi. I know you didn't know they'd be here, but do you think they could have a little?"

"Absolutely," I replied. "I brought way more than I could eat myself."

Dana called the boys over and told them I had sushi. They were excited and each picked out a tray. Mack was smiling as he leaned over to me.

"You just made friends for life, Steve," Mack said in a quiet voice. "They rarely get the chance to have sushi."

After the boys demolished their sushi trays, Cody asked for another. I told him as long as there was more left, he was welcome to it. Ned had a second tray, and Cody ate three. I polished off my beer and decided to eat the only remaining tray of sushi before it disappeared. I opened the Majorette. I offered Dana a glass, and she accepted.

When everybody had their fill of lunch Mack pulled out one of his killer blunts. He handed it to Theo to spark up, and Theo handed it to me once it was brought to life. After taking a hit, I handed it to Dana. She waved it past.

"I don't touch that stuff," Dana said. "Well, I touch it to trim it. Mack can smoke, and I'll enjoy this wonderful wine. Where did you get this?"

"Anselmo Vineyards over on the road to Lassen."

"It's great stuff," she said holding her glass up.

I refilled her glass with the remainder of the bottle. Theo beckoned me into the rickety RV with Mack. I was shown the lineup. There were twelve pounds of prime bud from Mack. No surprise there. There were two pounds of Blue Cheese from another of Theo's connections. Then I was presented with four pounds of something that thoroughly shocked me. It was garbage.

It was sub-standard. It wasn't even trimmed well. It was brown. It was not acceptable.

"What is this?" I asked.

"It's OG Kush crossed with Sour Diesel," Theo replied. "It's really good stuff."

"I'm sorry man but I can't buy any of that," I said. "It is not something I could sell. I've had OG Kush and I've had Sour Diesel and this doesn't look anything like either of them."

"I told my guy that these were sold," Theo pleaded "I can't go back to him without the money."

"That's tragic, but it's not my problem Theo," I said. "If I brought that back to Minnesota, I would lose my shirt and damage my reputation. I know you know good weed when you see it, so I'm stunned you took this from him."

"I know it's not the best trim job, but it's pretty good quality," Theo said "Just smoke a little with me and you'll see."

"That's fair, I guess," I said.

Theo rolled a joint with the pot in question and passed it to me to light. I sparked it up and was even less impressed after I tasted it. It was harsh and tasted like burnt pepper. It didn't even remotely resemble the look, smell or taste of the pot I was used to. I offered the joint to Mack.

"That smells terrible," Mack said. "I'll pass."

Theo was getting visibly upset. I felt bad, but I had to hold my ground on my decision. In my opinion it wasn't even pot adjacent.

"I'm sorry, man, but I don't even need a second hit," I said. "It's not something I can justify buying."

"If you don't buy it, I'm going to be put in a bad spot," Theo said. "Would you consider taking it at a reduced rate?"

"I can't," I replied. "I would kill any further business with anybody I would try and sell this to. You're making it out as if I'm being unreasonable. What's unreasonable is you assuming I would be happy with this shit. I don't travel out here for garbage pot. I'm surprised you thought I would even entertain the idea of taking this home with me."

"I don't know what to do," Theo said. "I need to pay this guy, or he's going to be pissed."

Mack chimed in. "The guy can't hold it against you because you can't unload crap like this for him. You should be pissed at him for assuming you would try."

I couldn't gauge whether Theo was more angry, embarrassed, or scared. He seemed to be equal parts of all three.

"Brother, I hate to see you like this," I said, trying to bring the temperature down. "Do you have anything else we can look at?"

"No. I can maybe arrange to get something else before you leave. Can you stop back out on Sunday?" Theo implored.

"Yeah, I can do that man."

We all went back out to the fire, and Mack pulled out a blunt leaf and began to roll another log. Before he had it rolled, a customer pulled up in front of the store. Theo went to the shop to help the customer with his cigarette purchase. When Theo was out of earshot Mack spoke up.

"I can't believe he expected you to buy that ditch-weed," he said. "Hell if you would have bought that I would have lost respect for you. That, or I would have thought you lost your damned mind."

"There was zero chance that was coming home with me," I replied. "Theo said I was putting him in a tough spot. What did he think he was putting me in? I am short of what I need to purchase. If he doesn't find me something else I am going to lose money on this run. I can't afford that."

"I have a little over a pound of my personal stash I would part with," Mack said. "It's my favorite. It's Blue Dream, and it turned out perfect. That's what's in this blunt. How much do you have trimmed of the Durban Poison, Dana?"

"Less than a half a pound," Dana said "I can get to work on getting as much trimmed as I can before Sunday."

"Looks like I'm putting you to work again, Dana," I said.

"That's ok. You brought me some good wine," she said with a smile.

"I appreciate all of that more than the two of you know," I said. "I feel bad taking your personal stash, Mack."

"Don't worry about it, Steve," Mack said. "This relationship has been good for both of us. Also, I have more of the Blue Dream at the house. It just needs to be trimmed. I like you, Steve, but I wouldn't give up the last of it."

"Well, be that as it may, I appreciate it," I said. "Also, I have a little something that may lessen the sting a little bit. I brought a special treat for dessert."

With that I went to the car and pulled out the smaller cooler I had packed prior to leaving Mankato. I brought it over to the fire as Theo was rejoining us. I pulled out the Snickers bars and gave one to Mack and one to Theo. I explained what a hit they were back home, and I cautioned them. I warned them that they should not attempt eating the whole thing. My warnings were ignored, and both of them ate the whole bar. I joined them. I pulled out two Ziploc bags. Each bag was loaded with a variety of suckers, gummies and hard candies. I explained the potency of each variety. It was my gift for all they had done to make the trips possible.

As the Snickers took effect, Theo's mood began to improve. At one point Mack got up to go find a tree to relieve himself. More to the point, he tried to get up but had to steady himself before finding his legs to transport him to the tree.

"Jesus Christ, Steve," Mack said "Snickers really satisfies!"

"I told you they were a head-wrecker." I said laughing.

We had a great afternoon, and Theo went back to being the Theo I had come to enjoy so much. We all laughed, smoked a copious amount of Mack's blunts, and Theo, Dana and I enjoyed several beers. It was an afternoon I wished would never end. The sun went down, and we continued to enjoy each other's company until Dana suggested we call it a night. We made our plans to meet again at the same place on Sunday, and I agreed to bring lunch again. I packed up, and Candy brought me back to the hotel.

I was so tired when I got back to my room that I didn't bother to order any food. I had the munchies in a big way, but I had zero motivation. I sprawled myself under the covers and crashed hard.

When my eyes opened again they opened fast. I awoke in a panic. I don't recall the details of the dream I had, but it involved the sound of prison cell doors closing. My heart was pounding out of my chest. With my eyes open, I heard the same sound. I knew where I was, but had a hard time shaking off that single image of the doors of my cell closing me in. I heard it again. It was coming from outside my window!

I got up and walked over to the curtains and pulled them open. It was a blindingly sunny day. When my eyes adjusted to the brightness, I saw the source of the sound that caused my fear. Somebody in maintenance was fixing the steel entry door to the pool area right outside my room. It was evidently not latching correctly. He would mess with the hinges and pull the door closed, then mess with them some more and try it again. I thought *what the hell is he doing working on something so noisy so early*?

Then I looked at my watch. The Snickers combined with the beers had pulled me into a sleep marathon. It was one in the afternoon. I guess I won't be getting my free breakfast. What is it about California?

I heard a knock at my door. As I walked across the room to answer it, I was hit with a little more panic. The whole room smelled like the pot I had picked up at Theo's. I was so tired when I got back that I didn't process the weed. I had just flung the bags in the bathroom and went to bed. I opened the door hoping it wasn't law enforcement or the hotel manager. It was the maid. I told her I didn't need room service but grabbed some clean towels and closed the door.

I was hungry, but before I could think of eating, I had to vacuum seal the bags and bleach them down. Those were the kinds of mistakes I simply couldn't allow myself to make. When my chores were complete, I answered the call of my moaning stomach.

On one side of the hotel was Logan's Roadhouse. On the other side was my target...Marie Callender's. I had to pay for it, but I got the breakfast I missed and deeply craved. I didn't eat my breakfast as much as I inhaled it.

I got back to the hotel and decided I had to give my head a bit of a rest. I was feeling less than social so I went to the small convenience area by the office and rented a couple movies to take with me back to my room. I spent the rest of the day stepping outside to smoke a one hit here and there but for the most part I behaved myself. It was movie night and I relaxed. It was a horribly needed respite. I had a calm night followed by a good night's sleep.

I awoke to the sound of a knock on my door. Shit! Did I sleep past breakfast again? Was it the maid? I went to the door and opened it up to see Gordy standing in the hallway.

"I'm sorry, buddy," Gordy said. "Did I wake you?"

"That's ok," I said. "What's up?"

"We never set a time to get together for the game," he said. "Thought I'd see if you wanted to join me for breakfast and make a plan. If you want to go back to sleep, that's ok. I'll be out by the pool this afternoon. We could talk then."

"No. Breakfast sounds good. Give me ten minutes, and I'll come down and join you."

"I'll see you in a few," he said and walked away toward the lobby.

I threw on some sweatpants, freshened myself up a bit, strapped on my sandals, and went to join Gordy. We made plans to meet at the bar at six o'clock to "get prepared" for the game. That sounded a little familiar. He said that his plan for the day was going to be pretty much sitting by or in the hot tub and having a few drinks. At one point he looked around to make sure nobody was within earshot of us and said in a whispered voice that he had a little pot we could step out and smoke later if I was somebody who did that kind of thing. If he only knew how funny that was to me. I told him that would be a nice treat. So there it was. The plans for the day were taking shape.

It was a great afternoon. Sun, hot tub, beer, scotch, sun, pool, beer, scotch, hot tub, sun, beer, pool, scotch, sun and, oh yeah, a joint out back with Gordy constantly looking around to make sure nobody was watching. I don't know why, but I let Gordy think that smoking pot was an occasional indulgence for me. It was kind of fun. I even pretended I was as paranoid as he clearly was. I couldn't blame him for the paranoia because after all, this was his actual workplace.

We needed to make a run to the liquor store late in the afternoon to pick up supplies for the game. I suggested running to the grocery store. I wanted to pick up lunch for Theo's the next day. He agreed, and we jumped in the Camry and made the trip. Gordy liked his bourbon and beer, so we each got our separate bottles and decided to split a twelve pack of Great White at the game.

With the exception of a half hour to shower and get ready for the game, Gordy and I spent the whole day together. He was a funny guy. He asked me why I decided to get a George Carlin tattoo. I told him I had a friend that offered to do it for free. I couldn't really tell him the truth which was that I had the chance to get it done cheap in exchange for some candy. I told him Carlin was one of my dad's and my favorite comedians. I told him that my wife and I were lucky enough to see him perform in Vegas a few years before he died. He thought it was cool that my dad and I shared a favorite comedian. He also asked why I picked the quote under the Carlin tattoo. The quote read "When you're born, you get a ticket to the freak show. When you're born in America, you get a front row seat." I told him I was a bit of a political junkie, and I agreed wholeheartedly with the sentiment.

When we were all primed up and ready for the game, we walked down the couple blocks and checked in. I recognized a few of the faces from the last time I was in the room, but there were mostly new faces. My nemesis from the night I suffered the bad beat was not there. I hoped he would be there. I wanted the chance to carve him up.

Gordy and I sat at the same table, and we both spent the time grinding it out. No big chip swings for more than an hour. Gordy was up a few bucks, and I was up maybe fifty.

After that disciplined hour, I finally caught a golden hand. I was holding a ten of clubs and a Jack of clubs. The flop (the initial three cards) was a King of clubs, a Queen of clubs, and a nine of diamonds. I had a straight, a chance at a flush, and a chance at a straight flush. I checked. Another gentleman put a medium sized bet out, two others called, and I called as well. The turn (The single fourth card) was a Queen of hearts. I was a bit nervous. My straight didn't improve, and now there was a possible full house on the board. I checked. The same gentleman increased his bet slightly. One of the other players called, the other folded, and the bet was small enough that I called it. The river (fifth and final card) was the nine of clubs. I had my straight flush! When the hand you are in possession of is the highest possible hand on the board, it's called the nuts. I had the nuts. I checked. The same gentleman that bet before went all in for $340. The other player folded. I only had $130 dollars left, so that's all I could call. I called. My opponent had flopped two pair. He had a Queen and a nine. The river gave him a Full House with nines over Queens. My straight flush took the hand and put me up over $300. I just wish I had more chips before that hand.

The rest of the night was more grinding. At the end of the night, I was $380 up, and Gordy gained a little over a hundred. It was a hell of a good night. On the way back, Gordy pulled out another joint, and we smoked and walked. It felt like a victory lap.

When we got back to the hotel, we made plans to meet for breakfast the next morning, said good night, and went to our rooms.

My tongue was glued to the roof of my mouth when the wake-up call startled me awake that morning. Water. I needed water. I don't know how many glasses I drank, but my guess is the hotel saw an increase in their water bill that morning. It was a high bar, but I think I drank more than I had drunk any day of my previous days of California debauchery. What the hell is it about California?

I went down to meet Gordy for breakfast. He wasn't there. I waited about twenty minutes before I went up and retrieved my food. I was halfway through eating when Gordy finally made an appearance. He looked like death warmed over. He was walking slowly and his eyes were tiny slits. He was wearing shorts and had a large button down shirt with one side tucked in and the other hanging free. His flip flops barely rose off the ground between steps. He didn't even get breakfast before coming over to my table and slowly lowering himself into the chair.

"Somebody ran over me with a Mack Truck," he said. "I hope somebody took down his license plates."

"I hear ya, man," I said. "I am moving a bit slowly myself this morning"

"I can't even stomach the idea of eating anything," he said, "I'm going back to bed, but I wanted to come down to say good-bye. You're leaving tomorrow morning right?"

"Yeah, I'll be hitting it early, so it's gonna be an early night for me."

"It was great getting together yesterday," he said. "Maybe we'll run into each other another time. Take care buddy."

"I will. You too," I said.

With that Gordy slowly pushed himself away from the table, stood up and did a zombie walk out of the room. That was the last time I saw Gordy.

I rarely require any hangover remedies. That morning was an exception. I went to the convenience area next to the lobby desk and bought a couple Advil. I was starting to gain a little ground when it came time to head to Theo's.

I took off and made my way through my favorite three letter towns and arrived at Theo's a little after noon. When I pulled in I saw Mack's car and a truck I had seen a while back. Mack was sitting in his car. That instantly seemed odd to me. I parked next to Mack, and he got out. As he approached me, Theo came out of the store with two of the toothless hillbillies I had met before.

"You got a fuckin' problem with my pot?" one of them said. "It's good stuff. You need to reconsider."

The hangover served me well. I was in no mood to take any shit from that hillbilly meth head. My wife once called my anger face "Black eyes". She said my eyes get a possessed look, and my pupils dilate to the point that they look black. I went there instantly.

"You best back the fuck down before I bust out the few teeth you have left!" I thundered at him though my blackened eyes. "Calm down, or prepare to go down...hard!"

He stepped right up to me and got face-to-face. His lack of brains were a counter to his over-abundance of balls. I figured it was going to get ugly and physical right away. I was ready, and I was in the perfect frame of mind to unleash some serious ugliness. At that close distance his nose would be the first casualty. It would be the recipient of a vicious head-butt. I am not one to instantly jump to violence as an answer, but in that situation it was the only answer. We squared off while his friend attempted to flank me. I kept his friends movements in my peripheral vision. If he disappeared from view, I would have no choice but to make the first nose flattening move. I wanted the situation to come to its conclusion, one way or another, so I pushed.

"If you're feeling froggy, leap motherfucker; otherwise, step off," I said. "If I were you I would be embarrassed trying to sell that noxious bud, you hillbilly son-of- a-bitch!"

He was shaking. His friend saw that this was going to bust loose and recognized that I was far too much for his buddy to handle. He decided he didn't want any part of it. When the attempt to flank me was abandoned, I could see the courage draining from my antagonist's face. He just shook, flexed and huffed short breaths. He backed down and stepped back. He stepped toward his truck, but to save face he had to say one more thing to Theo.

"Don't offer my bud to any more people who don't know good weed!" he said as he climbed behind the wheel of his crappy pickup.

I didn't bother with any reply. My eyes tracked him as he backed out of his spot. He avoided giving me any eye contact as he switched the rust bucket into a forward gear.

As a last show of bravado, he spun gravel in the air on the way out of the lot.

"What the hell, Theo?" I said.

"I didn't invite him out here, Chopper. He just showed up," Theo replied. "I was hoping he would be gone by the time you showed up, but he insisted on waiting for you. I told him it wasn't a good idea."

"I hate those guys," Mack said. "They're always trouble."

"I agree," Theo said. "It's my old lady's cousins. I wish they would just stay away."

"I'll tell you right now," I said to Theo. "I love you Brother, but if I ever see those toothless pieces of shit out here again, I'll stop dealing with you. It's not worth the headache."

"I'm sorry, Chopper. It won't happen again."

"So were you able to come up with some other alternatives?" I asked.

"I could only get another half-pound of Blue Cheese," Theo said. "The other guy I get the good stuff from is out of town for a couple weeks, and I can't get ahold of him. I'll make sure if you come out next time that I have it set up better."

Mack was able to cover two and a half pounds. I was going to be short. Nothing I could do. I was angry, but Theo and I found our way back to the friendship we had established. I didn't want that one incident to change everything. I thanked Mack and asked him to say thank you to Dana.

"You can thank her yourself," Mack said. "She's right there."

Dana had been sitting in the car the whole time. I didn't see her there when I pulled in, and she was not willing to be any part of the heated confrontation that had been taking place. I went into the back seat of my car and pulled out the remaining two bottles of Majorette and brought them over to the passenger side of the car. Dana was visibly upset. She was shaken by what had taken place. I handed her the two bottles, and she gave me a smile and thanked me for thinking of her. I thanked her. The whole visit lasted less than forty-five minutes, and I took off without pulling lunch out. I didn't feel much like eating.

When I got back to my room, I was all business. I prepared for the trip home, placed my wake-up call for four o'clock in the morning, ordered some food to pick up at Logan's, ate it, watched an hour of TV, and put the day behind me when I hit the pillow.

I spent more time on the way home worrying. Yes, there was the usual worry about law enforcement, but that wasn't the worry that consumed me. I worried whether this whole idea was over. I worried that I had perhaps misread Theo. I worried because I was three pounds short of what I was supposed to be bringing home. I worried I may run into the hillbilly again someday and worried how that would play out. I drove. I worried. I made it home, and the worry did not go away. I was happy to be back with Sue. I was happy to be sleeping in my own bed. My happy was short-lived. I woke up to fresh worry.

What is it About California?

I was unsure of where to go. The fear of the future had begun to crush down on me. Too many things were beginning to set off alarm bells. On the other hand, there were many things about what I was doing that held allure for me. I loved travelling out to California. The open road was something I was weaned on and continually craved. When I was a little kid I remember many times teachers would ask for a show of hands from those who had visited specific places.

"Raise your hand if you have been to the ocean."

My hand shot up.

"Raise your hand if you have been to the mountains."

My hand shot up.

"Raise your hand if you have visited another country."

My hand shot up.

"Raise your hand if you've been to our nation's capital."

My hand shot up.

"Raise your hand if you have been to George Washington's home at Mount Vernon."

My hand shot up.

"Raise your hand if you have been to NASA."

My hand shot up.

"Raise your hand if you have visited Disneyworld or Disneyland."

My hand shot up (twice).

"Raise your hand if you've been to New York."

My hand shot up.

Every time the questions were asked, I answered the same. What I noticed was how few other hands shot up. I didn't realize how lucky I had been to be able to experience all those places. I took it for granted. My father was the chairman for his department at the University located in my hometown. Every year he would attend a convention in a different state. Instead of jetting off to attend and leaving the family behind, he and my mom made plans for two week vacations coinciding with the dates of the conventions. By the time I had entered high school, I knew about American history on an intimate level. I didn't just read about it in books; I visited the actual locations. From the civil war battlefields of Gettysburg, Antietam, Manassas, Bull Run, Fredericksburg and Fort Sumter to the revolutionary war sites of Lexington and Concord, Bunker Hill and Saratoga, I had visited them all. I walked the grounds, stood by and had my picture taken with cannons that had fired volleys during those turbulent times. I had seen where Jack McCall shot Wild Bill. I had visited the home of Lincoln in Illinois, his birthplace in Kentucky, and the memorial to him in Washington DC. I had been to Mexico and Canada and had traveled to all of them with my four brothers and my parents via the open road.

When I was a young man, I drove a semi-truck and racked up over one and a half million miles. I had experienced the adrenaline rush of recovering from jackknifes as I navigated 80,000 pounds down mountain sides. I had smoked my brakes and had to consider runaway ramps as my only possible escape from death. I had drunken bar fights in half the bars next to truck stops across the country. I had been mugged twice. I even had a beat cop in Brooklyn direct me to intentionally run over a Volkswagen bug which was in my way and double-parked. The good, the bad and the ugly experiences were all part of the life. The road was in my blood.

I loved my travels with Lucas though Yellowstone and out through the high Sierras. I loved the feeling of barreling down the road on Interstate 80 on my way to California. Okay, I wasn't thrilled with the trip home but not because of the travel.

I had come to really enjoy the friends I was making out west. With the exception of Theo's girlfriend's cousins and Carl, they were all very cool people.

I had fallen in love with California. Wine, weed and great weather. I truly loved it.

All of it was now in question. I was short on my intended weight coming back from California on my last trip, and I was forced to question my relationship with Theo. The three pound shortage meant I had to squeeze every dollar out of that batch and would have to make a return trip much earlier than I would have liked. It meant I would be farther behind on what I owed Slim. He was being paid back more than he had invested, but his steep percentage of my profits was making it difficult to make significant gains. The recent shortage made it worse. I could pull the plug on the whole thing but that would leave me in debt to Slim. I didn't want all I had risked to count for nothing. Less than nothing - a loss.

All of that was bad enough, but it seemed as if a bit of California was coming home with me. It wasn't just the stellar weed; it was the drinking. Before I went out to California, I would drink every couple weeks, and, though I would get drunk, it wasn't flat-out blotto drunk. I had started to drink at least a couple nights a week.

Golf leagues every Thursday night became a drinking marathon. Me and my golf partner Brad would meet down at a local park a good hour before league started and throw back several beers. Another six-pack would be consumed while golfing. Another couple beers at the meal served afterwards. Then it was off to The Wine Café for Karaoke night where it would be scotch and beer to the point that I would get up and sing *Big Balls* by ACDC. When I actually got up and sang, it meant I had way too much to drink. I was never asked for an encore.

On Friday or Saturday it would be a night out with Sue. We didn't want to spend too much at the bar, so we loaded up on vodka-infused energy drinks. I would eventually drive us to wherever we had decided to go. When the night came to an end, I would drive us home. I was always way beyond any standard of legally drunk. I always loved the term legally drunk. Was I breaking the law until I reached that threshold?

During the summer months, Sue and I would take in an occasional festival or music event in the park. Those were the days when the wheels really came off. It would be pre-drinks, drinks at the event, then often times we would have people over after the show to have cocktails by our fire pit. What is it about Mankato? It didn't have the same ring. I could no longer blame California.

I hadn't really allowed the drinking to bother me a whole lot, but it was beginning to become a question. Most days were spent nursing a hangover, consuming a little of the hair of the dog, or planning the next round.

After a few months of Minnesota drunken nights I was getting to the end of my reefer supply and knew I would have to plan another return trip. I was looking forward to seeing Theo and Mack, but that took a backseat to the fact that I would have a chance to see Lucas.

As expected, the Carl-Lucas connection was dissolved shortly after Lucas, Chelsey, and Amy made the trip out to California. It didn't take long. It blew up in spectacular fashion. Lucas not only moved out from Carl's house but out of his life. He told me the whole story.

Lucas had sold most of his possessions before making the trip out. Carl put them up in his spare bedroom on the second floor of the house. According to Lucas, the first weeks went fairly smoothly then the slow burn began. It started with small things. Of course Carl made sure it was known that he was being a great guy for letting Lucas and his family stay with him. Soon after moving in, Lucas started getting the feeling that Carl viewed them more as intruders than as actual guests.

The first piece of the nightmare that was Carl, which dug under Lucas's skin, was Carl's unbelievable level of frugality. Frugal sounds like a compliment. He was a cheap-ass. Lucas and I had always known Carl was cheap, but he began taking it to a whole new level. Lucas got a big dose of it. The initial indication of just how unconscionably cheap Carl could be, was summed up in a story relayed to Lucas by Chelsey.

Chelsey was out getting some shopping done with Kathy. Carl had told Kathy to go get some basic supplies for the house and Chelsey went along. At some point during the trip Kathy came across a small house plant. She really liked it and showed it to Chelsey. It was obvious how much she wanted to buy it. Kathy put the plant back on the shelf and started walking away when Chelsey asked her why she didn't buy it.

"Carl would kill me if I spent that much money on something we didn't need." was her reply.

Chelsey went back and grabbed the plant and paid for it. The cost came to a grand total of three dollars and ninety-eight cents. When Chelsey told Lucas about it, the blinders began to slip. With all they had riding on the venture, Lucas let it go.

A couple weeks later, Kathy was preparing supper for the crew. The meal was stuffed green peppers. Everything was going fine until Carl saw the rice to hamburger ratio. Carl wasn't just upset. He threw a fit and berated and lectured Kathy in front of Lucas and Chelsey. Carl ranted about how during the depression people would stretch their food budget by putting very little hamburger in with an abundance of rice. He actually used the depression as his guide post! The same person who was robbing everybody at the trim site blind, was making huge bank from those he was screwing, was acting like a pauper rather than the robber baron he actually was. The blinders were slipping a bit further.

Lucas told me that over those first few weeks, Carl was generally just being an asshole. He continued to keep his cool, but Lucas was starting to get a bit uncomfortable with the feelings he was having. He forged forward and kept his eyes on the prize. He was there to grow some girls out on the site and create a new opportunity for his family. He swallowed Carl's abuses as a means to an end. The ends promised were considerable. Lucas was promised a share of the profits from the year's harvest. Only Don knew how empty that promise really was.

Lucas floated an idea to Carl which Carl liked. As long as they were utilizing the grow site to grow pot, why not plant a vegetable garden as well? It would take advantage of the watering system and sun drenched area that the site already had in place for growing the weed. The only thing missing would be a spot with decent soil. The plan was to dig a squared off area and layer it with soil, compost and nutrients. With the exception of the minimal startup costs it would be free food. That was a concept Lucas knew Carl would be behind...free. Carl loved the idea.

Lucas was excited to work on the new project with Carl. Soon the day rolled around to get to work. Lucas and Carl loaded various shovels, hoes, picks, and other implements of destruction to break through the dry, rocky ground to create the garden space. They rode out to the site and parked near where the girls would soon be growing. They unloaded the tools and Carl jumped into his truck to leave. Carl had no intention of helping. He expected Lucas to do all the work. Lucas was dumbstruck. He couldn't believe it. He voiced his displeasure with Carl, but Carl left anyway. He left Lucas in the middle of nowhere to work with tools. If Lucas was hurt, he would have no vehicle. For that matter, if he needed anything, he was shit-out-of-luck.

As Lucas watched Carl climb his truck up the hill, he stood there among the tools in disbelief. The garden was meant to benefit everybody and, until that moment, Lucas thought the effort to create it would be shared. When the anger subsided enough to start tackling the work, Lucas did just that. He worked. With every swing of the pickaxe his anger grew. With every shovel full of coarse unforgiving ground, his temper flared. He worked the whole day while getting more and more aggravated. Carl came back to pick Lucas up, and the blinders had not only come off, they had been shredded, never to be put on again. It was a face-to-face blowout, and Lucas trashed any chance of working with Carl again. Lucas had no *desire* to ever work with Carl again. Their partnership was dissolved along with their living situation. Lucas, Chelsey and Amy moved into a small one bedroom apartment in Redding.

Carl's loss was my gain. I was given the opportunity to finally see my friend on my upcoming trip to California. That would be a new and welcomed addition to my return. I also thought I would try a change in where I would lodge while out west. I loved the hotel, the people I met, the card game down the street, Logan's Roadhouse and all the wonderful amenities afforded me at that location but it had proven to be far too convenient for my urges to get California level drunk. A change would do me good.

I searched Airbnb and found a perfect place. It was located on the side of a mountain a few miles north of Redding. From the description it sounded just right. It was a guesthouse completely detached from the owner's house so I would have a modicum of privacy. It boasted a beautiful view along with all the basic necessities.

I called Theo and told him I was coming out and for him to expect a similar sized purchase as the last two visits. I called Lucas and told him I would be out and made arrangements to get together. I got the directions to his new place. He had actually only moved a few blocks from Carl's house...and a few blocks from Meth Park. I booked my stay on Airbnb and did my due diligence so I was prepared to run the gauntlet back home. I was, once again, excited to get on the road.

I met with Slim and had to borrow enough for the trip even though I had not paid him all of his thirty percent. He was not thrilled. I was a little irked at the fact that I was doing all the work; he was thousands of dollars up at that point and I was being berated because it wasn't enough. If I could have told him to blow it out his ass I would have. But I needed the money.

When I last left California I was mostly dreading the idea that I would need to return. In all respects it was not a good trip. From the run in with the cousins to the shortage of weight it was a trip that should have given me the message that it was time to hang it all up. With the salve that time can put on the wounds of a bad experience I found myself ready and honestly excited to get back in the saddle.

Giddy up!

From the Frying Pan into the Fire

The weather was perfect the day I left home. It was warm and sunny with a few rolling clouds ambling across the sky. I was leaving home with the disadvantage of being financially behind the eight-ball. My shortage from the last trip meant that zero of my dollars were being used to make the purchase. I had twenty-six hundred from Big Mark to make a single pound buy and I had seventeen thousand secured from Slim. What I had personally scraped together was enough to cover some of my expenses. I had to acquire seventeen pounds. Any less and it would be a bust of a trip. Even with the full seventeen I wouldn't get completely back on track from the last run but it would get me rolling in the right direction.

Despite the pressure put on this trip, and the lack of confidence I had in its success, I was oddly happy. Despite my last words with Theo being tense and somewhat terse, I was looking forward to seeing him again. Despite having to go close to Carl's house on this trip, I was looking forward to the apartment I would be visiting in the neighborhood. It had been too long since I last had the chance to see Lucas.

I turned on the stereo as I was leaving town and cranked up *Wanderlust King*, as had become my tradition. My trips out west had come to include a series of traditions, and I adhered to all of them on my way to California. Fill the tank and my mug in Mankato and drive to Grand Island, Nebraska. Fill the tank and my mug and drive to Laramie, Wyoming. Fill the tank and my mug and drive to the truck stops by Mills Junction, Utah. Fill the tank and my mug and drive to Lovelock, Nevada. Fill the tank and my mug and drive to Susanville, California. Get my room at the High Country Inn, get my Mediterranean pizza, and get a good night's sleep. Grab my Depth Charge for the run over the mountains to Anselmo Vineyards, eat and drink lunch, buy some Majorette and take an inebriated cruise to Redding. At that point the traditions took a new turn.

Instead of going to the Oxford Suites I went north on Interstate five for about ten minutes, then turned off and followed the directions I'd been given; north and east through several small subdivisions and up the side of a small mountain to my reserved Airbnb guest house. I had arranged to have the owner leave the door unlocked with the key on the kitchen counter. True to the owner's word I had a private driveway and enough of a parking area to be able to drive in, turn around, and back up to the door. Perfect.

I backed the car up to the entrance and went in to check out my new place. Walking through the front door put me in the kitchen. It was not a full kitchen but plenty for my needs. It had a full-size refrigerator, a sink in the middle of the counter area, a microwave, a toaster oven and was stocked with cooking supplies including an electric frying pan. It had everything but a stove and oven. Beyond the kitchen was a small round table with four chairs. The dining area opened up to a living room with a big screen TV, a large comfortable couch, a recliner and a few nice chairs, a DVD player and a bookshelf filled with DVDs. At the far end of the living room was a nice, large bathroom with a toilet, sink, shower and a Jacuzzi tub. Also off of the living room was the bedroom. It was a beautiful bedroom. Large wooden doors with glass windows covered by long drapes opened up to a king-size bed, a walk-in closet and a large window covered by white silk drapes.

The place would have hit it out of the park even without its best feature. When I opened the curtains at the south side of the living room I saw the view. It was spectacular! The house looked down over some forested areas with a few sporadic houses. It opened up to give a view of Redding itself. When shifting my gaze from the city of Redding to the southeast I had a perfect view of Mount Lassen off in the distance! I could not believe I had found such a treasure on Airbnb. I would have gladly paid $200 a night to stay at that wonderful spot. I was only being charged $350 to stay there for five nights. Oxford Suites would have cost me close to seven hundred.

I unpacked all my things and opened up a bottle of the Majorette. I bought six bottles this time. I was determined to bring a couple bottles home for Sue to enjoy. I filled a glass and went to relax in the living room. I was so enamored with my initial survey of the place that I had not noticed there was a door slightly to the right of the window from which I had seen the picturesque view. I opened the door and it led to a deck with a couple small tables and a few chairs. The place went from being perfect to somehow, even better than perfect. I stepped out to my Camry, grabbed the smokeless ashtray and brought it out to the deck. I called Lucas.

"Hey man, what's up?" Lucas said as he answered the phone.

"I am in Cali," I said. "I am sitting on my deck having a smoke and a glass of wine. You wouldn't believe the place I found online. I am looking down over the valley with a view of Mount Lassen."

"Wow. That sounds awesome."

I let Lucas know that I would be heading out to Theo's the next day and asked if he would be able to join me. Unfortunately Chelsey was working that day and Lucas had to watch Amy so it wasn't going to work out. I told him I would swing down to his apartment late the next morning before heading out to see Mack and Theo. When I got off the phone I decided I would run into town to hit the Holiday grocery store to buy some supplies to utilize in my mountainside cottage.

When I arrived at the store I got a shopping cart. I was going to make sure I was stocked up for my stay. I loaded it with several microwavable meals prepared from the deli, some subs, several trays of sushi and, of course, some Great White and a bottle of Glenfiddich 18 year aged single malt scotch. What is it about...never mind.

I brought my foraged supplies back to the guest house and unpacked them. Nothing remained in my coolers or my luggage by the end of that first day. I made the place feel like it was my new home.

I enjoyed some sushi as an appetizer along with the remainder of the bottle of Majorette. I opened a Great White and threw some barbequed tri-tips over egg noodles with a side of green beans in the microwave. I enjoyed my meal at the table and watched some news on the big screen.

When I was done with supper I pulled out my small, portable humidor, grabbed a fat cigar, poured a half glass of scotch, cracked open a beer and went out on the deck. My laptop had already been placed on one of the small tables earlier. I put on some Miles Davis. There were very few moments during that period that would have rivaled the feeling I had that dusk. I was smoking a good cigar, with a glass of single malt, listening to the smooth sounds of Miles, while watching the sunset. It was sublime. I had no idea at the time, but it was the calm before the storm.

I awoke the next morning to my alarm. I wanted to be up early enough to watch the sun rise over Mount Lassen from the deck with a cup of coffee. I started a half a pot of coffee brewing and took a quick five minute shower. When the coffee was done I poured a cup and went out to the deck to watch the show begin. It was dark, but soon the clouds over Lassen started to come to life displaying wonderful shades of oranges and purples as the sunlight struggled to make it over Lassen's peak. Half the horizon was painted with multi-colored clouds which gave way to deep blue patches of sky with the moon, and some of the brighter stars still refusing to go unseen. That was the second time that looking up from my small spot on California's landscape had me in awe. That was the first during the daylight hours. It was magnificent.

I threw a breakfast sandwich into the microwave and ate it while finishing the last cup of coffee. I grabbed a bottle of Majorette in case Dana decided to visit with Mack, jumped in the Camry and took off to visit Lucas. I could hardly wait to see the friend I had missed for several months.

I followed the directions and missed the final turn I was instructed to make. After running back over the directions I finally found the elusive street. It looked more like an alley than a street. The houses on both sides of the street were in various states of disrepair and tightly packed together. After traveling almost the entire block I saw the place Lucas had described. It had a gravel parking lot next to a wooden fence. I parked and approached the building. It was two small rambler style houses facing each other with a small brown patch of lawn between them. Each rambler was divided into two apartments. Lucas was living in the apartment farthest from the parking lot on the west side. I knocked on the door and Lucas appeared. Amy was at his feet.

"C'mon in, man," Lucas said. "Excuse the mess; we've been in the process of unpacking for a while. There's not a lot of space to put everything."

He wasn't kidding. Inside the door was a small kitchen with a smaller bathroom in the back. Through the kitchen to the left was a tiny living room with a door to the single small bedroom.

"We were pretty limited on places to choose from in the short time after Carl and I had our blow up," he explained.

"You really are close to Meth Park aren't you?" I said.

After the gravel lot the block actually ended on the edge of the park that had become known for its tweaker population.

I could see Lucas was not real happy with his surroundings, but in true Lucas form, he was rolling with whatever life threw his way.

Lucas told me about the neighborhood and specifically told me about the neighbor that resided on the other side of the fence by the parking lot. The man who lived in the tiny house was named Hank Farmer. He was actually originally from Mankato. Small world. Hank had just recently been released from prison. He moved out to California in the late sixties and became a member of California's infamous Hell's Angels bike club. Hank had a run in with one of the locals and ended up taking him out. Hank was charged with, and convicted of murder.

While Lucas was talking about Hank he took out some of the finest looking indoor grown pot I had seen in quite some time. Any connoisseur of cannabis will weigh in on whether they like indoor or outdoor weed better. I personally love aspects of both. If pushed I would say I like the indoor grown slightly better. Outdoor weed is usually a bit less colorful and the taste is slightly earthy. Indoor grown is almost neon in its coloring and gives the distinct taste of the variety itself. It's pure. When smoking a bud of outdoor Blueberry Kush you can taste small hints of the fruity flavor combined with its earthiness. When smoking the same strain of indoor, the fruity taste is distinct. It is anything but subtle.

Lucas loaded a pipe full of Cherry Pie. When he passed it to me to light I could instantly taste the fruit flavor. It was sweet and very slightly piney.

"Holy shit that's good man," I said. "Where did you pick this up?"

"At the dispensary," Lucas replied with a smile. "I have my medical card."

California was in a chapter of its pot history where all citizens who had a doctor's prescription could purchase pot at one of the many dispensaries throughout the state. Redding had a few of them. One of them, the one that particular gem of a strain came from, was only a couple blocks from the Oxford Suites. The medical cards were known to be a joke of sorts. Any ailment would assure you a card. I think a hangnail would have qualified.

When Lucas was ready to get his medical card he went to a doctor's office with Hank. Hank knew the doctor. It was the doctor's uncle that Hank had murdered back in the seventies. According to Lucas the doctor held no animosity for Hank because, in his words, "My uncle was an asshole."

Lucas talked about how awesome it was to visit the dispensaries.

"They have everything Steve," Lucas said. "They have a bunch of strains of good indoor weed, they have varieties of hash and even edibles."

"If I have some cash left after visiting Theo and Mack could you grab me a few things?" I asked.

"Of course." he said.

We enjoyed catching up, and smoking up, and made plans for my return the following afternoon. By then, Chelsey would be home and Lucas would be able to get away for a bit. After turning a few bowls to ash it was time for me to go to Theo's. I stepped out, said good-bye and jumped in Candy and directed her west.

When I pulled into Theo's, there were two other cars parked up next to the store. Neither was Mack's. I was not comfortable with there being two other vehicles in the lot. If this became another hillbilly situation, I would be outnumbered. The rust bucket pickup wasn't there, but that didn't put me at ease. I slid my hunting knife down the back of my jeans and covered it with my flannel shirt, just in case. I stepped up to the sliding door and eased it open. I was keeping a vigilant eye on my surroundings and keeping myself hyper-alert and ready for whatever the situation demanded. I was pleasantly surprised to see a young woman and two gentlemen who looked to be in their seventies. All of them were there to purchase cigarettes.

"Hey, Chopper!" Theo exclaimed. "Come on in, Brother."

"Oh shit," I said. "I gotta grab my cigs."

I used the cigarettes as an excuse to go back to the car and slide my knife out from my jeans and put it under the driver's seat. I was embarrassed that I had assumed the worst, and I didn't want Theo to think that I was paranoid. I didn't beat myself up too much. After all, I had been given good reason for my apprehension after the fireworks I had experienced on the last visit.

When I approached the door the young woman was on her way out. I waited for her to pass through before sliding the door shut behind me. The older gentlemen were having a conversation with Theo about the upcoming harvest just a couple months away. They bought a couple cartons of cigs and took off.

"Mack was here, but he had to go back home. He forgot to grab the last pound that Dana trimmed. He should be back any minute." Theo said.

"Oh. okay," I said. "How is the weight looking this time?"

"I am still working on a few pounds," Theo said. "I have nine pounds for you right now."

With that Theo pulled up seven bags. There were five bags with a pound in them and two bags with two pounds in them. The first bag was the Blue Cheese. It was two pounds and I was happy to see it. Good start. The second bag also had two pounds in it. It was not the quality of pot I was hoping for. I told him I wasn't sure if I would be interested in it. He said it was Hindu Kush. It very well may have been, but it was not the high grade bud I was used to seeing. The third bag, a single pound bag, was loaded with popcorn bud. The weed itself looked decent but it was all tiny buds. My clients were partial to big, fat buds. That bag would be a hard sell. The remaining bags were bad. Small popcorn buds of less than desirable quality.

"Brother, I thought you said you had me covered," I said. "I can take the Blue Cheese, but I don't like any of the other choices. What are the few pounds you're still trying to set up?"

"It's more of the same Hindu Kush," he said, obviously a little embarrassed. "It's coming up on harvest time. All there is available are the remnants left over from last season."

"Dude, I can't go back with this," I replied. "I'll never be able to sell it."

"What if the Kush guy was willing to sell it cheap?" He asked. "Would you be able to buy it then?"

"Let's see what Mack has for me," I said. "I really don't want any of it. If you could get me a discount on the one pound of the popcorn bud I may be able to work with that. It would need to be a big discount."

I heard Mack pulling up and he brought the familiar rucksack through the door. It didn't look as loaded as I had hoped.

"Hi Mack," I said. "How goes life in the backwoods?"

"Better than life in the frozen north," he said with a smirk. "How's life in the tundra?"

"Frigid and crazy as usual!" I said.

Mack threw the sack up on the counter and opened it up. It was the quality I was hoping for but not the quantity. Six pounds and not a gram over. The math was not adding up in my favor. Six pounds from Mack plus two Blue Cheese plus one pound of popcorn bud. I felt my world going into a tailspin. Nine pounds, of which one was popcorn bud, left me short of the seventeen pounds of bud I was counting on by eight full pounds.

"I don't know what to say guys," I said. "I am going to lose my shirt on this run. This may honestly be the end of the road for me."

"Don't say that Steve," Mack said. "Harvest is right around the corner and you will have all the bud you can handle at that point. I'll keep as many pounds as you need reserved to fill your orders next year."

"I appreciate that Mack, but it doesn't help me right now. I have to survive this trip to even stand a chance of making it to harvest."

"I only have my personal stash but I will part with one more pound of my Blue Dream for you," Mack volunteered. "That will leave me short until harvest but I may be able to trim a bit off a few of the plants before they're completely matured. I think everybody I know is tapped out but I'll ask around to see if I can scare any up. Can you stop back out on Sunday?"

"I will also do my best to see what I can come up with Chopper," Theo said.

I took the six pounds from Mack and two pounds of Blue Cheese from Theo and brought them out to the car. I pulled out two Tupperware containers and gave one to each of them. They were loaded with every candy I made. Both containers had two snickers bars, two squares of black licorice, two squares of caramels, two large suckers, two chocolate chip cookies, a few gummies and several hard candies. I pulled out the bottle of Majorette and handed it to Mack and told him to give my regards to Dana. They both thanked me and Mack, of course, pulled out a Blue Dream blunt.

"I love all your candies Steve," Mack said. "I like the root beer hard candies the best. Can I pre-purchase a container of just those?"

"No Mack," I said "The candies are my way of saying thank you. If I'm able to survive this run and come back at harvest time, I will bring you a container of root beer candies, free-of-charge."

That brought a smile to Mack's face. As Mack's blunt made the rounds we stopped talking business and had some laughs. The men that I had the pleasure of getting to know were going to go to work to try to make me whole. I felt I was with brothers once again. We made plans to meet back at Theo's on Sunday, and I committed to bringing lunch. I jumped in the car and drove back to my cottage in the hills.

I prepared the bags in the bathroom of the cottage and had a couple Great Whites before microwaving a meal and eating it while watching *Caddyshack* from the selection of DVDs on the bookshelf. After supper, I went out on the deck with a glass of scotch and a cigar to watch the sun go down.

I set my alarm to make sure I could watch the sun make its return. I tossed and turned that night. Mack's promised extra pound brought me to nine pounds of good bud and one of popcorn bud. The consequences of coming up that short were hard to expunge from my brain. My alarm came way too early. The sunrise made the lack of sleep feel minimal in the grand scheme of things. It once again failed to disappoint. My entire morning was spent on the deck. I made a call to Sue to check in, I called Lucas to confirm our rendezvous that afternoon, and I ate my lunch all while sitting outside enjoying the beautiful weather and scenery.

At 1:30 I made the trek to Lucas's place. I stepped in and said hello to Chelsey. It was nice to see that she was doing well and had managed to recover from the Carl fiasco. She was not thrilled that on her day off she had to stay home while Lucas and I went to the dispensary, but she took it in stride and asked us to make it a quick trip.

I knew I was not going to be able to go inside without having a medical card so I gave Lucas $600 and told him to surprise me. He was in the store for about thirty minutes; when he came back out he was sporting a big, shit-eating grin. I knew it was going to be good and I was, for the second time that day, not disappointed. Lucas brought me some seriously colorful buds consisting of White Widow, Purple Urkle, Strawberry Cough, and Grape Ape. He also brought out two varieties of hash, one black and one white. Four gummies rounded out the purchase. I was thrilled!

We went back to Lucas's place and sampled the grab bag of goodies. While we were smoking, Lucas told me about the deal he had made with his neighbor for the next grow season. Hank had a small patch of dirt behind his house that was not visible from public view and had talked to Lucas about putting a small grow together. Frank knew nothing about growing pot, so he made a proposition. If Lucas did the work, and tended to the girls, they would split the harvest fifty-fifty.

I told Lucas about the disappointing afternoon I spent with Theo and what kind of a position the shortage would put me in. Lucas mentioned that Hank had a few connections, and we could see if he knew of any bud available. He suggested we go over and see if Hank was around. I agreed.

We walked over and knocked on Hank's door.

"I'm coming," the grumbling voice shouted.

When the door opened a large man stood in the doorway. He was large with respect to both his height and his width. Hank was a big guy. It was easy to see why he would have been a feared man back in the day. Age had caught up to him. He moved slowly but his rough edge made it feel like caution would be the smart angle when dealing with him.

"Hi Lucas. What are you up to?" Hank asked.

"Not much Hank," Lucas replied. "I wanted to introduce you to a fellow Mankato native, Steve. They call him Chopper."

"Chopper huh," Hank said "What kind of a bike do you ride?"

My normal answer to that question, because I got it a lot from bikers, was a Schwinn. With Hank I thought humor wasn't the way to go.

"I don't own a bike," I said. "I am a fan of as many tires as I can put under me. I'm more of an eighteen wheeler kind of guy."

"Ah, a trucker," Hank said. "My uncle used to drive big rigs. Why the hell do they call you Chopper?"

I stayed vague.

"It's a long story involving a machete and a hatchet."

It was fairly creepy seeing the grin of assumed acknowledgement on Hank's face. I had passed muster in Hank's eyes.

Lucas asked Hank if it was ok to show me the proposed spot for the next year's grow. Hank said it was fine. He stepped through the door and joined us as we went around to that back side of Hank's house. It was small and it was out of view of any neighbors just as Lucas had described. It wouldn't be a game changer but it was the perfect side-hobby for Lucas.

I asked Hank if he wanted to smoke a little weed. He was happy for the invite. We went into Hank's house. It was a very small house and must have been the maid's day off. It was cluttered and dirty. While we smoked we talked with Hank about the possibilities of him locating some weight for me to bring home.

"How much weight are we talking about?" Hank asked.

I didn't know Hank and considering his past and the connections he may still have I minimized my needs. I didn't want it to sound like I had thousands of dollars available to me...or to him. I made sure to answer quickly so Lucas would back my play and understand I had some reluctance.

"I have $1,200 cash and could get another five or six if I hit an ATM," I said.

Lucas knew what I was doing and did, indeed, back my play.

"Give me the day, and I'll see what I can find," Hank said. "Can you stop by later tonight?"

"Yeah, I can do that," I said. "What time?"

"Nine o'clock," Hank said. "and bring the cash."

I didn't like his demand that I bring the cash, but I also didn't want to offend Lucas's neighbor.

"I'll bring the $1,200 but I'm not running to the ATM unless I have to," I said. "But if you find something that justifies it, I'll hit one tonight."

"Where are you staying while you're in town?" Hank asked.

Another question I didn't like.

"The Oxford Suites," I lied. "Why?"

"Just curious," he said. "I thought maybe you were staying with Lucas."

We smoked another bowl, then Lucas and I walked back over to his apartment. I said good-bye to Chelsey and Amy and went back to my hideout to have supper and watch the sunset before heading back to Redding. I returned with exactly $1,200 and knocked on Lucas's door at five minutes to eight. We walked back to Hank's. Hank was sitting on his front steps.

"I wasn't able to find you any weed," Hank said. " But I did find you some really good hash. Check this out."

Hank handed me a bag that contained two ounces of the worst looking hash I had ever seen. Whoever made the hash didn't know what they were doing. It looked like furry coffee grounds. If it was anybody else showing that to me I would have told them to shove it up their ass. I had Lucas to consider. I had to be tactful and even perhaps purchase it, if it was indeed hash at all. I took the bag and took a whiff. It did smell like it had once been pot. It would have been better off staying pot. It was a really poor imitation of hash.

"Not the best looking hash Hank," I said. "How much are you asking for it?"

"I can let you have it for six hundred."

Christ! Six hundred is more than I would be willing to pay for good hash! I was being robbed. The man may have been let out of prison, but he was obviously still a crook. I had Lucas to consider. I had to stay calm and think this through as quickly and logically as I could. If smoking it produced a high, I could throw it in some Everclear and turn it into tincture. I could make a few dollars from it in the long run. Tincture should be a high dollar reward, but to keep Lucas in Hank's good graces and get myself out of the uncomfortable situation I would be willing to consider it. I asked Hank if we could smoke a little. He obliged. The taste was awful and burned my lungs, but it was, in fact, thankfully, able to produce a high. I paid Hank. I couldn't believe I paid him, but I did.

"I might be able to get some more lined up," Hank said. "Should I make a few more calls?"

"No this should do it for me," I said. "Thanks."

With my Ziploc full of furry coffee grounds I walked back with Lucas to the parking lot.

"I'm sorry man," Lucas said. "That was bullshit."

"Don't worry about it," I said. "I'll turn it into candy and make my money back. No harm no foul."

I jumped in Candy and returned to my mountain getaway. I set my alarm so I wouldn't miss the best part of my day.

The morning coffee, Jazz and cigarettes while watching the sunrise, was indeed the best part of my day. The rest of the day was spent worrying, and attempting to drink my way to muting the voices in my head. It didn't work. Unless Theo and Mack came through in a big way I was screwed. I managed to get a little food eaten between the Great Whites and the scotch…and, of course, another bottle of Majorette.

I woke up Sunday morning to the sun pouring in through the window. I had fallen asleep on the couch and I smelled like a bottle of scotch. When I passed out I had a half a glass of scotch. When I woke up it was upside down on my chest. So I reeked and I missed my sunrise. I hoped that wasn't an indication of how the day was going to go. It was late morning so I made a half a pot, threw a breakfast sandwich down my throat, loaded the cooler with lunch supplies and made a mug to go.

When I pulled into Theo's the familiar rusty truck was pulling out. The hillbilly glared at me as we passed each other. I glared back. I was a little early so I assumed the plan was for him to be gone before I arrived. Mack's Outback wasn't there. I parked at the entrance to the store and went in.

"So, any luck?" I asked Theo.

"Well, yes and no," Theo said. "I wasn't able to line anything else up. I did talk to the people with the other bags and they are willing to take a big hit to get rid of it."

"How much?"

"The pound of the popcorn buds can go for seven hundred," he said. "If you buy four pounds of the other weed they'll let you have them all for two grand."

That was not the news I wanted to hear. My last hope was that Mack pulled off some kind of a miracle. Theo and I stepped out and went over to the fire pit to wait for Mack.

"The four pounds belong to the shit-kicker right?" I asked.

"Yeah, he was pissed you didn't buy them for full price."

"I hate to tell you but I'm not buying them for two grand," I said. "I'd pay twelve hundred tops. The only way I can make anything off them is if I turn them into edibles. It's up to you if you want to even give him that offer. I'm sure that won't make him very happy."

"Screw him," Theo said. "He knows he either sells it to you, or he makes nothing on them. Pay me the twelve, and I'll deal with him."

"You got it, Brother," I said.

Mack rolled in and joined us by the pit. He pulled out his bag and gave me two pounds of Blue Dream.

"I wasn't able to find anything," Mack said. "I'm gonna have to curb my blunt habit until harvest time. Here's two pounds of my personal."

Ironically, that's when he pulled out a blunt and handed it to me to light. I lit it up and passed it on. We had a couple sandwiches, and I ate the last of my sushi. As crushing as the news was concerning my purchase, I was feeling good that they had made the efforts to do what they could. I spent a couple hours and enjoyed their company before thanking them and rolling back to my tranquil mountain cottage.

The weight I had secured was a joke. I now had only ten pounds of quality pot, four pounds of bunk, one pound of popcorn buds, and two ounces of furry coffee grounds. I decided to indulge in some of the smoke that Lucas had gotten for me from the dispensary. That gave me an idea. As big of pot snobs as some of my clients were, I began to wonder if I could turn a profit by getting some more treats from Lucas. It was costing me about seven dollars per gram at the dispensary, but I figured I could ask for fifteen back home. It didn't solve my problems, but it would help. I called Lucas. He was willing to make a buy for me but the dispensary would not be open until the next morning. I would be cutting the timing close for my checkout the next day, and I would be leaving California later than I wanted to, but I decided to do it.

I met with Lucas in the morning and made the run to two different dispensaries to pick up a few ounces. I gave Lucas three hundred for helping me out. He tried to refuse it but I insisted. I raced back to the cottage, vacuum sealed the new treats and jumped on the road.

As the miles rolled by the reality of my situation sunk in. I was going to be in a tight position for the next two months and would need to find a way to finance my trip back for the end of harvest. That would prove to be easier said than done.

Into The Mystic

I was in a jam. I had to figure out a way to make the substandard quality and reduced total weight pay decent dividends. I had to stretch enough profit to attempt a triumphant return to California at harvest time. The problem was compounded by the limited time I had available to pull it off. I also had to recover my losses in such a way as to not damage my reputation. I had a reputation for delivering primo weed. A large portion of what I had in my possession certainly didn't qualify. I had two obvious options.

First I needed to sell in smaller quantities. That would increase the weight-to-profit factor. Relying on smaller quantities created another issue. Smaller quantities equaled increased traffic. Increased traffic would increase my chances of getting on law enforcement's radar. The only other option was to convert the substandard weed into candies. The candies would not lack in potency but would require more pot to create the same effect. More pot meant additional care in covering up the taste of the pot itself. Nobody would want a snickers or a mint hard candy that tasted overly earthy. Ninety-nine problems, being rich ain't one.

With marketing having been one of my professional strong-suites, I put my mind to the task, couched in a marketing frame-of-mind. I had to continue to make multiple small sales but not significantly increase traffic. I needed to maintain the higher profit margins of those small buys. I needed to offer an enticement to those that already made visits for those smaller purchases. I needed them to increase their sales to the people they were getting orders from. Speaking in business terms, I would need to retrain my sales staff and offer them bonuses for achieving the assigned benchmarks. The five pounds of substandard weed was not terrible weed. The biggest problem was that four of those pounds did not look great. It was poorly trimmed and dry. The other pound was good quality but made up entirely from popcorn bud. I came up with a plan.

I took a half-pound of the ugly weed, mixed it with a half-pound of the popcorn bud and put it through a coarse grinder. That made it into perfect pot for rolling joints. I purchased a cigarette rolling machine and got to the task of rolling tight, perfect looking joints. I put seven joints into large prescription drug type containers and waited for my salesmen to come in with their orders.

Each time I had a visit, from those who purchased small amounts for multiple people, I gave them my sales pitch. I started by smoking one of the tightly rolled joints with them. Then I pulled out one of the containers with seven perfectly rolled joints. I explained that whatever amount they were there to purchase, if they could add to that total and get it over the five hundred dollar threshold, they would get the bottle of joints for free. I also told them, for every additional hundred dollar sale, they would get an additional joint. If they only sold four hundred dollars' worth they would get no free joints. If they made it up to a thousand, they would get an additional container of seven joints.

With my excited pot entrepreneurs updated on the new bonus structure, I sat back and waited to see if it would work. After the first week I had four returning purchasers. They had reached their goal and were there to get their bonuses. It was working perfectly. I was still only getting minimum visits but the average purchase went from three hundred to close to seven hundred. Some of the small dollar purchases had even grown large enough in quantity that I reduced the overall purchase price. That allowed them to keep a few bucks in their pocket. Most of those additional dollars went to candy purchases. I was still going to be damaged from the lack of good weight but the damage was not going to be catastrophic.

An odd thing happened as I was working toward the goal of justifying a trip back to California. Sue asked if she could join me on the next trip. I was thrilled by the prospect. I pointed out the risk she would be taking. She was aware of the risk, and it made her nervous but she wanted to do it anyway. I told her I always try to drive straight through to California. That also did not thrill her, but she wanted to do it anyway. I can't put into words how thrilled I was at the prospect of having my wife join me on a trip. I knew she would need to be versed in what to say if we were pulled over. Instead of going with the usual sales convention idea, we would have to have our new story straight, about the wedding we attended in Redding. To keep the story easy to remember we would make the wedding be that of people we knew, Lucas and Chelsey.

When the time rolled around to prepare for another trip west, I had managed to pay Slim his last investment money back. The problem was, I had only given him ten of the thirty percent profit. He was not happy, and it took some convincing to get him on board with another investment. By that point he had made well over $15,000 in pure profit and didn't have to lift a finger. That didn't stop him from bitching - loudly.

I was finally ready in early November to get myself set up for the run. I had my investment of $17,000 from Slim and another two pound purchase from Big Mark for $5,200. I was once again not able to bring any money of my own, with the exception of expense money. I had to make the run count in order to get on track. I needed everything to work perfectly for me to come out on top. A "get-rich-quick" scheme needs the rich part to kick in at some point.

I attempted to rent the cottage for the trip, but unfortunately it was booked for three weeks solid. It was no longer my little secret. I badly wanted us to stay there, but I could not wait that long to make the trip. I looked for other gems on Airbnb. Nothing came close. Instead I booked a room at the Oxford Suites. I didn't want to run into a no vacancy situation, so I prepaid for the room. I also booked the room at the Susanville High Country Inn in advance. I wanted to take no chances.

When the day came to leave, Sue and I packed the last of our things, went and got gas, and grabbed a couple mugs full of coffee for the road.

"Are you ready to sail into the mystic?" I asked Sue.

"Yep," She replied "Let's hit it!"

Unlike my other trips west, I didn't leave town to the sound of *Wanderlust King*. This time I had *Into the Mystic* by Van Morrison cued up on the stereo. It was a song Sue and I both loved. To me it described our life together in a broad sense. We embarked on our marriage journey not knowing where it would take us and had always managed to stay madly in love through trial after trial. We bounced around like a couple of gypsies but always felt like we were home no matter what or where that home was. In our time together we have stayed in apartments, bought a condo for a while, stayed in a run-down trailer and even lived on the road in a semi-truck for several months. Not one of them was a house but to us they were always home. It was the perfect song to hear as we hit the road at the beginning of the adventure we were embarking on.

The miles went by quickly. Having Sue with me made the trip fly by as though I had only covered half the distance. Thirty hours after leaving home we were pulling into the High Country Inn in Susanville. I had rented the double suite so we could have room to seriously relax. We enjoyed our Pizza Factory pizza and watched a movie together before getting a good night's sleep.

When we woke the next morning it was cloudy and drizzling. I was concerned. If it was raining in the valley, what was in store for us going over the mountains? Sue loves to take her time getting up and ready in the morning, and after the long run I certainly couldn't blame her, but I had to push to get going as soon as possible. If it was snowing in the high sierras it would be best to get underway as soon as possible. She understood and we made quick work of packing up. We got our morning brew at the Starbucks and pointed the Camry toward Redding.

As we started to climb the grade on the other side of Susanville my fears began to manifest. The higher we climbed the bigger the flakes got. By the time we reached the top of the initial ascent, the roads had gotten slick and the snow started to accumulate not only by the road, but on it. The first thirty miles of that road was always a slow run due to the reduced speed zones and sharp curves. That morning we had to take it extra slow. As we hit the steep grade leading down the other side of the main trail through Lassen, the same area where Hondo and I almost met our demise, the roads became snow-packed and dangerously slick.

I eased Candy down the hill at twenty-five miles per hour and kept a light pressure on the brakes. It was my hope that when we hit the valley, the snow would relent and go back to raining once again. It didn't. As we continued, the snow came down harder. Even though we were on flatter ground the speed at which we were traveling required a decrease. On one straight piece of the road a huge four wheel drive pickup sped by us as if he didn't have a care in the world. He looked at us like we were crazy for going so slow. I was a veteran of over thirty-five years of driving through Minnesota winters. I knew slick roads when I saw them.

My plans before getting up that morning were to take Sue to Anselmo Vineyards. Those plans were no longer on the agenda.

"I thought we were going to sunny California," Sue said. "We left dry roads in Minnesota to drive out to a blizzard in California. What the hell?"

"Trust me, Baby, this will change," I told her. "Pretty soon we'll be seeing palm trees."

"Yea, right," She said in disbelief.

We continued on, and unfortunately had to pass by the road leading to Anselmo. We hit a long, fairly steep, straight grade. The road was almost pure ice. It was a testament to the wisdom of our caution. We passed several vehicles in the ditch who had obviously thrown caution to the wind. We had the pleasure of passing by the same four wheel drive pickup that had passed us earlier. A little schadenfreude kicked in.

Ten miles later we hit the final long grade and watched the snow turn to rain; then the rain begin to slow. The forests of Lassen had been replaced by the brown tall grass leading up to Redding. By the time we reached the hotel, the rain had stopped completely. The sun was making an effort to make its presence known. I pointed to the palm tree-lined median down the center of the street, out in front of the hotel.

"Palm trees as promised my love!"

The smile on Sue's face was priceless. She had been going to school and working part-time at an accounting office earlier that year. She needed a break, and she finally got it. We checked into the hotel, unpacked, and got changed. I took her to the bar by the lobby and grabbed a couple cocktails in plastic cups. Minutes later, we were in the hot tub. It was a long and stressful drive from Susanville, and we were in full-on relax mode.

Sue and I had our share of drinks that day but she had a calming influence on me. I was not on my way to becoming California level drunk.

We were set to go to Theo's the next afternoon and I gave Sue a bit of a warning. I told her that there would most likely be plenty of pot smoking going on. Sue was an occasional smoker. I told her part of meeting Theo and Mack would most likely (ok definitely) involve large quantities of weed being smoked. She assured me she would be up to the task.

We enjoyed an afternoon in the hot tub and just being generally lazy around the hotel. When suppertime rolled around I introduced her to Logan's Roadhouse. We each devoured a wonderful hamburger and enjoyed a couple drinks before wandering back to our room. It was a wonderful day and I slept like a baby that night.

Waking next to Sue in California was surreal. I could have sworn it was the remnants of a dream. I considered myself to be as lucky as any human has the right to be. I brewed a cup of coffee and woke her with the hot cup of java at the ready. She smiled at me. Could we be enjoying the same dream?

I guided Sue down by the lobby to get our free breakfast and we took it out by the pool to enjoy the warm sunny morning. It was as if the snowstorm we had traveled through the day before was a distant memory. We enjoyed each other's company and took our time getting ready.

Our first stop that morning was a quick visit with Lucas. Lucas had a pot of coffee and a bowl of his recent dispensary acquisition ready for his anticipated visitors. Sue had not seen Lucas since before I had left with him to do the trim. They spent some time catching up as I kept Amy entertained...or maybe she was doing the entertaining. It was an extension of an already wonderful morning.

After leaving Lucas's place we drove to the Holiday grocery store to get lunch supplies, beer and wine. As we parked the car Sue looked over at me a bit dazed.

"I am really stoned," she said. "Give me a minute before we head into the store."

"I hate to say it Babe, but that was just a taste of the day ahead of us. Buckle up!"

"Oh God," she said. "I'm strapped in. Let's do this!"

We got our supplies and made our way toward Theo's. I went the back way through Igo so she could see the scenery that came with that route. The road passed through a suburb then a long winding road along the side of a few mountains. Shortly before hitting Igo the road crossed a bridge that overlooked a beautiful stream a long way below. It was a breathtaking view. We had plenty of time to get to Theo's so I gave her a tour of my previous trip when Lucas and I had come out to trim. I brought her through the washed-out roads, along the pine cone littered dirt paths they call roads and actually brought her to the gate that led down to the camp. We stepped out and I showed her the site from high up above.

"I didn't realize how high up this place was," she said. "The pictures you brought back didn't really do it justice. I can't believe you stayed out here that long. You really are crazy!"

We jumped back in Candy and started weaving our way back through the washed-out roads.

"I can't believe the Maxima lasted as long as it did considering the abuse it went through with these cow paths," Sue said.

We made our way out to the blacktop and snaked through the mountains and valleys on the way to Theo's. When we arrived there were no vehicles in the parking lot. We arrived about 20 minutes after we had planned to be there, but there was no sign of Mack's car. That was odd. Mack was usually pretty prompt. I showed Sue in through the sliding glass doors to Theo's smoke shop. Theo had already smoked before we arrived. The smell of freshly smoked weed hung in the air.

"Hey Chopper!"

"Hey, Brother!" I said. "I want you to meet the love of my life, Sue."

Theo dispensed with the normal handshake and came out from behind the counter and gave Sue a hug.

"I've heard a lot about you," Theo said, then turned in my direction. "She doesn't look insane to me. I assumed she had to have a few screws loose to stay married to you."

"Thank you very little," I replied. "Where's Mack?"

"He said he wasn't going to be able to be out until Sunday. He left me four pounds and some samples of each of them. He said if you want you can take the four pounds but asked that you sample the varieties and put in an order with me. He will bring out your order on Sunday. He has plenty of all of them."

"Sweet," I said. "Let's get to the sampling."

Theo pulled out a sample of Mack's famous Blue Dream. He commented on how, of course, we knew how that variety tasted. We had smoked so many of Mack's Blue Dream blunts that we could do a blindfolded taste test and pick it out of a lineup. We smoked it despite our familiarity. Sue was given the honor of sparking it up. She lit it and passed it around. It was a fairly large bowl. I could see the look of disbelief as it dawned on Sue that this was just the first of four samples. Theo pulled out a sample of Strawberry Cough and again handed it to Sue to do the honors. Like a champ, Sue made it through round two. Theo then loaded a bowl of Pineapple Kush and kept Sue on top of the lineup. She made it past round three. She was giving me glances that made me think she would refuse the next bowl. Theo pulled out the last sample. The smell upon opening the sample bag was pungent.

"I saved the best for last," Theo said. "Well, almost last. Mack left us a blunt to smoke after lunch."

Theo put the last sample in the bowl. It was Northern Lights. It was light green with long white hairs and so covered in trichomes (little specs on the surface of the leaves that holds a large quantity of the plants potency) that it looked like snow on a Christmas tree. He handed it to Sue who, trooper that she was, lit the bowl and passed it on. I had never seen Sue that stoned during the decades we had been married. She made it to the last draw and sighed with relief when the ashes were tamped out from the final bowl. She made it through all four rounds and was now peering through eyes the color of cherries and eyelids that were barely separated from each other.

We stepped out from the shop, and I took the chairs out of my trunk along with the cooler. We ate some sub sandwiches and had a couple beers. Sue was silent as she ate her food. I think the taste at that moment was better than any plate of food she had ever enjoyed before. When the sandwiches were devoured, Theo handed Sue the blunt Mack had left for us.

"Really?" Sue said.

"You don't have to, Babe," I said. "You don't need to prove anything."

Sue looked at me defiantly and grabbed the blunt from Theo's hand. She struggled to get it lit. Struggled but succeeded. We passed that log around for a good twenty-five minutes until it had dwindled down to a nub.

I told Theo that I would leave the four pounds at his place and pick everything up on Sunday. We made plans to be back to have lunch so Sue could meet Mack and I could pick up my load. I put in an order for three pounds of the Strawberry Cough, three pounds of the Pineapple Kush, six pounds of the Blue Dream and eight pounds of the Northern Lights. The twenty pounds would put me on my way to being made whole again. Again? Hell, it would get me close for the first time!

We packed up the chairs and started on our way back to Redding. I took Sue on the alternative route to show her a change in scenery. About a third of the way between Ono and Redding there was a nice rest area that sat alongside a fast running creek. We stopped to take in the view.

"I can't believe how stoned I am," Sue said.

"I can't believe you hung in there the whole time," I replied. "You didn't have to."

"Screw that. I'm in California...when in Rome..."

God I love that woman! She was embracing the adventure in front of her and doing it without reservation. Her enjoyment was making the trip all the more enjoyable for me.

When we eventually made it back to our room we changed our clothes and went to the hot tub, me with a Great White and Sue with a plastic cup full of wine. Sue checked out the weather forecast on her phone and announced that it would be a nice sunny day the next day. She suggested calling Lucas and Chelsey to see if they would like go for lunch somewhere outdoors. I liked the idea and took it one step farther.

"We never got to stop at Anselmo Vineyards on the way in. Maybe we could swing out there for lunch. It's only about thirty-five miles. It would be a nice cruise."

"Yes. Definitely!" Sue said with a smile.

I called Lucas. Unfortunately Chelsey was scheduled to work both Friday and Saturday so they could not join us. Sue and I decided to make the trip by ourselves.

Our trip to Anselmo was great. The weather was so nice that they opened up the deck. We sat and laughed and drank wine for several hours. Sue tried their flight and to my surprise, the Majorette was her least favorite.

"Do you think the house is still in one piece?" Sue asked over a glass.

"I hope so," I said. "I wouldn't lay odds."

Hondo was old enough to be left at home for a week but that was the first time she had been left alone for that long. We had every confidence that she was fine but we called to see how she was doing. Everything was fine, and she was looking forward to our return. Hondo said she wanted to be the next to make the trip with me out west.

The rest of the day Friday was spent at the hotel. We were being every shade of lazy. The most ambitious we got was to wander out to the hot tub. We ordered some take-out from Logan's and ate it in our room.

Saturday was much the same with the exception of stopping in to visit with Lucas and Chelsey after Chelsey was done working her shift. The plan, of making no real plan, was the best plan. It was fun, relaxing and had a few sprinkles of alcohol around the edges.

Sunday morning we had our breakfast early and lounged around until it was time to go to Theo's. When we pulled into Theo's drive, I didn't see Mack's car. There was a pickup truck over by the fire pit. It wasn't the hillbilly's rust bucket, but I was cautious as I approached. As I pulled up next to the pickup, I saw Mack sitting by the fire pit with Theo. I parked, and we got out. The pickup was Mack's other vehicle. We walked over to Mack.

"Hey, Grizzly Adams!" I said to Mack. "This is my wife Sue."

"Nice to meet you, Sue," Mack said with his hand extended for a handshake. "You're a brave woman for putting up with this fella."

"Yeah, Theo said he thought I was insane," Sue said smiling.

"Well, there's that thought, too," Mack said shaking Sue's hand. "Otherwise, I would have assumed you were blind, deaf, and dumb."

"You see why I like it out here, Babe?" I said to Sue. "It's all the love and respect I get that keeps me coming back."

Sue was enjoying my ribbing. Usually, it was her that dished it out. If I didn't know that was the first time they had met, I would have mistaken Mack and Sue for longtime friends. Sue fit right in with the crew. We had some lunch, some laughs, and took care of business before Mack pulled out two blunts. He passed the first one to Sue, and her memory from the last visit to Theo's served her well. She immediately drew long and hard on that monster joint and got it going like a pro. It was the familiar Blue Dream blunt. After passing it around and bringing it to completion, Mack handed the second blunt to Sue.

"You obviously like the Northern Lights, Steve, so I rolled a blunt from that."

"You spoil me, sir." I replied to Mack.

Sue again sparked it to life, like a veteran.

We stuck around until late afternoon then went back to the room to get the bags ready for transport. Mack knew I would have limited time, so to save me the task of vacuum sealing the bags, he had them sealed before bringing them out. I still had to bleach them down.

We got up early Monday morning and ate our complimentary breakfast. We stopped for fuel and a cup of coffee and jumped on the road to make our way back home. The trip was uneventful with the exception of stopping at a casino in Winnemucca, Nevada and taking a few extra dollars home with us. We made it back safely. We made it back on time. We made it back with fabulous bags of decent varieties. Maybe my luck was beginning to turn in the right direction. I could always hope.

Double Edged Sword

Sue and I made it back to our humble abode. The house was in one piece. Hondo did a great job of looking after things while we were out in California. I was glad to be home and grateful to have made it back with high quality weed in tow. Had all my trips to California been as successful as the last one, I would be on my way to realizing the rich part of the get-rich-quick scheme. I felt I could finally rectify some of the damage that had taken place. I had paid Slim his original investment back several times over, but I was behind on the thirty percent I had agreed to. With the current acquisition I was hoping I could get Slim paid in full and be on my way to being able to cut him loose and be self-financed. It was a big goal, but the math worked out - in theory.

Every strain was a hit. They were selling like mad. For the first month, I was sending it out the door as fast as I could bag it. I did a basic inventory and found a hole in my plan. I had sold almost half the weight I had available, but my profit was only about two-thirds of what I had projected. It wasn't hard to figure out where the deficit took place. I had been making too many high-weight sales. My profit margins were taking a hit. I was not making the number of small item sales that were accompanied by the higher margins. At the rate I was going, I would fall short of being able to pull away from Slim. I couldn't raise the rates. They were in line with the market. The candy was flying off the shelves, but I was using full-priced, high quality weed to create the ingredients needed. It was reducing my inventory and putting a dent in the profits.

I had an idea that seemed sound, but I needed to get in contact with Mack to see if it was plausible. I called out to Mack's house, and Dana answered the phone, on perhaps the last actual land-line in existence.

"Hello?"

"Hi, Dana. It's Steve. How are things out west?"

"Same as usual. I'm just trimming away, getting ready for you to come back out and visit us."

"Glad to hear it," I said. "Shouldn't be long, and I'll be on my way. Is Mack available?"

"He's out by the garden. He should be back in an hour or so."

"Could you have him call me when he gets back?"

"Of course. I'll let him know you called. Have a great day Steve!"

Dana hung up the phone, and I made another call.

"Hey, what's up Steve," Lucas said.

"Not much, man. I have an idea I'm throwing around and was wondering if you would be interested."

"What's the idea?"

"You said to me, a while back, that Carl showed you how to make hash right?" I asked.

"Yeah. I already knew how but Carl helped me with some techniques," Lucas said. "I know this will shock you but Carl showed me how to do it cheap."

"Such a shocker!" I said while laughing into the phone. "If I brought you some materials to work with could you produce a fair quantity over a few days?"

"Sure, it takes a day to prepare then a day or so to dry it out. What are you thinking?"

"I don't want to count my chickens before their hatched. Let me game this out and call you back."

"Sounds good," Lucas said. "I'll be here."

I hung up the phone and waited for Mack to call me back. I was surprised the idea hadn't occurred to me before. The best way for me to make the tincture, which was the base ingredient for many of my candies, was to start with hash. Hash was also a pretty good seller all by itself. Hash did not require high dollar pot to make. Low quality pot could be used to produce good quality hash, if enough raw materials were available. My cell phone rang and the picture of an old prospector displayed on my screen.

"Hi Mack," I said. "Find any gold out in them thar hills?"

"It's all green out here Nanuck," Mack replied. "Are you calling from inside your igloo?"

"Yes I am. At least I have cell service here in the frozen wasteland."

"Dana said you needed to talk with me," Mack said. "What did you need?"

I explained my plan to Mack and he was more than helpful. I thanked him for his time and told him I would be out in about a month's time. I also had him reserve as much Northern Lights as he could spare. It was nice talking to Mack. It was always nice talking to Mack. After hanging up I called Lucas.

"Hey, what's up Steve," Lucas said.

"I think I have the plans set up," I relayed. "I just got off the phone with Mack and he said he could supply me with a hefty sack full of trim scraps and popcorn buds. If you're up for it I will bring those to you next time I'm out and we can split the hash you produce right down the middle."

"Jesus, a hefty sack?"

"Yeah Dana has been busy," I said. "Mack said he would charge me about fifty bucks for a fifty gallon bag stuffed to the brim."

"I'm going to need to pick up some supplies to make the hash," Lucas said. "But we'll hash that out when you get here."

"Nice pun," I said. "I'll be out in about a month and we'll give it a shot."

I hung up the phone and patted myself on the back for having come up with a plan that benefited both me and Lucas. I couldn't believe I hadn't thought of it before.

I put myself to the task of liquidating my wares and it went quickly. I sold everything I had but I was still short on getting Slim the entire thirty percent. I attempted to renegotiate but I was doing it from a less than desirable position. Not only was he not willing to work with me to get a more mutually beneficial arrangement, he wanted to start adding to what I already owed him. He, in essence, wanted to tack on late fees. I had no leg to stand on. If I wanted to make a significant purchase on the next run I would need the influx of his capital. I managed to head off any late fees and attempted to arrange a twenty thousand dollar advance for the next trip. He wouldn't do it. He had profited thousands of dollars and I still owed him a mound of money. I began to get the feeling that the only reason for his refusal, was to keep me earning, and in arrears. That made it more difficult for me to get clear of the debt. It kept me on the treadmill of earning him even more. I was demoralized when he offered me eighteen thousand. It wasn't the reduction of two thousand that hit me so hard. It was the fact that he was calling the shots and I was powerless to do anything about it. I knew I had to take Slim out of the equation if I was ever going to realize any true profit.

On the next westward adventure I had the eighteen from Slim, fifty-two from Big Mark and four thousand from scraping together my own profits. If I watched my expenses I could purchase twenty-two pounds. I managed to do exactly that.

I ran to California and it was much the same as my other runs, with the exception of getting two ounces of hash, from the scrap trim purchased from Mack. Actually, it wasn't even a purchase.

Mack gave me the hefty sack for free. It produced a little over two ounces and Lucas insisted I keep it all. My California brothers had my back in a big way.

When I returned home I gave Big Mark his share and that left me with nineteen and a half pounds to sell, a half-pound to turn into butter and two ounces of hash to sell as hash or to use to make tincture. I finally had the enterprise running in the right direction.

After running through my inventory I had enough to pay Slim the eighteen and pay him an additional four thousand. It was short of what he wanted, and I owed, by a long-shot. The inventory was gone in six weeks. I decided I had enough to make a run without getting any additional funding from Slim. He was making more money from my efforts than I was, and I began to toy with the idea of simply telling him I was done. It didn't sit well with me. I made an agreement with him and I had good intentions of holding up my end of the bargain. If something didn't change, I would be working for the next year just to pay him back what I owed. He talked a big game about friendship but he knew he was taking complete advantage of the situation. He was in the way to me breaking free and actually realizing any profit. He initially said he was risking it all by giving me the first infusion of cash. He was right. I could have been busted and he would have lost his initial investment. I would have lost my freedom. It went against my very being to back out on an agreement. I had not decided to back out, but the idea was tempting. I could walk away. What could he do, report me? To who? He was several thousands of dollars richer from my efforts. That seemed to me to be fair recompense in and of itself.

After paying Slim the $22,000, I had sixteen of my own ready to make another trip west. I hit up Big Mark, and he was up for another two-pound purchase. I had my sights set on a seventeen-pound buy without any assistance from Slim. I didn't even make him aware of my scheduled trip. I needed to break free of his grasp.

I made my arrangements, booked the cottage on the mountain, alerted everyone that I was heading out, and packed the Camry. *Wanderlust King* damaged my eardrums as I pointed Candy west and hit the road!

Dancing with the Devil

My trip out west followed all traditions. The trip was becoming clockwork. Thirty hours after departure I was pulling into Reno to do my due diligence. I made my normal lap down to the La Quinta and, within a few blocks of pulling up to it, I ran into slowed traffic making its way around construction. I didn't bother to finish the reconnaissance. I opted to go to the other La Quinta and follow the route to the convention from there. After the brief deviation I was back in tradition mode. I pulled into Susanville shortly thereafter and had my Mediterranean pizza, a movie and a good night's slumber.

As tradition dictated, the next morning I was nursing my Depth Charge on my way through Lassen. I made my usual stop at Anselmo Vineyards for lunch and supplies. Majorette may not have been Sue's favorite but it was still mine and I knew Dana had become a fan. With the exception of my visit to Anselmo with Sue, I always sat at the small bar next to the dining area. I usually sat by myself but that time there was a couple sitting at the bar. As I have been known to do, I struck up a conversation with them.

Jack was a tall man with a well-groomed, red beard and dressed from head-to-toe in western-wear. Black cowboy boots, jeans, a dark green t-shirt under his flannel shirt and, what I assumed was his cowboy hat, sitting at the end of the counter. His wife Janie was a thin, short, blonde version of her husband. The outfits matched in style but instead of a hat Janie had her long hair pulled back tightly and tied together with a red bandana. They were on their way to Red Bluff California. Red Bluff hosted a well-known rodeo and they were scouting talent for a new show they were involved with, a project for A&E called *Rodeo Girls*. The couple was, in fact, scouting the talent for the show, which was set to be debuted later in the year. As luck would have it, their next stop after Red Bluff was to be the convention in Reno that I had chosen as my faux convention. It was a convention for new and upcoming cable channel shows. I asked them if they had ever visited Anselmo Vineyards. They had not. I told them I was a veteran.

"What wine would you suggest?" Janie asked.

"My favorite is the Majorette," I replied. "But since I picked the wrong one for my own wife, I would suggest you try their flight."

Jack ordered a flight and was kind enough to order me a Majorette. My intention was to stop for lunch and a couple glasses. As we talked, those plans changed completely. There was no lunch and there were several glasses. I stayed and enjoyed their company until their appointment with the rodeo organizer drew close. Six glasses of wine would have led to seven had they not left. I paid my bill, purchased five bottles and drove west toward Redding.

Instead of going directly to my mountain rental I made the detour to the Holiday grocery store to pick up my microwaveable meals, scotch and beer for the next few days. When I arrived at the cottage I unpacked everything to make myself feel at home. I poured a glass of scotch, cracked open a Great White, lit a cigar on the deck, and called Lucas. Since my last visit, Lucas had added a new member to his family...his son Brandon.

"In town?" Lucas said immediately upon answering his cell.

"Yep," I said. "I had a thought about getting together this time. Instead of coming into town and visiting, why don't you, Chelsey, Amy and Brandon come out where I'm at? I just got back from Holiday, and I picked up several meals."

"That sounds like a good plan," he said. "I'll have to check with Chelsey to see what her work schedule looks like."

After talking for twenty minutes, we hung up, and I went to retrieve my laptop. Tunes on the deck were what that moment called for. The sunshine of California, the view of Mount Lassen, and some Mozart, Beethoven, and Tchaikovsky floating through the air made me feel at peace. Those were the kind of moments that made me fall in love with California.

The news went unwatched that day. I had no contact with the outside world, other than a call from Lucas to set plans to join me on Friday afternoon. I enjoyed the entire day on the deck and went to bed early, so I was rested and ready for my alarm to go off in the morning. I would not allow myself to sleep through a single sunrise.

When the alarm went off, I got up and started the coffee. I was wrong about missing a sunrise. It was raining. The sun was being held at bay. I grabbed a shower and turned on the news to pass some time. As I was finishing my third cup, the rain relented. I took a towel out to the deck to wipe down the chairs and tables. I poured my fourth cup and went out to relax on the deck. The clouds were breaking up and allowing beams of sun to strike through. Soon the light blue backdrop overtook the dark clouds, and the sun made its full-throated announcement that it was going to take over the skies. The last act of the moisture in the air was the creation of a rainbow stretching from Lassen over the skies above Redding. My sunrise was missed, but I was happy with the replacement show put on late that morning.

I made my trip out to Theo's and was surprised to see neither of Mack's vehicles. Instead, there was a Fat Boy Harley Davidson sitting next to the entrance to the store. I was pretty sure Mack wouldn't have that as part of his collection. My assumption was correct.

I slid the door open to the store and stepped in. Theo was next to the counter with a man wearing a leather coat, jeans, and a pair of black leather boots.

"Hey, Chopper," Theo said motioning for me to join him at the counter "I want you to say hello to Fats."

The man must have been nicknamed Fats like a bald man gets the nickname curly. The man was not fat. He stood close to six feet tall and maybe weighed two hundred and fifty pounds. None of that weight would be considered fat. He had long, greasy, dark hair. He had a long beard and moustache that had evidently caught the wind on the way in. It was wrapped around the sides of his face and disheveled to the point where the beard and moustache were indistinguishable in the lower spots under his jawline.

"I guess I don't have to ask whose Fat Boy is parked out front," I said as I offered my hand. "that's a hell of a bike."

"Yeah," he said as he grabbed my hand and covered it with both of his "Gets me down the road. We were fixing to do a line. You're just in time to join us."

He pulled out a bag and I recognized its contents immediately. It looked like a bag full of shards of glass. It was Meth. I was not a fan of meth. I had that demon coursing through my veins several times in the past and it always ended poorly. As he pulled a chunk out and put it on the mirror I saw a look on Theo's face I couldn't quite identify. It could have been fear but I wasn't sure. I know, in the past, Theo had talked about how much he hated that his girlfriend messed with the shit. Now it looked like he was going to take a line. Was he afraid to refuse the line? Was he afraid of Fats? He looked at me as if to say "Come on man just do one and be done with it" but I was not able to get a solid read on him. Fats cut up three (pardon the pun) fat lines. He handed the mirror to Theo. I was glad I wasn't the first.

Theo vacuumed the line up his nose and instantly began rubbing his nostrils. Meth always came with a sting to the nose. Fats then handed me the mirror. I said I would do it, but asked him to hit it first. Without hesitation he consumed line number two and handed me the remainder. I took the rolled up bill from Fats' hand and started snorting the line. When Fats shifted his gaze to Theo, I blew the other half of my line off the mirror. I only did half the line but it felt like I had been punched in the nose. My heart rate climbed instantly to an old, familiar and feared degree. It was pure glass and I knew I was in for a long, wired trip.

Fats filled me in on the quality of the product. That was something I was already far too aware of. He began telling me about costs to purchase and how much profit could be made by selling it. The numbers dwarfed the pittance that pot brought in. Those were figures I was well aware of. While he was droning on about its profitability I stepped back and walked toward the sliding glass doors. As I was reaching for the handle Fats gave me an angry look.

"Don't you fucking walk away from me when I'm talking to you!"

"I'm stepping out to have a cigarette," I said in a tone to match his. "If you want to talk you can join me."

"What the fuck is this guy's problem?" He said to Theo.

"I don't have a problem," I said. "I just need a little air. It's your shit that blew my hair back. You can join me or not, your choice."

I stepped down the stairs and lit my cigarette. Fats saw my dismissal as a lack of respect. It wasn't. Well, maybe it was, but it was more about avoiding hearing the next words I knew were destined to come out of his mouth.

Fats said something to Theo that I couldn't make out and then he walked to the door. As he stepped outside of the store, I saw a look on Fats' face I didn't want to see. He was strutting like he was ready to lock horns with me. I had seen the look many times in honkytonks and truck stop parking lots.

"You best listen-the-fuck-up boy," he growled. "I have a deal to make with you and it's going to get done!"

"I already know what your deal is, and the answer is no," I said in a flat tone. "And if you call me boy again, we're on. I don't give a fuck what deal you think you can strike with me; if you disrespect me again, they'll need your dental records for identification!"

My angry words didn't have the desired effect. I was hoping he would back down, and we could force things to turn to a civil discourse. Instead, he pulled his jacket back to show me the sheathed Bowie knife strapped to his belt. I undid the buckle on my belt and pulled it through the loops in one swift motion. It was all I had at my disposal. It wasn't much, but I was ready to defend at all costs. That had the desired effect. Fats immediately knew this wasn't my first rodeo. He had the clear advantage, but he knew, at that second, I wasn't going to back down, nor go down, without a fight. He stopped advancing on me.

"Theo said you have people in Minnesota that can move some weight," he said with the anger still in his voice. "I need you to hook me up. We can make some serious cash together. You can't say no to hundreds of thousands of dollars."

"I can, and I am," I said standing my ground. "I have not dealt with the kind of connections you need for a long time. My connections in the drug game are potheads. They're not equipped for, nor interested, in dealing with glass."

"How about I just gut you like a deer?" he said trying to regain the alpha position. "Your belt ain't gonna stop shit!"

"If you're *able* to gut me," I said, "then I bleed out, and you're no closer to a deal. I'm not playing fucking games. Your call, Fats; you got the knife!"

Fats turned toward Theo, who had emerged through the doors during the showdown, and shoved him. Theo banged off the side of the store and went halfway down to his knees before catching himself.

"Don't you ever ask me to come out to meet any of your fucking friends again," he yelled at Theo. "Next time it'll be you and me dancing. Stupid motherfucker!" He punched Theo solidly in the gut.

Theo was bent over holding his stomach as Fats got on his bike and took off. Fats and I locked eyes as he tore out of the lot. When he was out of sight, I turned my gaze to Theo.

"Jesus Christ, Theo," I said with white hot anger. "You asked him to come out?"

"Yeah, Brother," Theo began to reply, "I thought,"

I interrupted him before he could finish "You don't get to call me Brother ever again, you son-of-a-bitch."

"I thought you might be interested in making that kind of money."

"I am interested in making that kind of money," I said. "just not that way. What the hell were you thinking? Why didn't you ask me before you set up the introduction?"

"I don't know," he said searching for an answer. "I'm sorry Chopper."

"That's the second time you've had to apologize to me for putting me in danger. There won't be a third. I'm done with you Theo!"

"Don't say that man," Theo pleaded. "I fucked up and I'm really sorry. I've been doing that shit lately and it's twisted my head around."

That's when the look Theo had earlier became clarified. He wasn't scared about doing the line, he was excited. I don't know why I didn't see it. Maybe it was the circumstances of the scary looking man in his store, combined with my memory of Theo saying he hated meth, which made me misinterpret the situation. I hated seeing Theo in that state. I have seen meth turn friends into fiends in no time.

"I have the bags Mack left for you," Theo said. "Do you want to take a look?"

"Fuck!" I exclaimed. "Yeah, I guess that's why I'm here. Let's get this done."

We went back inside. Theo was walking slowly. The punch, the shove or both took a toll on his body. He was in a fair amount of pain.

Mack had given Theo nine pounds of the northern lights and several pounds of his other strains. They were already vacuum sealed. I loved Mack. I took all nine of the Northern Lights, two of the Strawberry Cough, two of the Pineapple Kush and four of the Blue Dream. I had my seventeen pounds.

"I almost forgot Chopper," Theo said as he pulled the hefty sack from the back room. "Mack said this was yours at no charge. He also gave us a blunt to smoke together. I know you're pissed at me, but can we share this with each other?"

Theo had the look of a sad puppy and I had begun to calm down. Well, my anger had subsided. I was anything but calm. The small amount of meth I ingested was keeping my heart racing. Every fiber of my being was telling me to deny Theo my friendship at that point, but I truly considered him a brother. He had been there for me in the past and I valued his friendship. I didn't want that to be gone forever. I agreed to join him in smoking the blunt. Mack, in true Mack form, had loaded the blunt with my favorite, the Northern lights. Theo continued to apologize and asked me to reconsider putting an end to our friendship.

"Brother," I started, to Theo's delight. "I can't state this strong enough. If I see any meth when I'm around here or if you put me in any more tense situations, you will pay a heavy tax. Don't make me regret this."

"I won't Brother," he said with a smile. "Can I ask you something?"

"Sure."

"Do you still have the dreamcatcher I gave you?"

"Yes I do," I said. "I keep it in my living room to watch over my family."

"That's what it's for Brother," he said and repeated. "That's what it's for."

We had officially survived another encounter and ended up friends through it all. It would never withstand another hit but we were, once again, brothers from other mothers.

When I got back to the cottage I was still wired. The blunt hadn't really even taken the edge off. I hated meth. It was one of those drugs that gave me an hour of enjoyment followed by days of regret. That day I didn't even get the hour of enjoyment. Being threatened to be gutted was not my idea of fun. I knew I would not get much in the way of sleep that night. I applied liberal amounts of scotch to attempt to take the edge off.

I went to bed an hour after watching the sunset and stared at the inside of my eyelids as they danced with pulsing colors. Sleep was elusive. I tried for hours to no avail. I got up, threw in the movie *Dragnet* with Tom Hanks and Dan Aykroyd and hoped to fall asleep on the couch. No sleep. I threw in *Animal House* and sometime after the toga party I finally slipped into some restless sleep. The sun shining through the living room window woke me up. I was zero for two on California sunrises. I had a few hours of bad sleep and I was going to be entertaining Lucas, Chelsey, Amy and Brandon that afternoon. I felt horrible.

I went out to the car and grabbed one of the five hour energy drinks that I kept in the glove compartment *just in case* and downed it. After shivering from the awful taste, I got a jolt that seemed to reawaken the line I had done the day before. I was anything but sharp, but I was awake. I forced myself to eat a little lunch and waited for Lucas and his family to arrive.

When the Lucas clan showed up I showed them around and they were impressed with the place. We chatted, ate and enjoyed some Majorette and beer on the deck as Amy watched *Rio* from the selection of movies. I don't remember a whole lot about that night as my brain had turned to marmalade. Between the lack of sleep, the five hour energy drink, the wine and the pot we smoked on the deck, I was just longing to give my bed another visit. I gave Lucas the hefty sack and we arranged to get together at his place Sunday night. When they left I went straight to the bedroom and finally got the sleep I needed. I crashed hard and didn't wake up until after nine o'clock the next morning. Zero for three.

I spent much of that day recovering from the bat-shit crazy experiences I was having on that trip. I thought about my relationship with Theo and what that would mean going forward. Late in the afternoon my cell rang and displayed the prospector.

"Hey Grizzly Adams," I said upon answering Mack's call. "What's up?"

"Not much city slicker," Mack said. "Sorry I wasn't at Theo's the other day. Did you get everything you needed?"

"Yeah, I'm all set. What happened with you?"

"Dana and I had to run into town on Friday," he said. "We had some issues we had to clear up. I planned on meeting you, but things kind of happened all of a sudden and we had to go."

"Is everything ok?" I asked.

"Yeah everything is fine," Mack said. "I just wanted to make sure Theo got you taken care of."

"Can I ask you a question Mack?"

"Sure."

"Has Theo been acting strange to you lately?"

"Yeah," Mack said. "He's been hanging with some pretty unsavory people. I think he's getting into some shit he should steer clear of. It's not really my place to say anything. I am a bit concerned, but you know Theo, he'll be ok."

"Ok, I just wanted to get your opinion," I said. "It's concerning me too."

I told Mack about the encounter I had out at Theo's, and that Theo and I were on shaky ground, but that we were still working together. None of it came as a shock to Mack.

We got off the phone and I went back to my day of recovery. I ate supper on the deck and watched the sun disappear. I watched a little TV and then set my alarm before heading to bed. It would not be zero for four.

When the alarm went off I got the coffee ready and poured a cup. I brought the laptop out and selected some Miles Davis. I may have missed three sunrise opportunities, but it was all made up for in the show I got that morning. There were two long banks of clouds, one just below the peak of Mount Lassen and the other just above. As the sun made its appearance it lit the underside of the top layer of clouds with an array of orange, red and yellow. The lower level of clouds looked like it was there for the purpose of displaying Lassen. It was like the silk or felt cloth on which diamond jewelry is displayed. The moment the sun made it over the mountain it released a burst of light that shined down in tracts of beaming light. It looked like a fanned array of concert stage lights. It only lasted a few minutes before the sun was split in two by the upper layer of clouds. It was worthy of an artist rendering. It will forever be stamped in my memory. It was well worth the wait.

The rest of that day was spent preparing for the next. I intended to get an early start so I needed things in place before retiring for the night. I had picked up the hash from Lucas, vacuum sealed it and bleached down all the bags. I set my alarm for my last shot at the Cali sunrise.

I woke up about thirty minutes before my alarm was set to go off. I used the extra time to get shaved, showered and packed. The sunrise would be the last thing I witnessed before stepping out of the cottage. I grabbed a steaming hot cup of coffee to watch the sun arrive for my last morning in California. It was, as usual, spectacular. The sun made its way over Lassen to shine itself over the fog that had settled on the valley. I looked at it as an omen of sorts. I had risen above the fog of near war and emerged triumphant. I had a hard time stepping away from the deck. It was a beautiful day and I was feeling invincible.

As I was getting into the Camry the neighbor and owner of the rental, approached me and thanked me for the stellar review I had given him on Airbnb. I thanked him in return for the kind words he had left on my Airbnb profile. We chatted for a bit and decided the next time I came out to rent his guest house, we would have a meal together. Until that morning we had only waved at each other in the yard or talked on the phone. Noticing I was wearing my suit, he asked me what I did for a living. I told him I sold marketing materials and showed him some samples in the car. He seemed to be a nice man and I looked forward to the next time we met.

I set my sights east and drove until I entered Susanville where I got my tank filled and grabbed a Depth Charge for the run. The trip was the same as every trip home. I nervously kept an eye out for law enforcement and mourned the fact that California was fading in my rearview. As with previous trips, Reno was a bustle of heavy traffic as I passed through. I received a phone call from Sue and answered it, hands free, through my stereo.

As I was coming out from Reno I noticed a sheriff's vehicle pulling out on to the highway from an on ramp. It took him a little while to catch up to me but when he approached in the left lane he slowed his vehicle down. He began mirroring my car. He didn't gain nor lose any distance while we were snaking our way through the canyon. He followed me for several miles, during which time I noticed the emblem on the side of his truck said K-9 unit. I told Sue what was going on and she was instantly panicked, as was I. I started to catch up to the car ahead of me. I couldn't pass him due to the Sheriff trailing so closely behind me in the lane I would have to use to pass. I tapped on the brakes to slow down; when I did the disco lights came on. I was being pulled over. I was terrified. I told Sue what was happening and told her I had to get off the phone.

"Oh Christ!" Sue said. "Call me the instant you can!"

"I will Babe. I gotta go."

I hung up with my heart pounding in my ears. I honestly thought those were my last moments of freedom. Considering the weight I had on board it could well have been for the remainder of my life. Nevada is huge in the area of private prisons, which makes it one of the worst places to get pulled over. Kickbacks to officers who fed off the private prisons are a well-known hazard associated with Nevada. I struggled to take some deep breaths. *Calm down* I thought to myself *you've done everything possible to prepare for this eventuality.* The sheriff stepped up to the passenger side window and I rolled it down. I didn't have to worry about him smelling anything because the bags of weed and the hash were vacuum sealed and bleached. If he got the dog out of his truck, it would have been an entirely different story.

"Where are you coming from?" the Sheriff asked.

"I have been at the A&E programming convention in Reno for the last week," I said.

The sheriff then asked me a series of questions. "Where was the convention? When did you get into town? Where did you stay?"

I was prepared for those questions but I was terrified nonetheless. I had my fake itinerary including hotel booking, convention information and convention pass printed out and sitting on the passenger seat, opened, with some notes on a scratch pad (to give a reason for the book to be open). I answered his questions including telling him that I stayed at the La Quinta.

"Did you stay at the La Quinta over by the athletic field?" he asked.

"No," I replied. "The streets outside of that La Quinta are under construction and it's a mess. That is the one I usually stay at when I come to one of these conventions, but because of the mess, I stayed at the one by the airport."

"What kind of work do you do?"

"I sell marketing materials." I replied.

"What kind of marketing materials?"

"I sell anything you can put a logo on," I said. "I sold a ton of those hats." I said pointing to the line of hats that covered the bag the weed was stored in. "Those are for an insurance company but they're just samples. I sold three hundred of them with the logo of a new show which will be airing on A&E called *Rodeo Girls* premiering later this year."

"Interesting," he said. "I'm going to need to see your license and registration."

I opened the glove box and grabbed my registration and handed him my license. He took my paperwork and went back to his truck. The longest few minutes of my life was waiting to see what would happen next. If he came back with the dog I would be wearing orange in a matter of hours. I hoped my knowledge of the area and my response about the hotel and road construction did the trick.

After what seemed like hours, but was maybe closer to ten minutes, he came back to my car without the dog! He gave my license back and told me that the reason he pulled me over was because I had followed too close to the car ahead of me. He gave me a warning and sent me down the road.

I knew Sue wanted to hear from me the instant I could call, but I was shaking and unable to think clearly. The thudding in my ears wouldn't relent. I was conjuring up images in my mind's eye of how my return call to Sue could have been to tell her I had been arrested. My life as I knew it would have ended. As odd as it was, I had Slim at the forefront of my thoughts. It actually angered me that, had I got busted on that trip, it would have been all my money that was lost. I guess it wasn't odd to have such a thought. It was one of thousands of thoughts flooding my head. The blood pumping audibly in my ears was like a slide show clicker. Thud...screw Slim. Thud...Sue. Thud...my daughters. Thud...my mom and dad. Thud...prison. Thud...

I managed to get myself calmed enough to call Sue after I had passed through Fernley. It was only twenty-five minutes after I had been released but it seemed like forever. I couldn't wait any longer. I had to remind myself that she was probably waiting with a thud in her ears as well.

Profit at a Price

The two terrifying events I had just lived through caused my internal dialogue to shift into high gear. The fact that I was home safely with enough weed to start seeing some profit was one side of the conversation. The other was my rational self, screaming at me to reevaluate what I was doing. If sanity was a quality I possessed, I would have listened to the scream. I was not operating with sanity as my co-pilot. My interpretation was *I have to break free from Slim.*

My first thought, upon being released from the side of the Nevada road, was not how close I came to losing my freedom. That thought came second. I was angry it wasn't Slim's money on the line. I was on a treadmill that I had to jump off from. There was no longer any risk for Slim. I had made him his money back with thousands on top. If he staked me thirty grand and I got busted he would still come out ahead. For every ten thousand he had invested he was seeing close to six grand in pure profit. I was done feeding my profits to him. I decided I would attempt to end things on a good note. Not the kind of note he felt he had coming. The only impediment to telling Slim I was done, didn't come from the idea that he would be angry. It didn't come from knowing that the people from the poker game would only hear his side of the story, and thus, be angry with me. It was my own self-imposed morality. I had made a deal and I had a hard time justifying breaking it for any reason.

It was true that I had made him thousands of dollars without him sharing in the work. It was true that his initial investment was paid back with thousands in interest. It was true that I had risked my life, my freedom and my sanity. It was true that I had profited very little in comparison and did all the work.

It was also true that I had made a deal. I entered it on my own accord. Breaking my deal would have meant I went back on my word.

The internal dialogue began to set up its client's defense. It was true that Slim took advantage when he knew I was desperate. It was true that Sue was sharing in the risk and suffering, from the treadmill I had placed us on. It was true that I would never be able to get off that treadmill without breaking the deal.

I couldn't shut down the bickering in my head. I needed to make a decision. The longer I waited the less resolute I would become. It was time, as they say, to shit or get off the pot.

I made my choice. I would set aside a last five thousand dollar payment and hand it to Slim along with my notice of resignation.

The day I told Slim I was done working with him, and would be breaking the deal, went about as I expected. I was berated. I was banned from the game. I was told my name would be mud to those I considered friends. I hated every minute of it but I had to take the hit. I did break the deal. It was a deal I never should have made. If I had an inkling of an idea how much sacrifice I would have had to make, in order to get to that point, the deal never would have been struck. I didn't like the position Slim put me in but I couldn't lay any blame on his shoulders. He was shrewd, as usual, and I accepted the terms.

I was feeling depressed and ashamed, yet relieved.

It was not hard to fathom that I decided to pour massive quantities of scotch down my gullet that night. Scotch, in my world, is never unaccompanied by beer. Scotch and beer, in my world is never unaccompanied by clouds of California brush fires in a bowl. I was on a marathon. I went from Slim's, to The Wine Café, to the park to have a few pre-league beers, to several beers at golf leagues, back to The Wine Café, back home. Candy must have taken the wheel because I somehow made it home in one piece.

I was not handling the feelings from my backing out on the deal very well. That proved itself in many drunken nights over the next month. I was drinking almost daily and pouring myself into my car at the end of every night. I was losing my sense of self. It hit me hard and I knew things were spiraling out of control. The more I spiraled, the more I thought. The less I wanted to think, the more I drank. It was a new treadmill. It was an expensive treadmill. My internal dialogue had been muted. Only one side was given voice. *You broke a deal* was on a constant loop between my ears.

When my supply of California green was running low I made preparations to make a return trip. I had enough of my own money to make my purchase. I knew I could go without contacting Big Mark and could thus sell him his next batch at full price. Big Mark had been there since day one of my California adventures. I had no deal with him, but it felt wrong not to offer him the usual. I called and asked him for his order and he surprised me with a question I didn't see coming.

"I would like to come out with you to California one of these days," he said.

"You're welcome to join me anytime you want," I said. "Hell, you could join me for this run if you want."

"When are you leaving?" He asked.

"Next Monday."

"Any chance you could push it off a week?"

I couldn't believe it. I was excited by the idea of having somebody run with me. Big Mark and I had become pretty good friends over the years but I never thought he would be interested in making the trip out with me.

"Yeah I can do that," I said. "Are you absolutely sure you're up for it?"

"Yes!"

I explained the risks and I told him that as long as he was coming with me, I would charge him the same price per pound as before, but I would cover the lodging expenses for the trip. Mark already knew how much profit I was making from his orders but because the price still worked out over his normal costs, he agreed. He committed to his normal two pound purchase. I also made sure he agreed that my connections could never become his connections. The last thing I wanted was for somebody else getting into direct competition with me. We were on the same page and we made plans to head west together in less than two weeks.

The days of staying at my cottage or the Oxford Suites were over. Lucas and family had moved. Chelsey was given a transfer to Red Bluff California. I was happy that they were able to move away from the tiny apartment and that they were no longer in close proximity to Meth Park. Lucas got a job at a large hardware store in Red Bluff and between their two incomes, they were able to rent a small three bedroom rambler. As they were nearing the decision to move, Hank and Lucas had a falling out. Hank refused to honor his end of the bargain on the garden that Lucas cultivated for him. It didn't take a fortune teller to have predicted that one.

My new home away from home had become the Holiday Inn Express and Suites in Red Bluff. Chelsey knew one of the assistant managers that worked there and was able to get me a great rate on the rooms.

We had an uneventful trip out and Mark was thrilled with the Lassen journey and the amenities offered at the Holiday Inn. On Thursday we went out to Theo's to meet with Theo and Mack.

Mark was excited. I had told him a lot about both men. We went to the grocery store to pick up lunch supplies and beer.

When we pulled into Theo's I saw the green Subaru Outback over by the gutted trailer and the fire pit. It was going to be a day with Mack's family. Dana, Ned and Cody were all there. I was glad I purchased enough Sushi. It had the feel of a big family get together. I introduced Big Mark to everybody and they all made him feel welcome. I pointed out to Mark that Mack was the man behind most of the varieties he had been receiving, including the Northern Lights. You would have thought he was meeting a rock star or a movie star...he was in awe.

I pulled the cooler out from my trunk and let everybody know they were welcome to pick anything they wanted. The boys were elated to get some sushi once again. I apologized to Dana that I hadn't brought her any wine. I explained that I had not visited Anselmo and I didn't know she was going to join us. She said that was fine and opened a Great White instead. We all ate, enjoyed some laughs and took in the weather. It was warm but not hot, perfect weather for a pothead picnic.

After lunch I pulled out the gift containers for Theo and Mack loaded with their favorite candies. The Tupperware containers were full of gummies, suckers and black licorice for Theo, and fifty root beer hard candies for Mack. I then reached into the cooler and brought out the serious desert treats, the snickers. Theo grabbed one and began eating it immediately.

"I don't know about those snickers," Mack said. "Last time we ate those I was in a coma the rest of the day." He looked at Big Mark "Have you had the snickers?"

"I've only ever done a half of one," Mark replied.

"If you eat one, I'll eat one," Mack said.

Mack ate one. Mark ate one. I ate one. Theo's was already completely consumed.

"You brought the edibles," Mack said to me. "I brought the smokables."

Mack pulled a blunt out of his shirt pocket and handed it to Mark.

"Jesus," Mark said. "that's huge!"

After puffing it to life it got passed around and before it was done, Mack had another one rolled. As soon as blunt number one was ash, Mack handed me blunt number two. Mack went back to rolling duties and handed number three to Theo who sparked it as number two died. Mack repeated one more time and handed blunt number four to Mark. By that time the snickers hit their full effect. Mark was stupefied. He wasn't sure he could smoke another and just stared at the blunt in his hand.

"You're one of Steve's friends," Mack said. "I know you can smoke one more."

Mark sparked number four to life. He was not going to fall short of enjoying the California weed experience to the fullest. When number four was gone, Mack pulled out his ruck sack.

"I can't believe it, but I forgot to grab the last of the Northern Lights for you Steve," Mack said. "I have seven pounds sitting in the shed at home. I assume you want them."

"Hell yes!"

"Ok. If you want I can just give them to Theo and you can grab them before you go. I won't be able to join you on Sunday." Mack said.

"That works for me," I said to Mack.

I took five pounds of the Blue Dream, three of the Strawberry Cough and three pounds of the Pineapple Kush and would get six of the seven pounds of Northern Lights. Mark took a pound of the Strawberry Cough and would get one of the Northern Lights. Before leaving Mack rolled one more blunt. I thought Big Mark was going to die. We smoked the last blunt and said our good-byes.

Most of the way back to Red Bluff Mark was silent. He peered out through the tiny slits in his eyes at the scenery as it passed.

"I didn't think it was possible to get this stoned," he said.

"Yeah Mack rolls a hell of a blunt. Do you want to swing by and meet Lucas?" I asked.

"Can we just go back to the motel?"

"Of course," I replied "a bit too stoned?"

"I wouldn't say a bit," Mark said emphasizing the word bit.

That was the only conversation we shared the entire thirty-five minute ride back to the Holiday Inn. When we arrived Mark went to his room and announced that he was probably going to just relax for the night. I ordered some food delivered to my room and spent the night in my own version of relaxation.

The next morning I called Mark's room and we met down by the lobby for our free breakfast. Later that morning we went to Lucas's place and I introduced Mark to Lucas, Chelsey and the kids. We spent most of the day just kicking back and smoking a bit with Lucas until supper time rolled around. We stopped for some fast food on the way back to the hotel. We repeated the same schedule on Saturday and took advantage of our hotel amenities for all they were worth.

On Sunday we made the trip back out to Theo's and picked up the remaining seven pounds. We paid Theo and returned to the hotel room to get ready for our trip back home the next day. The bags were bleached and most of our packing was done so we could hit the road immediately following breakfast early Monday morning.

Everything was going according to plan. As we made our way through Lassen I quizzed Mark about the convention we were at in Reno. He had the story down and I was ready to tackle my sweat-inducing run through *The World's Biggest Little City*.

The traffic was insane as usual. As Reno receded from behind us I noticed, once again, a sheriff's vehicle pull onto the highway from the on-ramp and accelerate to our spot. When he caught up to us he lingered behind us in the left lane. It was frighteningly familiar. I didn't want to alarm Mark so I kept it to myself. I was being mirrored and, though I couldn't see the man behind the wheel, I had the feeling it was the same vehicle that had pulled me over on the last trip. I kept quiet and for a few miles Mark was blissfully unaware of its presence. It worked until Mark glanced over his shoulder.

Mark's face went white and he did his best to speak without moving his lips. "There's a Sheriff's vehicle behind us."

"I know," I said as I used my hand to look somewhat obvious that we were having a discussion "he's been there for a while. Just try to relax. Make him think you couldn't care less."

"It says K9 unit on the side," Mark said through pursed lips.

"I know," I said. "Seriously, don't act paranoid. Speak normally. Move your lips," I said again using small hand gestures hoping he would catch on. "Smile and act like we're having a fun conversation. The last thing we want is for him to think we're nervous about getting pulled over."

Mark certainly didn't get less stressed but he did start to act the part. He smiled a very strained smile and even feigned a laugh. I started talking to him about Winnemucca, and how we would soon be pulling over for gas, and anything else I could think of to calm him down. I asked a couple questions to get him to respond and look like he was a part of the conversation. The vehicle had been following us for at least fifteen miles since Mark took notice and it became obvious to me that he was running my plates. That was actually reassuring.

I had a clean record and the car had been pulled over and dismissed on the same road. I thought that played to our favor. I tried to maintain my calm but it was getting difficult. I knew one driving error could mean the difference between jail and home. I kept driving as perfectly as I knew how. I was surprised at how long the mirror was going on. I thought at that point I would have been pulled over or given up on. As we entered the outskirts of Fernley the Sheriff pulled off on the first ramp and disappeared. He had followed us for almost thirty miles.

"Don't look around," I said to Mark. "but he just exited behind us."

"Holy shit," Mark exclaimed "I don't know how you do this!"

"I'm on an all stress diet," I said. "I think that was the same one who pulled me over on the last trip."

"God man," he said. "I don't know how you kept it together that long."

"Fear of incarceration is a good motivator."

We continued down the road with the goal of driving straight through. We were doing well until we hit the Nebraska border early the next evening. The sun was beginning to fade when we pulled into a gas station in Sidney Nebraska. As I always did, I made a visual check around the car to make sure my lights were all in working order. It would be a shame to sit in a cell because I didn't change a taillight. I had Big Mark go around to the back of the car to check my brake lights. All of the main lights were working but thankfully Mark found one that wasn't. I had missed it on my lap around the car.

The tag light that illuminated the license plates was not working. That would have been an easy reason to get pulled over. I went inside the gas station to see if they had a bulb that would fit. They didn't. We went to the other gas station a block down the road to see if they had anything that would work. They didn't. On a normal night, doing normal things, I would have blown it off and continued down the road. Carrying several pounds of pot in the car changed that. We were stranded. The risk was too high to go anywhere.

We were both extremely tired and the idea of getting a hotel did not sound like a horrible option. We got a room at the Country Inn and Suites. I called Sue to tell her what was happening and not to expect to see me when she woke up the next morning, as had been the plan. Mark called home and made the same proclamation. As we were getting ready to get some sleep an idea struck me. I had two decent flashlights with me. I went out to the parking lot and lifted the lid of the trunk. There were access points under the plate that would allow the flashlights to shine through. With the aid of some duct tape I was able to attach the flashlight to shine over the license plate. Mark and I stepped back and after a few tweaks, it looked like it would have looked with a functional bulb. We had already paid for the night so we went back to the room and set a wakeup call for four in the morning to get a jump on the next day's travel.

We got up early, went back to the gas station to get a breakfast sandwich and a mug for the road and took one more look at the lights before pulling out onto the Interstate. We were quickly shown how important the lights were. The sun had not risen yet when we passed two vehicles within fifty miles of our rejoining the Interstate. They were pulled over with red and blue lights strobing as we passed. The second one had three law enforcement vehicles and dogs going to town on some poor guy's minivan. Had Mark not caught the fact that my lights were out we might have suffered the same fate.

Tumult

I began making profit for the first time. The profit was smaller than I had hoped, but it was a small taste of what I had envisioned. I was also losing myself further into the bottle. The stress of looking down the barrel of another trip, the self-deprecation from having broken a deal, my run-ins with knife wielding crazies, hillbilly cousins and a convicted murderer, the stress while in California of what may lie in wait for my return trip and the fear of getting a visit from local law enforcement while at home, were all taking a toll.

On top of the stresses of the life I had chosen was the loss of my brother Theo. He had been warned that I would not allow another misstep and continue to work with him. On the trip that followed my run with Big Mark, I prepared to make another round in the usual manner. I called to talk with Theo about my projected timeline. I called him several times and he was not answering. I found that to be odd as Theo always answered, or called back within minutes. He didn't answer. He didn't call back.

I called out to Mack's house and talked with Dana and asked her to have Mack call me back. There was no call back. Mack was always one hundred percent reliable to call back on every previous occasion. Had something happened I was not made aware of? I was perplexed. It was days after I had first attempted to get ahold of Theo when I got a return call from Mack. I was happy to see the prospector appear on my phone.

"Hey Mack, what's going on?" I was so concerned I didn't bother with the joking banter we usually shared.

"I need to ask you a question that I think I already know the answer to," Mack said with more seriousness than I had ever heard from him.

"Go ahead," I said. "You know you can ask me anything."

"Did you pay Theo for the seven pounds of Northern Lights on your last trip out?"

"Of course I did," I said "seventy-three hundred and fifty dollars to the penny. Why?"

"Theo told me that you took the pot and didn't pay him."

"No Mack," I told him. "That's complete bullshit. Big Mark can back that up. What the hell is he trying to pull? I've been trying to call him and he doesn't call me back."

"I'm actually sorry I even had to ask you Steve. I knew you wouldn't rip me off," Mack said. His voice changed to a mournful tone. "He's been messing with that meth shit and screwing around with those unsavory people I told you about before. I think he's in debt to them. I don't think you're going to hear back from Theo. He has five more pounds of my bud, but when I went to talk to him about getting the money he owes me for them, he said he was waiting for payment from somebody he had sold them to."

"Oh Jesus Christ Mack," I said. "What are you going to do?"

"I hate to say it but I think I have to let go of anything to do with Theo. With the state of mind he's in and the people he's got hanging around his place, I don't even want to try and collect on my bud. It's not worth it. When Dana told me you had called I went to Theo's so we could use his cell to call you and straighten everything out. He had a bunch of scary looking people out there and told me he lost his phone. He still insisted you stole the pot. I hate to say it but I can't work with Theo anymore."

"That's all right Mack," I said. "You and I can just work together."

That was how our new paradigm came into play. I made one last call to Theo to leave a message. It was brief. When the recording began I left five words. "Fuck you Theo. We're done." Those were that last words I ever spoke to him.

The stresses were building up and I was dreading each trip more and more. I knew the odds were, continuing would eventually result in something I couldn't pull myself out of. Instead of welcoming the trips as a way to have time to myself, I welcomed anybody who wanted to accompany me on the trip. It was a way for me to pull myself away from having hours inside my own head. I even let my own daughters come with me. In retrospect I could not have lived with myself had any harm come to them. I was not thinking clearly, and by adding liberal amounts of alcohol, I was making sure I never thought clearly...about anything.

When Hondo joined me we had a great trip and I enjoyed having her with me. She always had a way, of not only taking my mind off of the danger of what I was doing, but making me laugh along the way. Instead of the usual convention ruse for our trip, it was a father daughter camping trip. We memorized the name of the campgrounds we stayed at, and instead of marketing materials being loaded in the car, it was filled with camping gear. The trip out was smooth sailing and the trip back was interesting.

Because I had no need to go through Reno to back up the usual convention story, we instead drove a completely different route back. We drove north and went by Mount Shasta on our way to highway 395 which cuts through the east central part of Oregon. The road was fifty-five miles per hour for hundreds of miles. Considering the freight on board I had to obey it. It seemed to take forever but the scenery along the route was unusual and worth seeing. At one point it took us along a very curvy track following the side of a huge plateau of rock. The other side of the highway overlooked a long expansive lake with such high alkaline content that its water looked like turquoise stone. That led to a long stretch of rolling desert which was followed by green farmland.

It was one of the quickest breathtaking changes of scenery I had viewed on my trips out west. We also ran right through the heart of the Grand Tetons and Yellowstone where we were able to see a bear wandering by the road. Toward the end of the trip we drove through a myriad of motorcycles as we made our way through South Dakota during Sturgis. It was a wonderful trip...thankfully.

One of the most memorable adventures was much longer than my normal westward trips. It involved my older daughter Cassie. I had a nickname for her. I had always called her CeeVee. Both my daughters allowed me to use my nicknames for them. I appreciated their indulgence.

The difference from all of the previous trips was the fact that the California part of the trip was secondary to its main objective. Instead of going directly to California we would spend a week in Portland Oregon. CeeVee was the owner of her own dance studio and was a huge fan of a world famous dancer who owned a studio in Portland. She had a chance to take a week-long training with that dancer and was excited for the chance. The classes were not cheap so getting a free ride out and back would help her to be able to attend.

I offered up the idea of her riding out with me. After she finished with the dance classes we would drive down to California. Two birds, one stone. Her stay was covered while out in Oregon because a friend of hers, Sara, would also be going along. Sara knew some people in Oregon that had volunteered to put the two of them up for the week.

There was not a spot for me at Sara's friend's house so I started looking on Airbnb for a place to have a *Portlandia* experience.

I didn't want anything run-of-the-mill. Any offers of ordinary, normal, or quaint accommodations would be a deal breaker. I had a couple weeks to search for the right place. I had places boasting "great views" or "quiet neighborhoods" or "close to the downtown area." None of that interested me...until.

Welcome to Aphrodite's Den!

Lounge and Retire in a Temple Fit for a God and Goddess!

GREAT Room in a GREAT Neighborhood!

Placed right in the Heart of the Awesome Hawthorne District!

Rent a short stay room in an awesome full spirited House in SE-Hawthorne District!

We would love to host you!

Calling all mature and responsible creative types! Well-mannered and respectful Artists, Writers, Lovers, and Bohemian spirits are invited and welcome to stay at a very reasonable rate.

The room and location are perfect for creative spirits that are traveling or visiting Portland!

Please Note: *This is a very spirited house! We are not a House for the "Faint of Heart" or those that desire a controlled and quiet environment.*

Boldness and Adaptability are a MUST at The Heart of Hawthorne House! We are a Friendly and Fiery Bunch.

It is very much a permissive "When in Rome" in this case "When in the Heart of Hawthorne" do as the Heart of Hawthorne-Landians do...a very go and groove with the flow kind of house dynamics.

The house and neighborhood is located in a very lively area of the Hawthorne District. It is an "urban" setting...it is NOT Quiet and Serene...and the spirit of the household follows suit—Both Hood and House are lively and boisterous, and have a constant flow of hustle and bustle and various activities.

This space and house is unique and can be utilized in a number of creative ways, beyond just basic lodging.

It would also be a suitable room for a lively creative type that needs a portable office space...unless that person needs quiet space to work!

It also is a perfect spot for adventurous lovers that need a warm room for a discrete rendezvous in a Bohemian Love Hotel!

The possibilities are endless...

I had found my adventure! I could not have written a better description for the type of adventure I was looking for. I would have a week to put their descriptions to the test. I submitted my reservation to stay at Aphrodite's Den for my weeklong stay.

As the day rolled close for our departure I was getting excited for the trip. Excited in the way I had been excited back at the beginning of my California trips. Running out with CeeVee and her friend and spending time at the Den was renewing my desire for travel. I couldn't wait.

When the day finally arrived I picked up CeeVee and Sara. We were all excited about the adventure that was beckoning us west. CeeVee already knew I was a "drive till you get there" kind of guy. She was ready for it and explained my driving proclivities to Sara. Sara was on board. I, of course, put *Wanderlust King* on the stereo as we pulled out of Mankato.

We hadn't left home until the afternoon so it took us through the night to arrive at the entrance of Yellowstone. On our approach to the gates we welcomed the sunrise from the side of one mountain, while watching its arrival over the mountains on the other side of a pristine expansive lake. We were tired but the sun gave us the boost we needed.

That was the first time either of them had been to Yellowstone. They enjoyed the scenery. We even became tourists enough to stop at Old Faithful and watch the geysers erupt.

CeeVee had just got her first high-end IPhone so the clicking of selfies was constant. She was determined to save the memories of the crystalline blue lakes, steaming geysers, lush green forests, towering mountains and of course us, as we made our way along our route through Yellowstone and The Grand Tetons. CeeVee had seen large mountains before while on one of our family trips out to Colorado but she had never seen the Grand Tetons. She was enjoying documenting the entire experience.

As we traveled through the area I told them about the adventures Lucas and I had shared, while disturbing the peace with the Maxima in Cessna mode, on our way to Kelly, Wyoming. We decided to veer off the beaten track and stop at the Kelly on Gros Venture Café. As we turned off the main road to head toward the café, the girls got to see their first wildlife of the trip. The road was blocked by a herd of buffalo. There was no choice but to stop.

We enjoyed sandwiches on the deck at the café. Before leaving we all loaded up on coffee treats for the road. We were getting pretty worn out but we pushed on to try and make it to our destination. All we had left was a small portion, maybe a hundred and fifty miles, of Wyoming followed by Idaho and then we would be entering Oregon. I was certainly a veteran of long distance driving, but I was starting to doubt the drive would end in Portland. The extra stops had added hours to the journey. I was confident there would be a hotel stay at the end of the day. I broached the idea of a hotel and was immediately regaled with cheerful agreement. We decided to push to get as many miles as we could, but resolved to get a hotel somewhere along the way.

As we entered Idaho, I had a choice to make. I had to decide whether we should stay on the Interstate and enjoy seeing miles roll by at seventy miles per hour or risk trying a road I'd never driven before through the heart of Idaho on two-lane. If we took the two-lane there was a good possibility there would be no hotels until we rejoined the Interstate. With my fabulous traveling companions keeping me company, I figured they would keep me awake and alert enough to risk the two-lane.

We began the long drive through Idaho and the scenery was taking on an odd turn. It had gone from the lush green forests and majestic mountains of Wyoming, to a barren dry landscape sparsely adorned with brown and dusky green tufts of brush. It was as though we were on another planet altogether. Another planet was almost the right description. I stood corrected as we came across signs announcing we were entering Craters of the Moon National Monument and Preserve. It couldn't have been more aptly named. The dry landscape deepened in its vast emptiness of all things green. Rusty red and dull grey rocks were jutting out randomly from the hard unforgiving soil, interrupted only by deep cuts and jagged furrows. The mountains were left behind, leaving nothing but a monochrome scenescape of rolling hills. The view was grey, followed by greyer, followed by still greyer expanses of rock and desert style foliage as far as the eye could see. I would not have been surprised to see the moon rover drive by. It was surreal. I was the only stoner in the car, but I decided to indulge in a few hits of Mack's Northern Lights to make my traverse through the moonscape even more enjoyable. I was stoned, tired, and more than ready to find a place to crash, when we finally hit the Interstate and soon crossed the border into Oregon.

A few miles after crossing the border we found a hotel and decided to make it our resting spot. It was my treat to cover the cost of the rooms. I purchased two rooms for the night. One room was reserved for CeeVee and Sara to share and one was reserved for me.

The liquor store across the parking lot was exactly what I had in mind to end the day. I went over and purchased three bottles of locally grown wine and we toasted our arrival in Oregon. My travel companions toasted along with me but after one glass CeeVee was ready to call it a night. To be fair, she was ready to call it a night before she indulged my whim but, being the trooper she's always been, she humored me. Sara stayed and enjoyed two more glasses before she went to her room. I finished the last full bottle, smoked another hit of my Mack stash and called it a night.

The next morning we were all up as the sun seeped through the cracks of the hotel curtains. The three of us were anxious to hit the road knowing that at the end of our drive we would be in Portland.

Interstate 84 in Oregon has long steep grades that are amongst such high rolling elevations that it can be deceiving how much of a drop in elevation is involved...that is, until your ears pop, and pop again. It's an interesting drive which takes motorists over the famous "Deadman's Pass" where they seem to descend for an eternity. It was my first time going through the area without the push of eighty-thousand pounds making my knuckles dig painfully into the steering wheel.

Back in the day, I had been on those dangerous grades in the dead of winter. I was having fun taking the tour at full speed, on a warm sunny day, with no need to note the runaway ramps placed along the way. I had no need to worry about smoking brakes, slick roads or the push and pull of a dragonfly load. This is the term truckers used to describe a heavy load going over the mountains...drag up one side and fly down the other, drag-and-fly.

Sara received a phone call from the folks who had promised to put them up for the week, informing her that they would not be ready to host them until the following day. It was unexpected and would mean CeeVee and Sara would have to find a place to crash for one night. I made the suggestion of calling the woman who had rented Aphrodite's Den to me and see if she had any extra space available. The woman, who went by the nickname Cha Cha, said she had a shed in the garden area that was set up as a bedroom and we could rent it for the night. I accepted the accommodations and had her charge my credit card. I was thrilled that the first night in the interesting venue I had chosen would not be a solo affair.

I knew Oregon had several vineyards but I was surprised to see the vast number of them advertised on the billboards along the Interstate. We decided with the ample time we had available to us that we would pick a winery somewhere near Portland and take in a few samples of the local elixirs. As we were starting to draw near to Portland we came across signs for the Maryhill Winery. We made it our target.

We followed the signs which led us over the Columbia River to the Washington side. It was a beautiful drive and brought us to an impressive winery. The building itself was nice, but the grounds and the large amphitheater were positively breathtaking. We arrived in the late afternoon and sat down to enjoy a flight of their finest.

We spent hours tasting samples, enjoying some light snacks, and trying to decide which bottles would be making the trip with us to Portland. The decision was difficult. They had a wide range of choices, and the more we drank the harder it was to narrow them down. We started by getting a flight, then getting a glass to have out on the deck overlooking the crops and amphitheater. We were still unsure. We split another flight, stepped out to admire the view, and walked through the racks of wine. When we found a few we hadn't sampled, we asked for pours of the new varieties. It was a long process which culminated in a rather large purchase. We left the winery with a full case of wine. No two were alike.

Once the wine was secured in the trunk, we made the journey back over the Columbia River and onward to Portland. We timed the drive perfectly. It was after the dinner rush but before the sun began to fade, giving us the ability to see Portland and allowing us to read the street signs. With minimal effort we arrived at the reserved Airbnb location. We noted several places along the way that would be visited over the next week. The neighborhood was exactly what I was looking for. Small shops and interesting boutiques lined the street on Hawthorne Avenue. There was lots of foot traffic with the vibes of a cool collective right in the thoroughfare of the bustling city. It was an island of cool in an ocean of chaos - my kind of place.

Parking along the street out in the front of our rental required deft parallel parking skills. I have always possessed those skills. We were able to find a spot a half a block away and took the first load of our luggage onto the porch, and, as advertised, there were two people on the porch relaxing and reading books. They were both guests staying in the house and welcomed us to "The House of Fun."

"Cha Cha went to the store," one of the porch-folk said. "She said you should make yourselves comfortable, and she'll be back very soon."

We thanked them and made mutual introductions. The two were an engaged couple. Holly was an author who had just recently published her first book. She had a look half-way between intellectual and hippie, not that they're mutually exclusive. She had long, straight, brunette hair and an inviting smile. Her husband Tom was an aspiring musician who played multiple instruments, including the sitar. From what I gathered he had some renown in the area.

When Cha Cha returned from the store, we were shown to our respective rooms and given a brief tour of the house. It was an older two-story house with several rooms being rented through Airbnb. There were two rooms on the main floor, one in the basement, and three on the top floor including the one known as Aphrodite's Den...my room.

The kitchen, half-bath and full bathroom were all shared spaces as was the living room, porch and garden area. The garden area was located in the back yard and had a large variety of flowers, a grill, a hot tub, a pear tree and the shed which would be CeeVee and Sara's room for the night. The whole place was cluttered but clean. I was satisfied that I had made the right decision for a location to spend the next six nights.

After putting my luggage away and CeeVee and Sara getting their spot set up for the evening, I went to the car and retrieved the case of wine. It seemed fitting that a few of them should be sacrificed to ring in the new adventure. A few? Well, actually four. We enjoyed one of each of the wines we had considered our top picks. When the three personal picks were done, CeeVee retired to her bed and Sara and I drained one more bottle.

When the morning arrived I went down to say goodbye to CeeVee and Sara who were being picked up that morning by the people who were hosting them for the dance symposium. I had only briefly talked to Cha Cha the night before but after my former travel partners were gone we had a chance to sit down on the porch and get better acquainted.

Cha Cha was a thin blonde with long straight hair and, though diminutive in appearance, did not loom small. She had a big personality coupled with a fair amount of drive. She truly seemed to enjoy using her home for transient artists, adventurers and the avant-garde. With so many rooms available to rent she had stories for days. She was even in the process of cleaning and fixing up a large camper-van, parked alongside the house, to host even more.

The "House of Fun" was exactly that. Over the next several days I enjoyed the people in the house over long conversations on the porch. There were a few evenings that included naked hot tub parties with weed and wine as accompaniment. I indulged in the weed and wine, I even contributed a substantial amount. I was not as devil-may-care as the rest of the crowd. It felt odd being the only one in the hot tub with shorts on. It didn't feel odd, to feel odd, everyone was very welcoming. I quite liked being the odd man out.

The neighborhood was fantastic in the area of food venues. Tom, Holly and I had, on a few occasions, visited a wonderful French bistro. We had become friends as much as could be done over the span of the few days we shared together. I even went to Powell's book store and bought a copy of Holly's book. She signed it "For Steve Kind, Wishing you good times, shady porches and party lofts!"

The food at every spot I stopped was phenomenal and the variety was epic. Every block boasted its own unique combination. One block was small venues with limited seating, the next was lined with large, high capacity joints, and the next was coffee shops and bakeries. If I wasn't in the mood for one style or type of venue, I just moseyed down the street until I found one that suited my mood. It was not hard to find any kind of food I craved; it was just hard figuring out which one to choose.

After a few days, I was visited by CeeVee and Sara. We went to a charming Thai restaurant run by one of the coolest owners I think I have ever met. The vegetable spring rolls were delicious, and I ordered two plates of them. When the owner asked if I was going to order anything else, I told her I was not real familiar with the food she offered. There were pictures on the menu, but nothing truly appealed to me. She began asking me what type of food I liked and started asking me my preferences of all kinds of ingredients. After writing down a few things, she said she would make me something special and if I didn't like it I didn't have to pay for it. Twenty minutes later she came back with a bowl of soup with vegetables, a large chunk of sausage, and two hard-boiled eggs. It was an odd-looking soup, which my daughter named "Cock & Balls" because of the layout of the meat and two eggs, but it was delicious. The lady was a pro. She had a great sense of humor and made us laugh the whole time we were in there. We enjoyed the experience so much that we made it our last meal before leaving Portland a few days later. I, of course, paid for the soup.

It amazed me how much Portland had to offer. In the small amount of time I was there, I got to visit a street fair. It was a monthly affair during good weather, and even though it was held in a metropolis, it had the feel of a small hometown gathering. Another thing I loved about Portland was the food pods. The food pods were unutilized areas that would attract several food trucks in a circle around picnic tables.

Saying goodbye to Portland was a tough thing to do. The day before getting out of Portland, Sara decided she did not want to go with to California and bailed on CeeVee at the last minute. What I didn't know until later was that Sara had been starting to back out on joining us on the trip to California the first night she arrived in Portland. Sara was one of the pieces to the puzzle that made the idea of our return trip more palatable to CeeVee. She was understandably upset.

After packing the car and having our last meal at the Thai restaurant we bid farewell to Portland and began the drive south to Red Bluff California. I was excited to be taking CeeVee to meet Mack, Dana, Chelsey, Lucas, Amy and Brandon.

I was excited but it seemed as though CeeVee was not sharing in my excitement. She was usually very talkative and almost always donned a smile but the further we drove away from Portland the less talkative she became and the smile had disappeared. I assumed she was just disappointed that Sara would not be joining us. I also thought, because she had enjoyed Portland to such a degree, perhaps she was mourning our departure. I gave her some respite from my chatter and put on some tunes. We made our way down Interstate 5 which was our sole trail from Portland all the way to Red Bluff. With the exception of laughing at the name of one of the towns in California we shared very little in the way of conversation. Seeing signs for Weed, California gave us a well-needed grin.

We pulled into Red Bluff late in the evening and instead of the usual Holiday Inn stay, Lucas had invited us to crash with him and his family at the house. When we arrived Lucas took us to a small bedroom with a mattress on the floor and a blow up mattress next to it. CeeVee immediately went to bed and I stayed up with Lucas for a bit, to enjoy a little smoke and a beer.

When we woke up the next morning I offered to take CeeVee, Lucas, Amy and Brandon for breakfast. It was a couple days before Lucas's birthday so I also offered to treat him and Chelsey to a trip to Anselmo Vineyards. I thought that would be a nice day for everybody and perhaps put the smile on CeeVee's face that was struggling to make an appearance. Her smile did break out while she was interacting with Amy. As I had said before, Amy reminded me of CeeVee in many ways and it was like they were sisters when they were together. I wasn't sure which one enjoyed the other's company more.

After finishing breakfast I asked CeeVee if she would like to join me to go meet Mack. She was on board with the idea so I called Mack.

"Hey Mack," I said as he answered the phone. "Are you up for a couple of interlopers to come visit you?"

"I am," he replied. "Dana is excited to have some visitors. Nobody ever makes it out this way."

"I'm bringing my daughter with if that's ok."

"Yes, of course."

Mack lived out between Ono and Platina, in other words the middle of the middle of nowhere. He explained that there was no way we would be able to find him without help. The plan was to drive to Platina and meet in the parking lot of the post office.

We made our way to the Platina post office through the wild, winding, mountainous roads and followed Mack from there to his house. He was right; there was no way we could have found his place without assistance. We wound our way back toward Ono for about twelve miles before stopping at a small dirt turn-off with a gate across the entrance. Once the gate was opened we followed Mack down a path, similar to the road I had previously had to take to get to the old trim site. Washed-out roads, inclines, declines and constant curves brought us past the only other house in the area before we finally turned into Mack's driveway. He got out of the Outback and took us into the house to see Dana.

Mack and Dana's place was much as I had imagined it. An old wood structure nestled in the valley that Mack had described to me in the past. Bleached deer skulls hung by the overhanging shed and tools of every shape and size were strewn throughout the place.

Dana was inside the house trimming pot and was thrilled to be introduced to CeeVee. Mack, of course, lit up a blunt and handed it to me. We talked for a bit, then Mack said we should go out and walk down to the garden. He cautioned us on the way that we should be vigilant and keep our eyes open for rattle snakes. That didn't come as welcome news to my daughter. Half way back along the trail, Mack stopped and pointed into a big white bucket.

"Came across that one this morning," Mack said. "It's a big sucker."

I couldn't resist pulling his prize out of the bucket to get an idea of its size. It was a rattle snake as tall as I was.

"Sucker crept up on me when I was getting ready to water the girls."

We stepped a couple hundred yards down the path and came across Mack's pride and joy...the garden. Mack had strung up an overhanging tarp next to the garden to have a place to dry the plants during harvest and showed us how the stream next to the garden had almost completely dried up. He was concerned that if California didn't get some rain soon, there would no longer be a water source to keep him in the grow business. That was concerning to the both of us.

After spending some time in the garden and back at the house talking with Dana for a bit, Mack and I got down to business. I purchased the pounds needed for the return trip. Mack mentioned to me that he tried stopping by Theo's a couple weeks before, and he was nowhere to be found. There was nobody at the store and nobody in the trailer. Mack left a note for Theo, asking him to call when he got back and had not heard from him. He went out to Theo's again the day before I arrived, and he said that nothing had changed. There was nobody at the site at all. Mack was concerned that something may have happened to Theo and told me he was going to see if he could find out what was going on.

On the way back from Mack's CeeVee was once again quiet. Something was not right and my attempts at conversation landed flat. I hoped that getting back to Lucas's place would bring her some joy by having more time with Amy.

We spent the afternoon and evening enjoying the company of Lucas and his family. The next day, Saturday, was Lucas's birthday and a sitter was lined up so Lucas, Chelsey, Chelsey's friend Callie and I could spend the day together. We all jumped in the Camry and drove out to Anselmo Vineyards. It was a very warm day and we decided we would enjoy a lunch and some wine out on the deck.

The smile I had so missed from CeeVee was back. We spent hours on the deck enjoying a few flights and several samples of the wines. Our waitress was fantastic and made an already special day even better. I told her that I was from Minnesota and that I often came to Anselmo. She informed the owners of our patronage and pretty soon the owner came out to speak directly with us about our experiences at the vineyard.

When she was made aware that it was Lucas's birthday she brought us a bottle of a special wine that had not yet been released for the public. It was a perfect afternoon and, though my funds were almost completely depleted I offered to treat everybody for a meal at a great Mexican restaurant in Redding. Lucas was not used to drinking so much wine so the trip to Redding became time for a drunken nap.

When we arrived at the restaurant Lucas got his second wind and it was Margarita time! The drinks were wonderful but we had more fun playing with the flags from the drinks than enjoying the drinks themselves. It was one hell of a fun birthday celebration. When we returned to Red Bluff everybody was exhausted from the day. We weren't so exhausted that it stopped us from opening two of the bottles of wine we had purchased. We drank them while smoking some of the weed that Lucas had been growing in his indoor grow. His indoor grow was a team project. Lucas did all the work but I helped finance some of the equipment. I didn't have enough to put out a big chunk, but doled out a little at a time from each trip I made out west.

Sunday morning I awoke excited to get ready for the trip home. My excitement was not shared. After a day of fun and smiles, CeeVee was back to being distant and quiet. It was obviously not missing Portland that was the root of the problem. I had asked her a few times over the last few days if she was ok, and she always replied that she was fine. She was not fine, and I was unsure what to do. I was down to my last $300 to cover the trip home with a little bit to spare. The last smiles I saw on her face, other than the vineyard trip, was having breakfast and enjoying her time with Amy. Though it would leave us tight for expenses on the way home, I decided to repeat the breakfast idea. We all jumped in the car and went to the same restaurant as we had dined before. It was the same restaurant but not the same result. CeeVee was quiet and, even though she spent time playing with Amy, the joy was not there. We finished our meals and when we arrived back at Lucas's house she disappeared into the room we were sharing. I expected her to come out, but she did not. After giving her some time to herself, I entered the room.

She was sitting on the edge of the mattress staring down at the floor. Her melancholy mood was palpable. I sat next to her, put my hand on her knee, and looked directly into her eyes.

"What's the matter?" I asked her. "Obviously something is bothering you."

She instantly broke down crying. "I'm scared." was all she said.

"What are you afraid of?" I asked.

"I don't want to be in the car with all that pot," she said sobbing. "I thought I would be ok with it, but I'm not."

I was instantly ashamed. It was not a subtle realization. Of course she was afraid. Had I really not taken her risk into account? What does that say about me as a father? I had always been proud of being the father I was, but in that moment all of the pride drained from me to be replaced with self-loathing, embarrassment, and shame. I broke down and began crying. I hugged CeeVee, and she hugged me hard.

"I don't want to go," she said. "but I don't want to abandon you."

The shame deepened. She was concerned about my feelings and my welfare, yet I discounted her welfare the minute I set the trip in motion. I had been oblivious to the obvious. I pulled back from the hug and put my hands on her shoulders facing her.

"Don't worry about me, CeeVee," I said sobbing. "I do this all the time. It's my thing, and I should never have even asked you to do it with me."

Trying to hold back the tears, she again showed her concern for me and not herself. "I know you don't have enough money to get me another way back."

"We'll find a way, CeeVee," I said. "If I have to, I'll try and arrange some kind of financing to get you an airline ticket. Maybe I can get Big Mark to float me a loan against some weed."

"I don't want you to have to do that," she said.

The more her concern for me escalated, the more my sense of shame grew. She was being selfless in the situation that I had selfishly put her in. She was truly the wonderful daughter that I had raised right. It was the only thread I had to hold on to. Her caring for others above herself is something I preached but was guilty of not practicing.

"No matter what happens," I said, "you will not be joining me on the way home. I love you and I will find a way to make this work."

We spent the next moments trying to recover from a well-needed cry. We wiped away the tears and gained some composure before leaving the room to sit down for a cup of coffee with Lucas. I explained to Lucas what was going on.

"I have an idea," Lucas said. "I have been thinking about selling my Suburban because I never use it and the gas mileage is terrible. If you can cover the gas to get home you could go in two separate vehicles and on your next trip you could maybe have somebody drive it back."

The words were a solution that worked even better than Lucas could have imagined.

"How much are you asking for the Suburban?" CeeVee asked.

"I was thinking about asking for twelve hundred."

"My boyfriend John is actually looking for a truck to haul his drums to his gigs," CeeVee said. "He may be interested in buying it."

"I'll tell you what," Lucas said, "how about you drive it home and if he likes it I'll take eight for it?"

"That just leaves gas money as an issue," I said.

"I've got a little room on my credit card dad," CeeVee said. "It's not a lot but it might be enough."

Lucas volunteered a hundred dollar loan to me until my next trip, which I accepted. In the space of a half hour we had a solution. CeeVee's smile returned. The weight had been lifted off her shoulders. It had lifted off mine as well.

The rest of that day I had my wonderful, smiling, happy daughter back. It was a good day. I think CeeVee probably had the first good night's sleep she had experienced in a while. I, on the other hand, did not sleep well at all. Thoughts swirled angrily around my head. Who was I? When did my selfishness override the thing I held as the most important role I had ever played? The role of father had been something I not only held dear, but considered myself to be very good at. My children meant more to me than life itself and I had just relinquished those ideals.

How could CeeVee look at me in a positive light ever again? She tried so hard to bottle her feelings up, in order to cover up my egregious choice, that she couldn't even broach the subject with me. When did I become someone to whom she didn't feel comfortable sharing her problems with? I didn't so much fall asleep, as had a pause between thoughts. I fell asleep to those thoughts and they were back the second I opened my eyes. I put on the façade needed to get ready for the road, but I had a hard time looking my daughter in the eyes. In my eyes, I had failed her, and myself.

As CeeVee and I prepared to leave from Lucas', we made a plan to travel with distance between us. She would travel in front of me, far enough ahead that she would not be associated with my vehicle. We would keep in touch when needed with our cell phones.

For nineteen hundred and fifty miles I continued to beat myself up. No matter how loud the tunes were turned up, my inner voice drowned them out.

We made it home safely and CeeVee and John bought the Suburban. All's well that ends well right?

It wasn't an ending. It was a beginning of sorts. I could not shut the voices down, and they haunted me constantly. The only way to shut them down was in the bottle that I had already become too well acquainted with. My drinking became continuous. I was able to complete a few more California runs, but it was getting more dangerous the more I succumbed to the drinking. I began to make small mistakes. The small mistakes in judgement in that chosen endeavor could have wound up with catastrophic results.

The few years running back and forth to California, after the trimming trip, had resulted in very little money being earned, huge risk being visited upon me and my family, near incarceration on multiple runs and violent confrontations that could have ended in injury or even death.

In the winter of 2015, I pulled the plug on the whole affair. I would no longer be the California weed guy. I would no longer be the Candyman. I would no longer be Chopper. I would miss visiting Lucas and his family. I would miss seeing Mack and Dana. I would miss blunts on a sunny day with Mack and Theo, although anything with Theo was over regardless. I was no longer going to be that guy. Who would I be? What would I do?

AWOL

The last few trips I made out west were strictly perfunctory. I had no desire to be on the road anymore. My wanderlust had been extinguished and my heart was no longer in any aspect of those trips. My expenses almost equaled the income I had risked everything to gain. I enjoyed seeing my friends out in California but everything had become a ghost image of its former self.

Theo was no longer part of the equation and according to Mack he was no longer on the right side of the turf. What Mack had gathered about Theo, was exactly what we had suspected, and hoped was not true. Mack did some digging around and was informed by more than one source that Theo had gotten in deep with people in the meth trade and owed them too much money for him to have possibly had any hope of paying back. He attempted to eliminate his debt by using the money he ripped off from good people like Mack.

Mack asked around only to find out that there were many people who had similar dealings with Theo. Theo would take pot on consignment and sell it in order to pay down his debt. When Theo's reputation was sullied to the point where nobody could trust him, his income dried up and the debt cost him his life. As angry as I had become with Theo, I never wanted anything like that to happen. I regretted my last words to him on his voicemail.

On the last phone call to make arrangements for my trip out to Mack's, I had to break the news to him that I was done coming out. Mack was very understanding but saddened. He honestly seemed more upset that we wouldn't be working together than by the loss of income. I shared that sentiment. On the last trip out, Sue wanted to join me. She enjoyed meeting Mack and wanted the chance to be there on the last trip. I was not comfortable with her joining me because of the risks involved, but she insisted. I told Mack it would be my last trip, and as a special offering, I offered to pay for a couple rooms to put his family up at the Holiday Inn. Sue, trooper that she was, didn't miss a single blunt Mack smoked with us out in the parking lot. I brought Mack two hundred root beer candies as a final parting gift.

We visited Lucas and Chelsey and invited them to bring the kids to the Holiday Inn to enjoy a day with Mack, Dana, Ned and Cody while we took advantage of the swimming pool and Jacuzzi. The trip was part celebratory but also solemn in that we knew it was the end of an era for us.

When the week was over we packed our things, said our good byes and rolled east for the last time. Thankfully there were no issues with law enforcement coming out of Reno. We had a hell of an ending, in that, when we were on our way through Yellowstone we were redirected. A mudslide had occurred along the roadway to the east gate, which led to Cody, Wyoming, so we had to turn around and follow the detoured traffic. It took me in parts of the park I had never seen, which was nice, but it added several hours to the journey. On the way around the detour a herd of bison blocked the road delaying our progress even more. By the time we made it over and around the detour and finally made it to Cody, we were exhausted and decided to stay there for the night. We were not the only ones with that thought. There were no rooms available anywhere. We checked several hotels and they were all at capacity. We finally gave up and continued heading east figuring we would get a hotel farther down the road. The fun didn't stop there. We rolled down the road until we got to a rest area and decided to take a bathroom break. We pulled in and parked. As we were getting out of the car a policeman came out of the bathroom. I was so tired that I had not realized I parked next to an unmarked police car. Those were the kind of mistakes I never would have allowed before. While sweating the fact that I smelled like the last hit I had taken on the road (another thing I rarely indulged in...standards had gotten too loose) the officer got in his car and stayed parked. I went in and relieved myself and hoped that he was gone when I came back out. He wasn't. When Sue joined me back in the car we pulled out and the cop followed us to the entrance to the rest area. I was relieved for a second time when he decided to turn west as we turned east. The fun didn't stop there. Ten miles down the road, I hit a skunk as it was crossing the road. It was only a matter of minutes before the whole car smelled like skunk. The smell of that skunk not only accompanied us the rest of the way home but took several days to dissipate from the car, even after several washings. The universe was screaming at me that I had made the right decision to give up the California runs.

Being on the last pounds I would ever be selling, I had to face the fact that I had to find a new direction. No get-rich-quick schemes. No illegal activity. Calm, boring, and steady was looking very appealing to me. But what would that be? What was my next chapter? I didn't want to drive truck again. I was burnt out on the idea of sales. I didn't want to do anything except perhaps win the lottery.

My recent years were highly dangerous and stressful, but at least I knew who I was. I was the pot guy. I was The Candyman. I was Chopper. I had a routine and had become fairly good at what I was doing, such as it was. I lost my identity. Hell, I was lost. I was scared. I was unmotivated and depressed. I was drunk more days than I was sober. I looked for every opportunity to drink. I didn't have to look very hard.

I eventually had to find something. The money was drying up quickly, and I needed employment. I eventually landed a gig with a property management firm and dove into some pretty heavy labor. I was enjoying having a job that took very little thought and had no risk of incarceration. I felt as though the rest of my life was going to be work, drink, repeat. I showed up every day ready to work and showed up every night ready to drink. I was on my new treadmill, and it didn't take long until I wanted off. I had only been working a few months when my wrists decided to throw in the towel. I had developed carpal tunnel in both wrists from repeated abuse tearing out carpets after renters were through abusing them. My employer refused to cover the costs of the surgeries I required, and I was not in a financial position to hire an attorney to make them do what was right, so I ended up paying for them. In retrospect, I learned that it would have been a wiser move to get the wrists repaired on separate occasions. Having eight weeks of no real ability to use either hand presented some challenges. Going to the bathroom was one of those challenges - enough said?

Being once again unemployed, I started looking for my next job. One day while looking through the want ads, my phone rang and displayed the picture of the prospector. It was just the pick-me-up I needed. Mack always made me laugh,nd I was excited as I answered the phone.

"Hey there old timer," I said "how are things out in the wild and wooly west?"

"Hi Steve. It's Dana. I have some bad news," she said. "Mack had a heart attack yesterday and died."

I was silent. I didn't know what to say. I tried to reply but the words refused come out.

"Steve," she said not hearing a response "are you there?"

"Yes Dana. I'm sorry it just took me by surprise. Are you ok?"

"Well I'm pretty shook up," she said. "I know it's a longshot but I wondered if you could make it out for the funeral. He would have liked that."

"Of course, when is it?"

"I don't know yet but I'll let you know. I want you to know that he died as he lived. Do you remember him telling you about his favorite spot overlooking our valley?"

"Yes."

"When he didn't come back to the house we went to that spot and he was there next to the pickup. You know Mack, he was most likely smoking one of his damned blunts."

"I'm so sorry for your loss Dana," I said. "Let me know if there's anything I can do. I will plan on coming out for the funeral."

When I got off the phone, I broke down. I had gone from the high of getting a call from Mack to the low of knowing I would never see him again. Of all the California natives I had met he was my favorite. A quick wit, a memorable smile and deep commitment to those he cared about. I considered myself lucky to have been among them. I called Lucas and told him the news. He was deeply saddened. Lucas committed to joining me for the funeral.

When I received the information from Dana I made my plans to head west. It was not to be an actual service but rather a memorial at a local dining establishment. Dana made sure to alert me to the fact that the venue served alcohol and that I would not be the only one taking advantage of that. In order to make the trip I had to drain my last dollar from my bank account.

It was, without a doubt, the oddest memorial I had ever been to. People from all the farms, ranches and grows in the area were there. I got to meet many of Mack's relations and, without fail, they all had kind words to say about the kind of man he was. Dana was putting on a strong face throughout the day. We drank and told stories about the man we had come together to memorialize.

It was well attended and I was surprised to see how many people Mack knew. It was not as mournful as I had anticipated. Everybody celebrated that they had the honor and privilege to have had him in their lives.

After spending a couple days with Lucas and his family I had the odd pleasure of driving home without any worries. Law enforcement was not a concern. A small part of me wanted to be pulled over just so I could pull to the side of the road without the usual panic. I made the best time I had ever made getting home. I managed to cover the 1,950 miles in twenty-seven hours. Amazing how fast things go when a speeding ticket is the only concern.

My return home was followed by a renewed job search. It was late in the summer of 2016, and I managed to mow some lawns and do some gardening to try and pay some bills, but it was tight. Late in August, I had just gotten home from mowing a couple lawns when I got a call from one of my old friends Weezy. Weezy was his nickname back in high school. My nickname in high school was Lucan. To this day it is how we refer to each other.

"Hey Lucan, it's Weezy," he said. "I am in town for a couple days and my brother and I are going to go to the Kansas concert tonight. I was wondering if you wanted to join us."

I was worn out and not really in the mood to go out but I knew it could be quite some time before I would see Weezy again. Weezy lived in Europe and only made it to town on rare occasions.

"Yeah man, I'm up for that. What's the plan?" I asked.

"We're all meeting down at the Midtown Tavern around six o'clock for some beers before the concert."

"Sounds good, I'll see you there."

Because I was tired and not really in the right frame of mind for the concert, I set to work getting my mood altered. Energy drinks, cranberry juice and vodka were what were called for, and I answered the call. I answered it several times. I asked my wife if she would like to join us, but she declined. In the couple hours leading up to our planned rendezvous I managed to drink a half a large bottle of vodka by myself. I ran down to the Midtown Tavern and had a few beers and bought some shots. By the time we left to walk the couple blocks to the concert, I was already blackout drunk.

The rest of the evening I can't swear to, but I pieced it together from others recounting it for me. First of all, I heard the concert was fantastic. I remembered none of it. Oh well, carry on my wayward son. At some point during the show I lost Weezy and his brother and ran into my golf partner Brad. He asked if I would like to play pool at the Oleander Saloon after the concert. I did. Beers and many shots were consumed while I lost at pool. After stumbling back to the Midtown Tavern to retrieve my car, I drove down to The Wine Café, you know, because I needed a nightcap. After finishing some scotch on the patio, I poured myself into the Camry and pointed it toward home.

I didn't get very far. The entrance to the bridge which crosses over the Minnesota River from Mankato to North Mankato was less than a block from The Wine Café. Before I made it to the other side of the bridge I was pulled over. According to the police report I was very honest in my initial replies to the officer who asked me if I had been drinking. I told him I had. He asked if I felt I had drunk too much to be driving. I told him I had. He gave me the walking sobriety test which I failed miserably. Candy remained on the side of the road as I was taken to jail.

I made two calls from the police station that night. The first was to a lawyer friend of mine to get some advice. The second, the one I dreaded, was to Sue. I was booked and put in a holding cell for the night.

When I awoke the next day I was more than a little confused. I had no memory of anything after leaving to walk to the concert. I knew only one thing...regret.

I stayed in jail for a few days until my father was nice enough to make my bail. I was embarrassed and ashamed. I was also broke. Years of risking everything on my California trips resulted in zero dollars in my account. A DUI is an expensive proposition and I had no way of paying for what was lying in wait for me.

When I made it back to Sue she was upset. She knew the financial toll that came along with a DUI and our relationship was immediately strained. I told her that I would get some help and quit drinking.

I only knew of one way to get sober and that was through Alcoholics Anonymous.

Powerless?

When I prepared to attend my first meeting at the local AA I was less than enthusiastic. It wasn't my first rodeo, or second, or third, or...

I dreaded it. I had read the Bible, as many people call it, many times. The Bible in AA is the Big Book. It is sworn to by members of AA as ultimate wisdom. It was a book primarily written by a man named Bill W. back in 1939 who had suffered from alcoholism and came up with twelve steps and several stories to help guide fellow sufferers to the promised land of sobriety. Henry Parkhurst wrote two chapters and Dr. William D Silkworth contributed to a section in the book, but it was mostly written by Bill W.

I had read the book in the past. I had practiced its principles. I had memorized the Twelve Steps. I was back to give it another try. What is the definition of insanity? Doing the same thing over and over expecting a different result. That was me.

My first introduction to AA came way back during my high school years. During my senior year I voluntarily put myself into an in-patient program. My girlfriend Anna and I signed up to go at the same time to the same facility. It was a thirty-day program and involved journaling, group therapy, and focus on the Big Book and its Twelve Steps. Being a Christian, I took its philosophies to heart. I read, I prayed, I journaled, and I didn't hold back when group therapy was in session. Both Anna and I had become the poster children of AA. When the local sheriff came to the treatment center to look for somebody to speak to the community, it was

Anna and I that were selected. Upon graduating from treatment, we both attended AA. Most weeks we attended four or five times. I was entrenched in it - until I wasn't.

AA offers medallions or pins to commemorate various milestones of sobriety. I had received my first medallion upon graduation from treatment. I received my ninety day medallion sixty-days later. I did not get to my six month medallion. I was back to drinking, and it picked up right where it had left off.

My second stint in AA was not really worth mentioning. Suffice it to say, I entered treatment on an out-patient basis after I was arrested for possession of marijuana with the intent to distribute. I stayed with one of my brothers up in Minneapolis while I walked to and from treatment. I had no intention of quitting. I went with the sole purpose of reducing my sentence prior to standing in front of a judge. It worked. To be clear, treatment didn't work; reducing my sentence worked like a charm. Anna and I celebrated my graduation from treatment with a bottle of rum and two liters of Coke.

My third time in treatment was, again, out-patient. That time I was determined. My drinking and drugging had gotten out of control. Not that there was ever a whole lot of control in the first place. My drinking scared me, and I was taking any drug I could come across. I came across a lot. LSD, coke, magic mushrooms, speed, and of course gallons of whatever alcohol was available. I entered treatment without any outside motivation. No judges were waiting in the wings, no family members prodded me and, other than my own self-realization, nothing pushed me to make that decision. I read, I prayed, I journaled and I didn't hold back when group therapy was in session. I knew the Big Book from beginning to end and quoted it like a bible salesman quoted the Holy Scriptures. I knew every cliché. "There but for the Grace of God go I", "One drink is too many and a thousand is not enough",

"Sick and tired of being sick and tired", "Have an attitude of gratitude", "My worst day sober is better than my best day drinking" and of course "Let go let God."

I was the walking, talking epitome of the self-righteous, better than thou, big book quoting, cliché spewing AA member in good standing. I was obnoxious. Instead of just living the program, I wore it on my sleeve. If I was asked to enjoy a drink with somebody I didn't just say no, I told them why.

I didn't get my six month medallion.

So there I was, getting ready to enter AA for the fourth time. The difference that time was that I had no belief in God. I had stopped being a Christian years before I became the Candyman. How does one work with a program that puts such a high price on one's faith in a monotheistic entity when I had none? Could I pick and choose the steps I felt comfortable with and ignore the others? Was there another way to look at the Twelve Steps that perhaps I had not considered?

I decided I would simply be upfront and honest and ask the advice of the members of the AA group I attended and get their take. I didn't want to introduce myself to the group in that way, so I went through the motions and kept quiet for the first few meetings. It felt uncomfortable to say the least. I am in no way a militant atheist. I don't wear my atheism on my sleeve.

Contrary to many who don't truly understand what an atheist is, I don't follow the tenants of atheism. There are no tenants of atheism. I am not a Satanist, I am not anti-Christian, I don't hold séances or drink blood and I don't sacrifice small children. I simply don't believe in a God. That's it. I understand Christianity, as I was a practicing Christian for most of my life. I understood the comfort it could bring and I always welcomed anybody who believed, without reservation.

My whole family was Christian. My mother was a God-fearing woman who practiced as she preached and I loved her for it. When she was on her deathbed, her faith gave me comfort. She welcomed her death as the gateway to a wonderful next chapter. As much as I would have liked to believe, I simply didn't. I couldn't simply "Fake it till you make it" when it came to my core beliefs.

So what was so uncomfortable for me in the meetings in which I held my views to myself? I felt false. I wasn't true to myself and that was the person I was there to work on. AA meetings often started with the serenity prayer "God, grant me the serenity to accept the things I cannot change, the courage to change the things I can, and the wisdom to know the difference. Amen." It was expected that all the members joined in its recitation. I omitted the word God from the "Prayer" and looked at it more as a self-affirmation. The next step of the meeting was to hear an excerpt from the big book. The meeting where I finally had to speak my truth came when the excerpt read was from a chapter called gratitude in action.

> *I believe it would be good to tell the story of my life. Doing so will give me the opportunity to remember that I must be grateful to God and to those members of Alcoholics Anonymous who knew A.A. before me. Telling my story reminds me that I could go back to where I was if I forget the wonderful things that have been given to me or forget that God is the guide who keeps me on this path.*

The discussion went in order from person to person and I was the fourth in line. The first three made fairly similar comments about how, without God, they would have never been able to reach the sobriety they were experiencing. Not a single one gave themselves credit for the accomplishment. It was all God's doing. If that was truly the case, I was in trouble. The only part they seemed to give themselves credit for was the fact that they had humbled themselves and given their lives over to be corrected by God.

When it came around to my turn to speak, I took a deep breath, steadied my nerves and spoke my piece. Whenever you start to speak in AA, you begin in the same way by stating your name and saying "I'm an alcoholic." That is another thing I have never liked, but when in Rome...

"I'm Steve, and I'm an alcoholic."

"Hi, Steve," the group replied in unison.

"I have been having a really hard time trying to get some things straight in my mind," I said, testing the waters. "Do you mind if I ask the group a few questions?"

"Of course not," the man running the meeting said. "This is the place to ask them, and you are among friends."

"Thank you," I said still trying to steel my nerves to speak. "The section that we read today talks about being grateful to God, and that he is what keeps you on the right path. I am not a Christian, and I don't believe in any God. I can't relate, nor use the information in that chapter, to help myself."

More than one person answered me with the same basic response. What was the consensus answer? I could substitute the word God with the term Higher Power. One even decided to give me a rundown of the third step's phrasing as "God as we understood him."

"But I don't believe in a God or any kind of a higher power. I could never understand something that I have no belief in," I said and decided to show the person quoting step three that I was well aware of the steps. "How do I humbly ask something I don't believe in, to remove my shortcomings, like it says in step seven?"

The group had heard this before and evidently the higher power substitution was the only general answer. I was given several examples of things that could be my higher power. "The group could be your higher power", "Nature could be your higher power", "Buddha could be your higher power" or the worst suggestion of the day "Anything can be your higher power even a door knob."

My intention in the discussion was simply to get some workable solutions, so I could attempt to work the Twelve Steps in earnest. What it became was me pointing out how those examples didn't work when you actually substituted them in the Twelve Steps. How could I humbly ask the group to remove my shortcomings? How can I admit to nature, to myself, and to another human being the exact nature of my wrongs? If I didn't out-and-out say that I was a Buddhist, what would make it a viable substitute for God? A door knob? Really? How would a door knob work with the Twelve Steps?

The Door Knob Twelve Steps

1. We admitted we were powerless over alcohol—that our lives had become unmanageable.
2. Came to believe that a Door Knob could restore us to sanity.
3. Made a decision to turn our will and our lives over to the care of the Door Knob.
4. Made a searching and fearless moral inventory of ourselves.
5. Admitted to the Door Knob, to ourselves, and to another human being the exact nature of our wrongs.
6. Were entirely ready to have the Door Knob remove all these defects of character.
7. Humbly asked the Door Knob to remove our shortcomings.
8. Made a list of all persons we had harmed, and became willing to make amends to them all.
9. Made direct amends to such people wherever possible,

except when to do so would injure them or others.

10. Continued to take personal inventory and when we were wrong promptly admitted it.

11. Sought through prayer and meditation to improve our conscious contact with the Door Knob, praying only for knowledge of the Door Knob's will for us and the power to carry that out.

12. Having had a spiritual awakening as the result of these Steps, we tried to carry this message to alcoholics, and to practice these principles in all our affairs.

It didn't fit. It didn't work. I gave up on trying to find a way to reconcile the disconnect. I attempted to simply try working the Twelve Steps by omitting the parts that were not relevant. My version of "fake it till you make it" was to continue going to meetings and half-heartedly work the steps that I could.

I was able to make it through uncomfortable meetings and kept my mouth shut. I had the support of my wife. My oldest brother and his wife were always in my corner, and even attended the meeting with me and my wife when I accepted my thirty day medallion. I stayed sober, attended meetings and continued to keep my mouth shut.

The night I was given my ninety day pin I was accompanied again by my oldest brother, his wife and Sue. I was filled with pride that I was able to get to that point working a program that didn't really fit me.

I was white knuckling the sobriety but I was staying sober. During one Saturday meeting I decided to open up my piece of the meeting by rehashing the same questions I had for the group a few months prior. The group was damned near hostile about my calling myself an atheist and, as usual, the misconceptions of what an atheist was, reared its ugly head. They were so hostile that, just for my benefit, they decided to end that particular meeting with The Lord's Prayer. That was the last time I ever walked through the doors of an AA meeting.

I did not get my six month medallion.

Grabbing the Third Rail

Early on in my limited sobriety I managed to find another job. An old friend from my Junior High days who was also a fellow golf league member, Wally, offered me a position at his property management firm as the Maintenance Coordinator. It was a good fit. When I initially took the job, I was unable to drive. The only way for me to change that was to get a device put on my vehicle to allow me to start my car after blowing into a machine designed to detect the presence of alcohol. Wally, a three time veteran of DUI offences, helped me jump through the hoops to get approved for the device. He also helped me financially to cover the costs involved.

The first few weeks of my job I had to do office work and had to rely on Sue getting me to and from work. Once I was approved to install the breathalyzer device I was off to the races. The job utilized many of the skills I had acquired over the years. Wally owned several units himself but the majority of the properties I was in charge of maintaining were owned by third parties. The third party owners paid the firm to do everything from routine maintenance and emergency repairs, to rent collection and accounting. It was a full service firm.

My previous maintenance position was helpful in giving me the understanding of the variety of labor required for the job. My past sales experience made my interaction with the third party property owners a breeze. I had to identify issues with the properties and find the right contractor to line up to complete the job. Some of the property owners were of the mind, that paying more for prevention and paying for solid workmanship on repairs would save them money in the long run. It also allowed them to charge higher rents. I had a list of contractors to satisfy them. Big Mark was on that list. Some of the property owners were in favor of low costs and minimal maintenance. Those property owners would prefer duct tape, bailing twine and bubble gum if it would push the problem down the road. Those owners catered to low income renters and often got paid through the county. I had a list of contractors to satisfy them.

Another part of my job was ensuring safety standards were followed and meeting with property inspectors to evaluate the properties. For the high-end owners it was a breeze. For the slumlords it became a scramble every time the inspection drew close. I created checklists and put together a system which successfully kept properties from being shut down or incurring high-dollar fines.

As the former owner of a website design and internet marketing firm I was also tasked with updating the website for the firm and doing some online marketing. It was the right job at the right time. For a little while I even did it while sober. Actually, I always did the job while sober. I never came to work drunk but eventually I did have days where I was hungover. I was very good at my job and was appreciated by most of the owners but my performance after a night of heavy drinking was less than optimal. I enjoyed working with the people at the firm and continued to improve the position for over a year. By the end of that year I had new systems in place that covered every aspect of my job. It became something I could do on autopilot. I was proud of the work I had done and I was confident that my role at the firm had improved and streamlined several processes.

Unfortunately I had done the job too well. Once I had the position running like a well-oiled machine, I was replaced. A new person was brought in to do my job at a fraction of what I was being paid. I was devastated. I was angry. I was unemployed.

Keeping in line with the stellar luck I had been having up to that point, my car died as I was nearing the end of my employment. The day I was given my two weeks' notice was the day my car was towed in, never to run again. When I originally bought Candy, I was in a position to pay for her with cash-on-hand. I no longer had that option available to me. I was facing unemployment, I had horrible credit and I needed a vehicle. Knowing I was about to be done working for Wally, I decided I would try to start up a lawn care business. Lawn care is not a business you can start without wheels. I began looking for a pickup truck. Lawn care would require it. I went back to where I had purchased Candy and found a Chevy Silverado that would fit the bill for $3,000. It might as well have been thirty thousand. I had no money.

Wally was feeling a bit guilty about giving me notice and had mentioned, if I did decide to start a lawn care business, he would give me jobs working at the properties doing lawn mowing and basic landscaping. I hit Wally up for a loan. He gave it to me. I've never underestimated the power of guilt.

The glorious day that I was legally able to remove my breathalyzer happened just prior to Candy dying. It was a minor silver lining - or was it?

Having the restrictions removed at the same time that I was no longer constrained by working for another person, proved to be far too much freedom for me at the time. My drinking was back at full strength. Oh hell, it was on a new level. If a friend wanted to go shoot pool during the day, I could do that. If I was too hungover, I could sleep in and let it dissipate before getting to work. If I wanted time to go on a bender, I simply arranged my schedule to accommodate it. I was unleashed. I was pushing boundaries I didn't even know existed. Little did I know, I was firmly grabbing the third rail but the jolt hadn't registered with me yet. I was a mess.

When I initially got sober, I stopped playing pool. It was not a game I considered conducive to a sober lifestyle. Playing pool was always accompanied by massive amounts of alcohol. Now that the leash was off, I was shooting pool most days. My typical days started with lawn work for a few hours, pool for several hours, and then I would show up at one of my favorite watering holes to drink scotch and talk stupid until I jumped in Rusty to carry me home. Yes, I named my truck. It didn't take long after the purchase for the rust to start showing through the concealing paint job. The truck was white but it quickly began to resemble the California rust bucket owned by my least favorite hillbilly.

My drinking was spiraling out of control, and it had become a topic of conversation between Sue and me. I knew my drinking was beyond dangerous, and I agreed with her that I had to stop. I detested the idea of going back to AA. AA does a lot of good for a lot of people. There are many who enter it and are able to give up the bottle forever. I am not one of those people. It didn't work for me. The idea of returning to it seemed like a hopeless proposition. The last meeting I had attended made me feel unwelcome and I swore I would never return. I couldn't do it. I wouldn't do it.

I attempted to quit drinking without AA. I slowed my intake and reduced the number of times I would drink each week. It didn't last. I would swear off it completely, and then get a call to play some pool. The days I went without drinking were becoming fewer and fewer and the sober days were filled with the desire to get to my next drink. Drinking never left my brain. I was always either consuming, or regretting the last time I consumed, or planning for the next chance at consumption.

The fact that my wife stayed with me through my drinking was something I had taken for granted. It was as if I knew she would stick by me so I didn't need to worry about that aspect of my life. She joined me drinking several times and I took it as a sort of endorsement. I could continue to drink without risking losing the love of the woman who had always stood by me. If I could continue to drink without her walking out the door, I had Carte Blanche to behave poorly. I truly had no constraints.

After months of going through the cycle of trying to quit drinking or at least attempting to curb my drinking, I stopped. I stopped stopping. I was back to daily drinking and often ended up blackout drunk by the time my head hit the pillow at night.

The times when I was sober enough to think, I was miserable. I had lost my California friends and was missing my talks with Mack, and to a lesser extent, Theo. I had put my family in danger and felt the shame that came with that. I was unable to keep a decent job. I was barely keeping the lawn care business afloat. I felt like a failure on every level. The bottle was the only escape I had from those thoughts. I always felt the need for escape. The more I drank, the more those thoughts intensified, the less I wanted to think them. I was on the treadmill from hell.

My pool games, golf leagues and pool leagues no longer held the allure they once did. They became things to do while attending to the main event of my drinking. It was possible for me to skip a pool game or a league night due to drinking but I never skipped drinking because of a pool game or league night. In high school I always joked that I had times when I had got out to the middle of the lake to do some fishing, only to realize I had forgot my tackle box or my pole, but I never forgot the cooler. It was no longer funny. I knew I had a serious problem but I did everything in my power to avoid doing anything about it.

I looked back at the other times I had attempted to quit drinking. The failure rate just reinforced the idea that it simply wasn't in the cards for me. Three stays in treatment and countless AA meetings had not stopped me from drinking. I always found myself getting back to drinking. I never fell off the wagon, I dove off. It felt like I was doomed to failure.

Just like step one of the Twelve Steps said, my life had become unmanageable. Step two had become my road block. I was not going to come to believe that a power greater than myself would restore me to sanity. I could not have foreseen the event that would break me through that road block, but it was indeed coming.

On a hot summer day early in June of 2018 my life was turned upside down. On that hot summer day I found myself in a place alcoholics know as rock bottom. It almost removed everything I held dear from my grasp and sent my life in a whole new direction.

What didn't kill me, made me stronger.

Liars and Lawyers and Cops, Oh My!

My days had become a blur. Occasionally I accomplished a bit of landscaping, but I was constantly smoking pot and early afternoons became drunken introductions to higher levels of drunken evenings. I had been following a pattern of self-destruction so profound that, though I wasn't suicidal, I was far from enthused about living. I didn't want to die, and I wasn't convinced I wanted to live. I was having a hard time looking at myself in the mirror. All I saw looking back at me was a beaten man. I had accomplished a great many things in my life, but during that time, I could recall none of them.

On a beautiful, warm, and sunny Friday morning, I awoke from my bed and went through the usual rituals. I started the coffee brewing, went to the bathroom to shave my head and face, checked my Facebook, checked my email, poured a cup, and sat down to read at the kitchen table while I waited for Sue to wake up and join me. As Sue made her appearance, I opened the window shades to let the sun in. I gave her a hug and a kiss and we sat down to enjoy our coffee together. Waking with Sue was one of the simple pleasures in life that I still clung to.

"What's your plan for the day?" Sue asked.

"I have to be over at Donna's to mow her lawn at 9:30, and then I mow Cindy's at 10:30," I replied. "I'm meeting Jerry to play pool this afternoon. Oh, I almost forgot, Troy called last night. He asked if I could go down to Wells and have a couple cocktails down there. Is that okay with you?"

"I guess," she said with her eyes rolling. "Just don't get all shitty."

"I won't."

Sue had reason for concern. Every time Troy and I got together, cocktails flowed like water. I have never left Troy's house sober.

My day went exactly as I had planned. Lawns were mowed, pool was played, and I was already well on my way to getting "shitty" before I left town to head to Troy's. Before getting on the road, I picked up a six pack of alcoholic energy drinks. My words to Sue were cast aside.

I finished off three of the six energy drinks while driving the forty miles to the town of Wells. I was two things; awake and drunk. Troy had just moved to Wells, and I had not yet seen his new house. When I pulled into his driveway, Troy greeted me with a cocktail, and gave me the tour. It was a nice two story home. It had plenty of room for a man who was suddenly on his own, after recently getting divorced.

I lost count of how many drinks I had at Troy's, but eventually we decided to go to one of the local bars to shoot some pool. Hopped up on energy drinks and my head swimming in a pool of alcohol, it didn't take long for me to get in an altercation with a local man who was itching for a fight. We had some tense moments and I was ready for it to break into a good, old fashioned bar brawl. I too had the itch and was hoping to scratch it.

When I put the challenge to him, to actually back up his bravado, he quickly backed down. As often happened when horns got locked, he bought me a drink to let bygones be bygones. Half the time that evening I played pool with Troy and the other half I played with my formerly itchy protagonist. I was having fun but decided to cut it short. I told Troy I was going to leave to get the drive over with before the bars closed. I didn't want to be on the road with all the drunks.

Yeah, I know, it makes me shake my head to this day how bent my logic was. Troy asked me to stay at his house overnight. He stated the simple and undeniably true fact that I was too drunk to be getting behind the wheel. My reason, or more to the point, excuse for not staying was that I did not have my CPAP sleep machine. He kept pushing the issue so when he eventually excused himself to go to the bathroom, I left. I left him without a ride home. I jumped into the rust bucket and pointed it towards home.

The trip was going fine, as far as I could tell, until I approached the outskirts of the town of Mapleton. The highway had a reduced speed zone which skirts along the edge of town. That night there was some commotion as I neared the lights of town. I slowed the truck down before the signs prompted it. There were people out by the highway and I saw police vehicles parked alongside the road. As I entered the hub bub I kept my eyes peeled for anybody who may have the inclination to wander out onto the highway.

The city of Mapleton had its annual fair that night and the derby had just let out. When I was about a hundred yards from the crosswalk, the last of a string of people had crossed and the area was open. I kept my speed steady at around thirty or thirty five miles per hour. As I entered the crosswalk area a police officer appeared out of nowhere and waved his flashlight at me. I had no ability to stop, and as I passed him, he quickly pulled himself away from my truck. The second I passed him he darted to his cruiser, hit the flashing lights and began to pursue me.

When I got to the other side of town, just on the outskirts, I pulled over. I knew I was not going to make it home that night. As I waited for the cop to walk up to my door I took the pot I had in my pocket and stuffed it in the cushion between the backrest and the seat. It was a quick interaction which resulted in me being placed in the back of his squad car and hauled to the tiny makeshift law enforcement building at the heart of Mapleton. It was a pit stop before taking the longer ride to Mankato.

On the way to the jail in Mankato I tried, to no avail, to appeal to his empathy. I told him I had been under extreme stress, that my mother was in hospice and that I lost a longtime friend just the day before. All of that was true. It wasn't why I was drunk but it was true nonetheless. Nothing changed his mind and I didn't really expect it would.

When I arrived in Mankato I was given the chance to make a couple phone calls. I made the same two I had made on my previous DUI. I called my lawyer friend and followed it with a call to Sue. I woke Sue up and I could hear the anger in her voice. I had obviously gotten "Shitty."

After going through the initial booking process I noticed something unusual. I was being treated in an overly hostile manner. It wasn't a misread, the officers were treating me like I had done something way beyond a simple DUI. I was brought to an interrogation room. I don't remember exactly what happened but one minute I was standing by the table in the room, and the next I was waking up on the floor with blood streaming from that back of my head. I had been knocked unconscious.

When I opened my eyes, I had two cops yelling at me to get the hell up and stop faking like there was something wrong. I couldn't stand. I was dazed and in serious pain. When I told them I couldn't stand up, I think it scared them a bit. An ambulance was called, and I was taken to the hospital where I had to receive stitches to the back of my skull. I wanted to say something to the doctor about how I suspected somebody had knocked me out, but there was a cop with me the whole time. The cop told the doctor that I had slipped. I knew that was wrong, but I also knew I had to go back to jail when I was done getting stitched up. I kept quiet.

When I was taken back to the law enforcement center (AKA jail) I was put in a holding cell. I slept that night on a concrete slab with no pillow and no blanket. I was cold and I was in pain. I could not get any real sleep. With no pillow it was very difficult to sleep on my side. With a fresh wound, sleeping on my back was impossible.

The next morning I noticed a bruise behind my knee. I couldn't say for sure, but I suspected it was where I had been kicked, to make me fall into the table the night before. I was taken to my cell in the main area where all the inmates were housed. The new shift was also treating me with an extra layer of contempt. I didn't get it. I had a DUI. I hadn't killed anybody.

It was later that day when I found out from another inmate, and from Sue, why I was being treated with such contempt. The officer who had arrested me, reported my DUI as much more than it was. He had embellished the report with exaggerations and outright lies. His report stated that when I approached the traffic area that night, I was revving my engine and accelerating as I neared his position. I'm pretty sure that, in and of itself, was impossible. How could anybody rev and accelerate at the same time with an automatic transmission? He said that I drove directly at him and that the other officer at the scene had to scream for him to get out of the way. He said that he had to dive out of the way and sustained minor scrapes from hitting the deck.

I was drunk. I was not so drunk that I had completely missed all of that. I had to replay it in my mind to make sure I was not imagining things. No. I was quite sure I remembered what had actually transpired. I did not remember every detail, but those were not details. I was certain he was lying.

After my father arranged to bail me out, my brother Arn picked me up, and I was brought to my parent's place. I was ashamed. I was humiliated. After bearing the righteous anger and disappointment of my parents and my brother, I was brought home.

Sue gave me a hug when I came through the door. It didn't feel right. There was no kiss. The hug felt obligatory not impassioned. She was angry, hurt, and unsure of her feelings for me. She knew what the costs of this DUI were going to be, and she was also well aware that I told her I would behave before I left the house. She had reason to be angry. She had reason to be hurt. Her feelings were amplified by the fact that the lying officer's report had been read on the radio and printed in the local newspaper with my name prominently included.

The next days were tense and I feared I might lose the love of the woman I would have done anything for. The mother of my two girls, the love of my life, was rethinking her desire to stay with me. I was scared. I was afraid she may actually utter the words. I was afraid, until she actually did utter the words. I was no longer afraid. I was devastated.

I was numb. The idea of losing Sue, and losing her through my own actions, hit me deeply. She said she wasn't sure she could stay with me. I had to cling on to the hope that there was a chance. Did I want, or even more to the point, deserve a chance? I wanted Sue but I also wanted her happiness above all things.

When Sue and I first were introduced, I loved the fact that, though I didn't know who she was, she knew who I was...sort of. She remembered me as the guy who stopped and waited so I could hold the door open for her. I didn't even remember the incident. We worked at the same company many months before our introduction and when I was on my way to the lunchroom I saw her coming and held the door open for her. Who would possibly remember that? Sue.

We began dating after our initial introduction. After weeks of dating I gave her the "Let's just be friends" speech and broke it off with her. A couple weeks after that I was on an impromptu vacation sitting on a beach in Florida with a friend named Laura. I was surrounded by beautiful women. Ten days of sunny Florida and all that kept going through my mind was how big a mistake I had made by breaking things off with Sue. The feelings I was having for her actually scared me. I didn't want a long-term relationship.

When I returned from Florida I wanted to reach out to her. How could I possibly do that after giving her the speech? A few days after my return, I got a knock on my door. It was Sue. She was there to pay me back the fifteen dollars that I had borrowed her. Kismet! I asked her to go play some pool and we hooked back up. The rest is, as they say, history. A little over a year later we were married and nine months after that we were parents.

I was about to lose that wonderful part of my life, because I could not say no to the bottle. Was I crazy? Was I unable to grasp the depths of the peril I had put us in? No. I was unwilling to confront the monster that was at the base of my misery. I used the alcohol to pour over my feelings in a desperate attempt to make them go away. It exacerbated the issues rather than alleviating them. I had to find my way through the wall that was separating me from finding happiness.

I was letting that wall come between me and my happiness, but it was also the structure that stood between Sue and her happiness. I knew she loved me. I knew that her anger shrouded any ability for her to see beyond the situation that I had thrown us into. I had been pressuring her to decide whether or not we should stay together and I had overlooked what was really important to me. I had overlooked the reality that she may have been better off without me. Her happiness had to be at the forefront of the decision for herself and for me.

I sat down with her on the couch and had the hardest conversation I had ever had to have with her. I had to tell her that she may have been right. I had to give her the out. If she was with me out of sheer obligation or simply to try to make me happy, neither of us would be happy. I let her know that her happiness meant everything to me and that if she wanted to call it quits, I wouldn't argue or blame her. I couldn't believe the words coming out of my mouth but I truly felt them to my core. I was already miserable. I knew the anger she had toward me made her miserable. Her leaving me would deepen my misery, but the consolation for me would be her happiness. I told her that regardless of her decision I would put myself into treatment. I would do whatever it took to make it.

The idea of getting back into treatment, attempting the Twelve Steps, and going to AA meetings was daunting. I didn't want to do it. I also didn't want to continue drink. If I was without Sue, I would still need to change the direction alcohol had been taking me. If she stayed, I would have even more motivation. I began looking for a treatment option in Mankato. I found one and set myself up for an intake interview with a counselor named Amber.

When I arrived for my interview I decided I had to be completely honest. There could be no holding back. The treatment center website talked about the Twelve Steps. If I just acted as though I was comfortable with that, it would be dishonest. I had to put my feelings about the religious aspects of the Twelve Steps directly on the table. If I was going to find the help I needed, I could not "Fake it till I make it." I could not afford to fake anything. My life was at stake. My very sanity was at stake. My marriage may well have been over, but without help, it was an assured casualty. It was time for a zero bullshit meeting.

When I was sat down, I was given some paperwork to fill out. There was a series of questions that I was quite familiar with. Why are you seeking treatment? When did you first start using alcohol or drugs? Have you been in treatment before? These were all pretty easy questions to answer. Then I came across a question that was hard to sum up. How had drug/alcohol dependency impacted your life? Where do I start with a question like that? It had impacted my life profoundly, and there wasn't enough space provided to write a book (that came later). I stared blankly at the page. I struggled with the reply. I finally wrote the truest statement I could have conjured up. The answer was revealing to myself and took very little space..."Drug and alcohol dependency has impacted every aspect of my life." I added, "without help, it will impact every aspect of my future."

When Amber came back into the room and read over my answers, we engaged in a long and serious discussion. When I was asked about my previous attempts at sobriety, I explained my feelings about the Twelve Steps and the fact that I was an atheist. I held nothing back. To my surprise I found myself speaking to someone who didn't judge me. She listened and made no assumptions. It was the first time I felt comfortable talking with anybody about those specific issues. What she told me changed my life.

Amber explained that recovery was not a one-size-fits-all proposition. She explained that while the Twelve Steps had been proven to help many people, it was not the only path available. She told me about an organization that she had heard a little bit about and suggested I take a look at it.

"It might not be for you," she said. "But it's worth exploring."

I was accepted to start treatment the following week.

The night after my entrance interview I went and looked up the organization that Amber had suggested I investigate. The name of the organization was SMART Recovery. SMART was an acronym for Self-Management and Recovery Training. I was instantly intrigued. Self-management was something I could get behind. It said that it was based in cognitive behavioral therapy, rational emotive behavioral therapy and centered around four points. The four points were;

1. Building and maintaining motivation
2. Coping with Urges
3. Managing thoughts, feelings and behaviors
4. Living a balanced life

There was no mention of reliance on a God to remove my addiction. To the contrary it was based on self-management. It was based on scientific principles. It put me in the driver's seat. It was something I wished I had come across long before. There could be no looking back; I just had to be satisfied that I came across it at all. I jumped on their "Find a Meeting" link and searched in my area. There were none available in Mankato. The closest meeting I could find was seventy miles away in Minneapolis. There were, however, online meetings. I took note of the times that would work and set my phone to give me a reminder.

When I entered my first virtual meeting I was welcomed and the meeting began with a check in. The check in was a moment for each member to speak about what brought them there or how things were going in their life. The first thing I noticed was that nobody identified themselves as an alcoholic or an addict. As somebody who had always hated that aspect of the meetings I had attended, it was a breath of fresh air. The second thing that stood out was that others in the group asked questions or engaged with the person speaking.

Cross talk rarely happened in my AA meetings. More fresh air. When it came to my turn to speak I didn't hold back. I asked questions and received answers from several people in the group. There was a main facilitator but everybody felt free to speak. At the mid-point of the meeting, the facilitator began talking about conducting a cost benefit analysis. The group actually joined in, talking about a cost benefit analysis about their addictions. The exercise was similar to doing a CBA for business expenditures or any other business decision. It was wonderful. Spoiler alert; the CBA sided with abstinence.

When I started my first week of treatment I told Amber about the meeting. I told her about the CBA and generally how comfortable I was with the group dynamic and the lessons they were giving me. It was at that moment in time when I give Amber credit for changing my life. I will never stop looking at our initial interview as a turning point in my view of addiction and as the point where I first truly experienced hope. I no longer had to fake anything. I was able to work on myself with an earnest sense of finally being on a road I could travel. Amber allowed me to veer off the normal curriculum established at the treatment center and, though I was an active participant in the group sessions, I was not going by the Twelve Steps. I was involving myself in the four points. Without having had such an open and trusting counselor I would have been back to white knuckle sobriety.

I had one thing going for me at that point. I had a new way to attempt sobriety. Unfortunately life didn't relent. I was still facing DUI charges. My mother had been put on hospice care and the entire family was dealing with the fact that she was nearing the end of her life. Sue had not given me a decision about whether or not we would continue to be married. I was, again, dealing with the added expenses of hiring a lawyer, getting a breathalyzer for my truck, and the added joy of having to buy my truck back from the county. Did I mention I was pretty much unemployed? Lawn care was not going to cover the bills that were headed my way.

The temptation to drink was excruciating. The fact that I had a new way to attempt sobriety didn't make it magically go away. The urges were there, the opportunities were ever-present, and I would be lying if I didn't say that the bottle seemed like the only way out on several occasions. There were times I looked at the bottle as the only thing that would relieve the pressure. I didn't know if I could make it. I was almost convinced I wouldn't.

I struggled. I went to my treatment sessions and received a lot of support. I even ventured up to Minneapolis and went to my first in-person SMART Recovery meeting. It was two weeks into treatment when I received the best news I could have hoped for. Sue was willing to give us another try. She had seen a change in me. Her decision, however, did not come without a stipulation. If I said hello to the bottle, I would say goodbye to Sue, forever.

Carpe Diem

With the mounting pressures of my court date looming, my marriage finding its way off the rocks, my mom suffering and bed ridden, the financial costs of, well, everything and getting in the ring to take another swing at sobriety, my world was a virtual pressure cooker. I made my way up to Minneapolis for a couple SMART Recovery meetings and was on the verge of completing treatment when an idea occurred to me. Travelling seventy miles each direction to attend meetings on Saturday mornings was difficult, and with my finances being what they were, even the cost of gas made it prohibitive.

I decided I would do some investigation into the idea of starting a local meeting in Mankato. Could I just announce it and find a place to hold the meetings or was there more involved? As it turned out, there was more involved. A lot more. As a matter of fact, I could not even announce a new meeting until there was a certified Facilitator to run the meetings. OK, it made sense. Unlike other meetings, the facilitator would have to have some kind of understanding of the basic concepts of the therapies involved.

Understanding the Twelve Steps of Alcoholics Anonymous, and putting them in action as the meeting moderator, took some skill and devotion. Learning the core concepts of cognitive behavioral therapy, rational emotive behavioral therapy and motivational interviewing, all concepts used in SMART, would take a bit more training. I made the decision to drive up to

Minneapolis and pick the brain of the facilitator who ran the Saturday morning meeting to see what he suggested.

The facilitator of the meeting suggested something that made me pause. He suggested that I apply on the SMART Recovery website to get a scholarship to become a facilitator. I wasn't aware that such an option existed. I knew there were courses but they came with a cost. I was broke. The scholarship would make the idea feasible. I was unemployed and in the process of looking for work. Until I found a job I would have the time needed to take the courses. As a bonus they were offered online so I wouldn't need to worry about travelling.

The following Monday I put in my application and announced at my treatment meeting that I was perusing the idea of starting meetings in Mankato. I think part of the reason for my announcement was to be held accountable. Once it was spoken out loud I knew I had to move forward.

Three things happened the following week. I was accepted for the scholarship, I graduated from treatment and my lawyer called to tell me he had some good news.

My lawyer had managed to get the dash footage from the arresting officer's cruiser. He said I was going to want to see it as soon as possible. I set an appointment to meet with my lawyer down at his office that afternoon.

When the dash cam video was run on my lawyer's computer it began with footage of people being walked across the street. The audio was so sharp that you could hear the people chatting as they walked. In the distance was my white rust bucket slowing down. No weaving, no revving and no accelerating. The audio even picked up the hum of the truck as it neared the crosswalk. The officer appeared in the video seconds before I entered the crosswalk and, just as I remembered, he appeared, waved his flashlight and backed away from my truck.

There was no scream from the second officer and the arresting officer never had to dive out of the way, nor did he scrape himself up, as he had reported. There was no indication that he had any reason to pull me over in the first place. That was fabulous news. That meant that the arrest itself was without basis and should be thrown out of court.

I was ecstatic! It was the best news I could have asked for.

Unfortunately the video continued. It was embarrassing. It showed that, though I had no reason to be pulled over, no probable cause, I was indeed drunk. The video showed me stumbling around and talking with a definite slur. That wasn't the most embarrassing part. On the way from Mapleton to Mankato I was pleading with the officer to turn around. I was telling him I normally didn't drink like that but that I had lost a friend and was losing my mother...all with a slur. That was also not the most embarrassing part. The most embarrassing part was my singing. Singing at the top of my lungs, poorly, in the back of a squad car, on my way to jail, was not a great venue for the performance. Seeing it in full color was hard to bear. I asked my lawyer to give me a copy of it on a flash drive so I could whip it out if I ever contemplated a repeat performance.

I left the lawyer's office humbled but happy. There was a good chance that I would be able to beat the charge and not have any more costs outside of the lawyer himself and the breathalyzer for my truck. Unfortunately, it would be months before I would get my day in court. I had to continue moving forward.

With treatment in the rearview, I put all my time and energy into getting my Facilitator's certificate and was able to complete the course in a little over six weeks. Once I had acquired my facilitator's certification it was time to find a venue and get the word out that Mankato was going to have an alternative to AA. I decided to start two meetings.

The locations were chosen with care. The first location was a coffee shop called The Fillin' Station. There were three reasons for choosing that particular spot. First, I was able to get the time slot two hours before a regular AA meeting that met in the same location. My hopes were that I would get some buzz going among the crowd as they were waiting to start their meeting.

SMART Recovery is not only an alternative to AA; it fits well in conjunction with AA. I was truly hoping to have some of the AA members give it a try. Another reason was having coffee available for a 9:00 AM Saturday meeting. It didn't hurt that their private room was free to the public.

The second location was chosen for its discreet nature and professional surroundings. The thought was to have a meeting for those who may have reasons to keep their recovery out of the public eye. Doctors, Lawyers, teachers or anybody who may have professional concerns, would find a safe haven to get sober. I found a meeting room at a local business park which had a great view, a large comfortable conference room and the privacy needed for a 6:00 PM Tuesday night meeting. After 5:30 the building was pretty much empty with the exception of the cleaning staff. Also, after 5:30 the elevators only went to the seventh floor, where the meeting room was located. The only way to stop at another floor was to have a key. The drawback to the location was that the only way you had access to reserving a meeting room was to rent an office in the building. I had to raise some money.

I created a GoFundMe account and went to work promoting the idea. I reached out to several friends and posted it on my Facebook account. Believe it or not, the first one to donate was Anna, my ex-girlfriend from high school. It didn't take long and I had enough to commit to a one year lease. With the donation from a friend I had completed treatment with; I took out an ad in the local paper and advertised the meetings. I had brochures that I had purchased from the SMART Recovery website and distributed them at local halfway houses, treatment centers and anywhere else I could think of that may benefit from them.

The first Saturday meeting rolled around and I made my way down to The Fillin' Station. I bought a cup of coffee and waited for the first people to arrive. I had purchased handbooks for those that wanted to buy them. I laid them out on the table along with some brochures. I sat nervously waiting, and waiting, and waiting. Nobody showed. Pretty soon I heard the AA crowd gathering to get their first cup of coffee consumed before their meeting. I waited until the hour and a half I had reserved the room for had expired. I gathered my things, put them in my duffle bag, and walked out. I was disappointed. I didn't expect a full-house, but I was hoping at least a few people would have shown up. I had resolve, and I was not going to give up easily. I went to the front and put in my reservation for the next six weeks. I was not going away anytime soon.

The following Tuesday night I made my way to the business park and put the handbooks on the table along with the brochures. I waited, and waited, and waited. Nobody showed. I pulled out my laptop after forty-five minutes of waiting and played some Miles Davis, as I watched the sun go down with a fantastic view of the Mankato River Valley. A sense of calming peace settled over me. It wasn't the same as the sunrises and sunsets I had experienced in California, but it was beautiful. I was disappointed, but I was content. I had my music. I had my sunset. I had my plan set in motion. I had resolve. I would be back the following week. If the meeting didn't work it wouldn't be for lack of trying. After the hour and a half expired, I gathered my things, put them in my duffle bag, and went home. The following week I repeated my efforts. No one showed up at either meeting. I kept showing up. Week three

I repeated my efforts. No one showed up at either meeting. I kept showing up.

That was repeated weekly. There was a modicum of embarrassment after a few weeks as I put in my order for coffee and made my way back to an empty room. I had occasional conversations with people waiting for their AA meeting to start but could not convince anyone to give it a try. Finally, six weeks after the first meeting, I had two people show up for the Saturday meeting. Both of the attendees had similar stories. Stories of feeling that they had no place to turn, other than AA, and needed a new direction. I had finally found someone like myself. I was excited and looked forward to the next week. Nobody showed up at the meeting in the business park that week, and the following Saturday I was once again alone. The two from the previous week did not return, until the following week.

The word began to get out, and pretty soon I had several people in the Saturday meetings and the Tuesday night meetings also began to thrive. Two months after my first Miles sunset, I had a functioning meeting that began to grow. I never had another meeting by myself. I had done it. I was proud of what I had accomplished. I was on a new high. I was happy for the first time in quite a while. Then, as often happens in life, the other shoe dropped.

The Bottle Beckons

With the meetings picking up momentum and holding strong with some who had become regulars, I began to get comfortable in the role of facilitator. I was on a weekly email thread with other facilitators and had the support I needed when questions arose. The more meetings I had under my belt, the more I grew into the position. The pressure cooker of my life continued but through the new focus of running meetings I was able to forge on. What I knew was coming, but didn't want to admit to myself, turned the pressure cooker to a whole new setting.

In the final days of October my mother's health had taken a turn for the worse. The family had been informed that they should make plans to say goodbye. I had been visiting my mother, almost daily, while her declining health had restricted her to her bed. She had the care of a wonderful staff and they made her as comfortable as possible. I enjoyed my visits and almost without fail, my mother would find a way to take the dark reason for my being there, and turn it into questions about my life. She was truly amazing in the way that she always considered others before herself. She was truly amazing in many ways. I couldn't imagine my life without her being a part of it. Even on her worst days she was able to keep her sense of humor, which was ever-present throughout her life.

The toll her condition was taking on my father was also very difficult to see. My mom and dad had been through tough times, raised five boys and overcome countless setbacks as a team. The fact that all five boys had strong marriages and never had a divorce was a testament to the profound examples set forth by my parents. They had been together over the span of several decades and I could always sense how much they still loved each other. They were more than husband and wife. They were partners, they were friends, they were each other's support system, they were often the brunt of each other's jokes and they were a team that supported and encouraged the five of us boys.

Her declining condition made every visit feel like it may be the last. The pressure was turning up and the bottle was patiently waiting for me to snap. It would be there to comfort me. I knew it had the power to temporarily remove the grief I was already feeling before her passing. I also knew that my mom would disapprove of my turning to it for comfort. That thought alone was a big reason that the cork stayed in the bottle. I loved my mother and did not want to shame myself in her eyes. She had sacrificed much of her life to raising me and my brothers. I couldn't let her condition be the excuse to throw away my sobriety.

It was on Thursday November first when I received the call I had been dreading. My mother had passed away. My sister-in-law was the one to break the news to me. It was not a surprise but it still hit me with a shock I had a hard time recovering from. It went beyond emotional. It felt like a physical punch to the gut. I had time to prepare for the news but felt woefully unprepared for how it affected me.

My reaction was the overwhelming sadness of knowing I would never see her again. I broke down and wept. It was a selfish cry. My mom was no longer dealing with the pain and I should have been happy for the end of her suffering. Instead, I was saddened by my loss, my brothers' and sister-in-law's loss, my father's loss, and the loss of her in the lives of so many people who she had touched over the years.

Once I had gained my composure, I called Sue. She had started a new job, so I had to interrupt her at work. She immediately left work to come home and be with me. God, I love that woman.

There was a sort of bitter irony that she died on November first, All Saints Day. My mother was one of the most God-fearing people I had ever known. If I was a believer, I would have considered it to be part of the plan. In my eyes, she was as close to sainthood as anyone could be.

Two days later, I found myself driving down to The Fillin' Station to facilitate a meeting. I didn't want to go, and I knew the members would forgive me for missing the meeting, but I felt I needed to carry on. It was where I needed to be. The outpouring of support and sympathy was amazing. A transformation had taken place. I was always there to help the members through tough times. That day the members had become my personal group of grief counselors.

The following Tuesday when I got to the meeting, the reality had sunk in. I broke down in group and was again given support and comfort. The group had started to become more than I had imagined it could be. It was no longer the group I had started in order to help others. It was the group that had, in fact, been made whole through their own sense of compassion and understanding. They had become the warm blanket that I needed to make my way through a cold time.

The shock of my mom's passing didn't push me toward the bottle. The day of the funeral was a different story. In the past, my mode of operations was, when anybody close to me died, I was drunk the night of the funeral. I was ok in the morning preparing for the funeral. The funeral itself was not pulling me to the bottle. My brothers all gave impassioned eulogies in front of the church. Each brother talked about specific aspects of my mother's life and personality. I spoke about her incredible sense of humor. I sought approval from my father to allow me to relate a story of her enduring sense of humor even at the end of her life. He gave me his approval and I did my best to give my portion of the eulogy while struggling to hold back tears.

"One of the greatest lessons I ever learned from my mom was not spoken to me at all. It was shown to me through her example time and time again. This lesson she shared, not only with me and my brothers, but with everyone who knew her. The lesson was just how valuable a good sense of humor can be.

Mom's sense of humor was not just used during the best of times; it was often what made the worst of times bearable. She always knew the right thing to say to lighten up the mood when that was what was needed.

One example I would like to share happened very recently. Being bed ridden and in pain, one of the nurses up at New Perspectives came in to give her some medication. The nurse asked my mom if she was experiencing any pain. My mom said that she was. The nurse then asked my mom to show her where her pain was....mom pointed to my dad.

It's not a coincidence that in the many pictures that have been displayed here and at the funeral home, whether posed for or taken candidly, the people in them are smiling. More often than not, she had a hand in putting those smiles there."

The funeral was followed by a light meal at the church and everybody shared their stories of their interactions with my mom. She was well loved and it was nice to hear. After the meal everybody departed and went to their cars. I sat staring at the steering wheel and couldn't move.

"Are you going to be ok?" Sue asked.

"Yeah," I replied. "I'm just having a hard time convincing myself not to stop and get a bottle at MGM."

Sue was stuck for a reply to that statement. I couldn't blame her. To her credit, she didn't attempt to say much of anything. She gave me the moment to get my thoughts together. I had an overwhelming urge to drink. It was then that the word *awefulizing* hit my head. Awefulizing is a term used in SMART Recovery to describe the irrational way of looking at urges as something impossible to overcome.

The idea, in essence, states that the urges you have to confront can be uncomfortable, they can even rise to the level of painful but, they are all bearable. They will pass. I took some deep breaths, grabbed the steering wheel and drove us back home, past the MGM without stopping for the bottle that was screaming my name. The urges came back several times that afternoon and evening, but they eventually subsided.

Over the next several days I had urges come up, challenge me for a short period and go away. Two things registered with me over that period. First, the urges reduced in frequency and duration. Some temptations were harder to resist than others but they all had an expiration date. Instead of allowing them to live in my head, I welcomed them as transient annoyances and cheered their defeat. Each one made me stronger in my resolve and added a layer of resilience. Second, I needed the group a whole lot more than they needed me. They had saved me when I was unsure I had the strength to save myself. I was lucky enough to have had them in my life when I needed them most.

As I made my way through my grief, life moved on. It wasn't long before I was hired as a customer service associate at Home

Depot and began working a forty hour week. It had been a while. I thrived on it and enjoyed working with the people on both sides of the counter.

Less than a month after starting I was asked to take over the manager position for the customer service and deliveries departments. Things were falling into place. I was happy. The bills were being paid. I had a job I liked and both Sue and I were performing legitimate jobs. It was a far cry from the wild and wooly days of the California runs. It was calm. It was legal. It actually involved a profit. It was fairly stress-free.

I continued to work and run the meetings. The idea of having a drink was receding with each passing month. Sue and I were in a better place. We had re-ignited the passion we had almost lost. Things were going well and I was about to get my day in court. I was excited and hopeful. I was looking forward to having the DUI overturned. It would reduce my costs and give me a sense of vindication. I looked forward to watching the officer get questioned in front of a judge. His lies would be a matter of public record.

Prior to the court date I was asked to get some character witnesses lined up. I did. I had the written endorsement of my counselor from treatment, I had a police officer friend of mine come in-person to testify, I had a friend that had been with me in treatment, I had my brother Arn, and I had Sue by my side. I had the video which spoke for itself. It was set up to be a good day.

The trial began pretty much as I had anticipated. I was sworn in and asked a few questions about the steps I had taken to get myself sober. The written endorsement from Amber was read into the record. I had a chance to speak about the facilitator's certification I had earned and the meetings I had started. My cop friend said some kind words as did my treatment friend, followed by Arn and Sue. After twenty-five minutes of character witness testimony, the arresting officer was sworn in and my attorney went to work. The written report was compared to the video. There was no escaping the falsehoods. The officer stared at me throughout his testimony with a glare. He was not happy to have been called out on his bullshit.

I was feeling great about where everything was going. It was all leaning my way. Then the judge spoke and knocked the wind out of my sails. It was like he had not witnessed the same trial I had just experienced. He commended the work I had done since my arrest but said, though I had made strides, I was still there for my second DUI. I was to be taught a lesson. Nothing was overturned, and I was pronounced guilty. Before arriving in court that day, I had the feeling my chances were better for me to be acquitted than to be found guilty. The more time that passed, I thought my chances were improving. I was not expecting what I was given. I was convicted and given a year in jail, all but thirty days suspended as long as I did two years of probation, paid a thousand dollar fine and a fifty dollar surcharge, attended a MADD (Mothers against drunk driving) seminar and completed one hundred hours of community service. I was almost as angry as I was stunned. My lawyer was able to get the judge to agree to amend the order to ten days in jail and allow the time I had already served to count against it. He also got it into the record that my time serving as a Facilitator would count against my mandated community service. I was given a period of time to arrange when I would serve my jail time and I was excused from the courtroom.

I left the courtroom stunned and Sue and I went to my rust bucket to head home. I had not driven more than three blocks when I was pulled over by a state trooper. I had done nothing wrong, my plates and tabs were in order, and I was driving with whiskey plates, so he had to know I had not been drinking, so why was I being pulled over?

The trooper walked up to my window and when I rolled it down his first words were "Have you had anything to drink?"

"No sir," I replied.

"I see you have a breathalyzer installed," he said. "I'm going to need you to shut down the vehicle and start the truck after the breathalyzer has had a chance to recycle. I also need to see your license and registration."

Sue and I were in disbelief. What could have possibly been his reason for pulling us over? The trooper waited for me to go through the process to restart the truck and took my paperwork back to his patrol vehicle. A few minutes later he returned, gave me my license and registration, and said I was free to go.

"Can I ask you a question officer?" I asked.

"Sure."

"What was the reason I was pulled over?"

"We received a phone call that a truck matching yours, with whiskey plates was being driven under the influence."

It didn't take a rocket scientist to figure out who most likely made the phone call. After the glares he had given me in the courtroom, I think the liar had decided to give me one more jackboot to the ribs. What an asshole.

An odd thing happened. I didn't notice it right away. As a matter of fact it didn't dawn on me at all. I was made aware of it when Sue made a comment.

"I'm surprised how well you handled yourself after your day in court," was all she said.

That's when it hit me. I didn't have my usual reaction. The bottle did not beckon me. The thought of getting drunk would most certainly have been my response in the past. It was the type of thing that had derailed so many attempts to stay sober in the past. The bottle would have been screaming at me.

The shrill voice urging me to drink would have been deafening. It wasn't there.

I was not deluded enough to think I had defeated the bottle, but I was well on my way to living without it.

Trial by Fire

The passing of my mother was one of the hardest challenges I had to my sobriety. The loss of my court case didn't help matters any. What did help is that I was beginning to dig in and get comfortable with being uncomfortable. My challenges didn't stop or even yield just because I wanted some relief. Hell, at times they seemed to pile on.

Life continued to give me bags full of lemons, but I never made lemonade. I made choices. I made hard choices. I made one choice above all. I had decided that no matter what difficulties life threw at me, I would step up, look the challenge straight in the eye, and tackle it as if my life depended on it. It did. The following year put that resolve to the test.

My job had been going fairly smoothly until one day when I went to help a customer load some bags of salt into their vehicle. My right arm did as it was told. My left arm refused. I was able to lift with my knees and get the salt up to waist level but when I attempted to lift it beyond that, all the strength in my left arm evaporated. I had no pain, and my hand was grasping the bag with ease. When I went to lift beyond my waist it was as though my left arm simply ignored its part in the chore. It just wouldn't listen to my brain telling it what to do. As somebody who had been somewhat obstinate his whole life, I took my left arm's refusal to listen as an affront. I chalked it up as a fluke.

The fluke became a regular occurrence. My arm was not weak, it was not in pain, and it was not accompanied by any other issues.

It simply denied me the ability to lift or pull once the task of bending my arm with weight was asked of it. The problem was not going away and began to impede even lighter lifts. Even a cup of coffee had become difficult to bring to my lips. It was a struggle. Once the cup was half way to my gullet, my arm would begin to shake.

I'm not big on doctors. I had always been one to attempt to walk things off. I was getting frustrated and could no longer wait for a spontaneous recovery. I set an appointment with my family doctor who referred me to a neurosurgeon. My neurosurgeon was pretty sure after our first visit what my ailment was, but ordered an MRI to be sure. I have always been claustrophobic, and the MRI was something I was not looking forward to. I had heard horror stories about the procedure. The horror stories proved to be accurate. I was laid down on the table and there were foam blocks put next to my head to restrict movement. The table I was on was barely wide enough for me to fit. I was given a button to hold in my hand during the procedure to allow me to alert the staff if my claustrophobia got the best of me. I was given headphones so I could listen to music. They asked what genre I preferred, and I selected funk, James Brown to be exact. The table then moved me head first into the MRI machine. My shoulders touched both sides of the unit and the top of the unit was inches from my face. I was already panicking, but I concentrated on *Papa's Got a Brand New Bag* and took deep breaths. That was when the fun began. Clang, clang, clang, whir, clang, clang, was all I could hear. The James Brown was completely obliterated by the loud noises emanating from the MRI. I refrained from hitting the panic button but, the longer the MRI took, the closer I edged to requesting that relief. It was an experience I never wanted to repeat. It felt like I was in the machine for hours but in reality it was closer to thirty minutes. I never hit the panic button. I was pretty proud of that accomplishment. All told, I was more comfortable with the MRI than I was with the news it brought.

My spinal fluid was being cut off by two of the discs in my neck. The doctor recommended surgery to remove the two discs and fuse the three corresponding vertebrae with a series of plates and pins. That sounded awful. I told the doctor that I didn't want to go through with such a radical procedure. I will never forget her response.

"If you don't get the surgery, it will continue to worsen and eventually you may be left with no ability to use your left arm at all."

"Can I have some time to think about it?" I asked.

"You can take your time to make the decision," She said. "But the longer you wait, the less your arm will be able to recoup its losses."

"What exactly does that mean?"

"If we do the surgery now," she said. "The best case scenario is you will regain somewhere around eighty percent of the ability to use that arm. The longer it is postponed, the lower the chances of recovery become."

That was not a statement I wanted to hear. The MRI was more than conclusive. It was easy, even for me as a layman, to see the obstruction. I was terrified. The thought of having my neck operated on and spending the rest of my life with plates and pins in my neck was a daunting proposition. What was more daunting was the idea of losing the use of my arm forever. Before leaving the doctor's office, I scheduled the surgery.

I had a few weeks before I would be under the knife but I had to tell my employer that I would be out of commission from a couple days before the surgery, until after the six week recovery period. Six weeks was the earliest estimate. It was very possible the recovery time would be more than that. I was told that I would still be able to come back but they could not hold my position for me.

I really liked what I was doing. I had to add the job I liked to the casualty list.

I was depressed. I knew the surgery was necessary but it was going to rob me of much more than I had bargained for. The job I was offered in lieu of my management position was selling appliances. I was good at sales but had no desire to get back in that field. I needed to keep it as a backup plan so I told them I might be interested in it. They said they would keep the position open for me.

The night after my surgery I was kept in the hospital, but much to my surprise, they let me go home the next day. I was clouded on pain medication and given prescriptions that would keep me stupid for several weeks. I weened myself off the medication after the first week. I was better off with some pain, than I would have been, had I slipped into a new addiction. Comfortable with being uncomfortable. It took four weeks before I could even lift my head off my pillow without using my hands to pick my head up and reposition it. I was miserable. I could barely see the light at the end of the tunnel.

It was almost eight weeks before I was in a position to make a decision about going back to work. I decided to decline the offer. I had to find something else. I continued my physical therapy and worked to regain the strength in my arm. The pain in my neck eventually subsided to a mere annoyance. I was feeling better and soon after making my recovery I lined up an interview for a job receiving tanker trucks at a cheese production plant.

The interview went well and I was asked to go to the local clinic to make sure I was physically able to do the tasks required for the job. I was asked to lift fifty pounds, climb stairs, climb a ladder, do repetitive tasks involving reaching and lifting various items and was monitored for heartrate. I was happy to have made it through with flying colors. Prior to my surgery I would not have been able to do several of the tasks asked of me. It was an endorsement of the surgery's success.

When I started the job, I saw exactly why they had me pass the set of tasks prior to being hired. I was working twelve hour shifts, walking up and down steep catwalks to access the tops of the tankers. I had to bend and apply pressure to open the top hatches on the trucks. I had to have ample hand strength to allow me to attach and detach the large hoses required for loading and unloading the trucks. It was a physically taxing job, but I considered it the perfect fit for getting paid to work out. I loved it. I wasn't thrilled with the twelve hour shifts, but I soon adapted to them. The job was a thirty-minute drive from my house and I had to be at my post at 5:00 AM. There was little time for anything but to get up early, eat, shave, shower, drive, work and repeat. The money was decent and I was looking at finally getting some cash built up in my bank account. It was perfect.

Two weeks after starting the job the world went into a chaotic change. Covid 19 had been unleashed on the planet and was spreading quickly. It was about that time that I also had an incident that was a larger issue than I first expected it to be. While unloading one of the tankers, I turned to grab a water sprayer to hose down the area. When I turned my body, my boot had gotten wedged under one of the large hoses, and I felt a pop in my knee. It was instantly painful. I grabbed a hand rail to keep myself from falling. It was painful, but I was the new guy. I didn't want to make too much of an issue about it. I reported it to my supervisor, but I was able to keep working.

Within days of the first reports, Covid 19 was given the status of a pandemic. I was on needles and pins. The last thing I wanted was for the plant to get shut down and for me to be out of work. The plant did their due diligence and began requiring masks, pushing handwashing and supplied sanitizer to both the truck drivers we were working with, and the employees of the plant. After a week of basic precautions, one of the neighboring plants had a minor outbreak and was forced to shut down. We were worried we would be next. To stave off a shutdown, more drastic measures were put in place. The drivers, who normally helped with the unloading process, were no longer allowed to leave the cabs of their trucks. That put more of a burden on the plant employees. We continued to do whatever we had to in order to ensure the plant stayed open. I kept working through the pain.

My knee and the top of my shin area of the same leg kept getting worse. I assumed it was from the long days standing on it with no real relief from constantly going up and down the catwalks. I kept toughing it out. At night I was applying ice and elevating my knee but nothing seemed to relieve the pain and swelling that had begun to take place.

About six weeks after starting the job I was working on a Sunday. I loved working Sundays as the plant payed double-time for Sunday shifts. My leg was killing me. I had been working for several hours when, after going up on the catwalk to work on a truck, I was on my way back down, and my knee gave out completely.

That time there was no ability for me to put any pressure on the leg at all. There was no way to continue the shift. I was helped to the office and there was an accident report filled out. I went home. I was scared. I did not want to be out of work and I certainly didn't need any more physical issues.

The next day I was taken to the hospital and had a series of x-rays done and an MRI scheduled. The MRI was much better than the previous one as my head stayed out of the machine. What the hospital concluded was that I had torn the meniscus in my right knee and, as an added bonus, I had contusions on the interior of my tibia. The damage I had done was not going to be a "walk it off" type of a situation. What I didn't know was that the injury was going to be an all-consuming issue for more than a year.

Initially the plan was to get physical therapy to see if the damage to the meniscus would settle down and the bone, which was shattered on the inside but had no outward breaks, would heal itself over time. I went to physical therapy three days a week and did home exercises to strengthen the leg. I went on bike rides and was lucky enough to have a personal trainer, who was a member of the SMART group, volunteer to work with me one-on-one. The leg was strengthening but the pain was not subsiding. The pain was getting hard to deal with. Sleep was becoming an issue. I was thankful to have a small check come to me once a week from the workman's compensation policy through work, but it was barely enough to cover my rent, let alone the other bills that continued to pile up. Sue eventually started working for Door Dash to try and cover all the added expenses.

After several weeks of physical therapy, my doctor suggested that the best course of action would be to undergo a surgery to repair the meniscus and drill small holes in my tibia to infuse it with a solution to help it harden and heal. I was not thrilled with the idea of having a second surgery less than seven months from my neck fusion. I felt like I was falling apart. The pain had become bad enough, that I was willing to consider anything that would give me some relief. Surgery was a better option than to continue with the PT, which had so far, failed me. I scheduled the surgery for mid-July.

I was not confronted with a powerful urge to drink before my neck surgery but those urges had become intense prior to the knee surgery. I don't know if it was the feeling of falling apart, the seclusion brought on by the pandemic or the feeling of being worthless while not working, but the urges were there. They were powerful. As urges always do, they subsided and lessened over time, but they kept coming back. By the time my surgery rolled around I had two years of sobriety under my belt. Two years and yet the bottle was still waiting in the wings to comfort me if I decided to give into its pleadings.

I began relying heavily on another of the techniques I had been taught in my certification courses. I gave my urges a personality. Not a generic personality, but one that I would hate myself if I gave in to. Some people use a pushy salesman as their urge image. Some people use a bully as that image. One person I know used his ex-wife. Any image of a personality somebody would not want to obey is the right image for them. For my image I imagined the nauseating, ear piercing, whining of a five year old trying to get what it wanted at the grocery store. My urge was a brat. My urge was loud. My urge was not going to get the sugar filled cereal. It would get the healthy snacks, and it would like it. The brat tried to wear me down, hoping that I would give in just to shut him up. I wouldn't give him the satisfaction. I named my urges Donny.

"MGM is open, and nobody would know," Donny said. "You don't have to go to work, so why not enjoy the time off? You deserve it."

Donny liked to tell me that alcohol would be a nice reward. He liked to trick me into thinking I could drink without consequences. The longer Donny stayed around without me relenting, the whinier he became.

"But SteeEEEve," he would whine. "We could just enjoy the time while you're not working. You could always quit again after the surgery!"

I knew if I gave in, he would know next time if he whined long enough and loud enough, I would crumble. I was not going to give in. I held firm. Donny is now almost a year older and he never got the sweets he demanded. Parenthood is full of tough love; I was just being a good parent.

I had my surgery, and after a couple weeks, I began physical therapy once again. The pain did not get much better. After almost two months of physical therapy I was finally released to go back to work with several restrictions. I was relieved to be going back and getting the chance to be productive. My restrictions limited me to four hours a day, no standing work and no stairs. I knew I was not going back to my former job, catwalks were out of the question, but I was excited to see what they would be assigning me to do. I was hoping it would be an opportunity to do something vital and perhaps even a chance to learn something new.

I was more than a little disappointed to be given the task of bagging up masks. Due to the Covid pandemic, all employees were required to wear masks at all times. My job was to open a box of masks, remove two of them, fold them, place them in Ziploc baggies, seal the baggies, and set them in a larger box. Not only was I not learning anything new, I was experiencing how four hours could be made to feel like eight. It was mind-numbing. The only challenge was trying to stay awake. I would split my day into two sections. I would work for two long hours, take a bathroom break, and finish the final two hours. The bathroom breaks were a nice break in the day. I would grab the bathroom key, hobble my way down the hallway, descend the stairs to the bathroom, do my business then enjoy an extra-long hand washing before going back to work.

After a few weeks of working, I was on my way to take my bathroom break when I had another incident with my knee. I was about a third of the way down the stairs when my knee buckled, and I felt another pop. Unlike the first time I felt that pop, there was no ability for me to get back up and go back to work. The pain was immediate and I was instantly unable to put weight on the knee. I was sent home that day and when I went to the hospital the following morning I was ex-rayed and told that I was in need of a complete knee replacement. That was not the news I wanted to hear. When would it all end?

Donny came back with a vengeance.

"You're going to have a long recovery from that kind of surgery," he said. "Plenty of time to sober back up. You might as well enjoy the time off. You deserve it!"

Donny is a conniving little shit. I didn't give in to his temper tantrums. Instead I did what I needed to do and set the surgery date for my total knee replacement. With plates and pins in my neck and whole new knee I was starting to look at myself as a cyborg...or better yet, the six million dollar man. "We can rebuild him. Better. Stronger. Faster!" Ok, maybe not better, stronger, faster but I was looking forward to being somewhere in the neighborhood of normal. My surgery was set for early in January. I was excited about the prospect of having the surgery behind me and getting through the twelve weeks of recovery by the time spring would roll around. Okay, I was not looking forward to any of it, but I was doing my best to maintain a decent attitude and I had decided to send Donny to his room...for good.

In order to prepare for major surgery I was set up for several appointments prior to the date of actually going under the knife. I had five weeks to prepare and I was doing my best to keep as upbeat about the prospect as I could. Christmas was just a few weeks away and I was going to do everything I could to enjoy the holidays. With the pandemic in full swing it was going to be an unusual celebration to say the least. It was about that time that I got two pieces of tough news. I was informed that the insurance company that had been handling my work injury was not willing to approve the surgery. They insisted that I would need to go to through an independent medical examination in order to get approval. I was also given a phone call from my brother Arn telling me that my father, age 88, had come down with Covid 19.

At the time I received the news about my father, the United States had over five hundred thousand deaths related to Covid and a large percentage of them were senior citizens. The memory of my mother's passing was still heavy on my heart and the idea that I could lose my father was more than I could bear. My father was more than just a father to me. He was a role model, a mentor and a true friend. He was so much of a friend, in fact, that he was the Best Man in my wedding. Losing him would be too much for me to handle. With the high mortality rate in his age group I practically started mourning before I even got off the phone with Arn. There was nothing I could do but wait and hope. Two days after receiving the initial phone call, my dad was admitted to the hospital. I feared the worst. Donny briefly made an appearance but I stared him down and he went back to his room. My father had been infected with the virus but, like the tough German he was, he defeated it and was back home three days later. One calamity avoided.

The other calamity needed to be addressed. My surgery was deemed necessary by a surgeon at one of the best hospitals on the planet. I didn't get the opinion from Bob's House of Knee Crap. It was the Mayo Hospital. How could that possibly not be enough of a recommendation to satisfy the insurance company? It didn't smell right. I contacted a lawyer.

The lawyer explained to me that the independent medical examination was an attempt to stop the surgery. It was, in fact, not independent at all. The doctor I was set up to see was most likely fed clients by the insurance company for the sole purpose of denying claims. There was nothing independent about it. Unfortunately, it was all part of the process, and there was nothing I could do but attend the sham of an examination. My lawyer gave me some advice about how to behave at the examination but informed me that I would need to go through with it no matter what. He said that I would most likely have my claim denied and that I should call him at that point. If my claim was denied, I could hire him to sue for the right to have my knee replaced.

With my knee surgery on hold, I had ample time on my hands. I decided to pursue something I had been encouraged to do months prior. I would attempt to get certified as a Peer Recovery Support Specialist. It was a designation that could help me get a career helping others trying to get sober. I had already been doing my best to do exactly that. Getting certified was my chance to actually get paid for doing it. It was by no means a get-rich-quick scheme. It was an honest career doing something that had given me immense satisfaction. There was no downside.

I applied for a scholarship to get my training and was accepted. I would need to pay back my scholarship by doing fifty hours of volunteer work helping people in the recovery community. I was excited for the opportunity. I was enrolled and scheduled to start my training the second week in January of 2021.

The pain in my knee had gotten so bad that I was averaging only about four hours of poor quality sleep at night. I couldn't think straight, and driving was a danger. On the day of the independent medical examination, Sue had to take the day off from work to give me a ride the eighty miles to the exam. It went exactly as the lawyer had predicted. It was a cursory examination, and the findings were a ridiculous set of arguments to deny my claim. Immediately after the exam report was written, the insurance company stopped sending my workman's compensation checks and informed me that they would no longer be paying for any medical treatments for my knee.

The independent medical examiner claimed that my knee problem was a pre-existing condition because three years before my work injury, I had seen a doctor about pain in my left knee. It was one incident three years ago in the wrong knee. I saw a doctor because I had hurt my left knee. I never had a follow up appointment because it had healed. That was one of the bullshit claims made; there were others. They claimed that because I was classified as obese, it was considered, again, a pre-existing condition. They said that because I had some arthritis it was, you guessed it, a pre-existing condition. They were grasping at straws to try and weasel out of the claim.

I hired the lawyer and he was amazed at the amount of false narratives incorporated into the IME report. We petitioned to get the workman's comp checks started again.

The following week I was set to start my classes for Peer Recovery Support training. One of the people I had been speaking with asked me to do an exercise prior to taking the classes. It was a simple task...or so I thought.

"Write a letter to someone you trust and explain why you have decided to help others recover from addiction."

I wrote that letter and it sent me on a wonderful journey. It was a journey that was filled with introspection and self-enlightenment. It was a journey that pushed me to complete my training for Peer Recovery Support. It was a journey that ended with me sitting in front of a computer, not just to write the letter to my brother, but to write in depth about the series of events which brought me to that amazing part of my life. The letter was written. This book was written. The journey continues.

Da Capo Al Fine

Da capo al fine, from the beginning to the end. While often used in musical terminology to signify a return to the beginning of a song and repeating it to the end, its true meaning is simply from the beginning to the end. The last thing I would want to do is repeat the events that have brought me to the end of this stanza. I would, however, gladly relive the events of the past if it was the only way for the journey to end in the place it has.

My life experiences have taken the good, the bad and the ugly and brought me to a place of profound appreciation. The Yin and the Yang of life is often filled with episodes that are easier to avoid than to confront. It's often that confrontation that develops the hard won lessons that allow the next step to come into clear view. I will always treasure the difficulties themselves as the catalysts of experience and catharsis. I have no wisdom to share, only observations.

When setting out on my journeys to California, I had the adventure in mind. The consequences were lost in the fog and obscured by the desire for the thrill. Sitting behind steel doors without basic freedoms was not the adventure I had in my sights but surely could have been the result. No Sue, no CeeVee, no Hondo, just the memories of what they once meant to me.

I have the chance to be there for all the events that make life worth living: my children growing into adults and making families of their own, vacations with Sue, even quiet moments of blissful solitude could have been replaced with the regrets of a man pacing his cell wishing the life he had taken for granted was still his.

As often happens in the throes of a full-on addiction, I, like most addicts, saw what I wanted to see. Was Carl the pot guru I had envisioned? No. He wasn't even a decent human. Was Theo a brother with my best interests at heart? Maybe in the beginning, but that went away all too quickly. Maybe the most important question of all was this: was I the only one taking these monumental risks? No. I had a moment of clarity watching my daughter suffer from my reckless abandon, but she wasn't the only one who could have been counted among those hurt by my decisions. I could have made Sue, either actually or metaphorically, a widow. I could have added suffering to my mother's already cataclysmic last few years. I could have been taken away from the time I now get to spend with my dad.

Imprisonment was one of the possible outcomes but certainly there was another glaring possibility - Death. Death was waiting for me on every turn. Hondo and I could have gone off the side of the mountain before I even encountered any of the pitfalls that were lying in wait for a misstep. I was lucky to not have perished under 80,000 pounds of steel on my drive back from trimming. I narrowly escaped being slayed at the hands of an angry biker or toothless hillbillies.

There was nothing that my lust for adventure could not have ripped away from me. My short-sightedness in retrospect cannot be considered surprising. It was that myopic point-of-view that nearly ended the life I was trying to achieve.

I have been fortunate to experience things that have not worked for me. The inspirational dissatisfaction of hitting road blocks along my journey pushed me to find the path that has allowed me to be sober, happy, and excited for the future. It's a future that would not have been possible from the cold confines of a prison cell.

There were things in my life that were unable to help me in-the-moment. Those same events have helped me immensely for the knowledge needed to work with others. AA did not work for me; I tried it with faith and without. I have also witnessed many who have taken the twelve steps to heart and have emerged sober and happy. That was their path. My path works for me.

Is my definition of spirituality different than that of others? Do I have true spiritualty without religion? The answer to both is a resounding yes! My spirituality, my connection to my community, and the world around me resides in the ability and desire to help others achieve successful sobriety. How can one stay sober without being happy? Perhaps the better question is why would anyone want to? I have seen people "white knuckle" their sobriety, and hang on with every ounce of strength they can muster but never get to a place of contentment. It can be done. Active addiction can be overcome by sheer willpower and dogged determination. The active part of the addiction can be conquered in that way, but if life revolves around the constant struggle not to give into the addiction; the addiction is still in control.

Donny still attempts to control me but he has become a minor annoyance. Soon I am hoping he will come of age, find his own place, and move out for good.

I have faced situations where I didn't know from moment to moment if I would keep my family, keep my sanity, keep my sobriety, or hell, even come out alive. Somehow I have managed to not only find a way forward but find happiness and a new direction to pursue. My days of get-rich-quick schemes are over. My days of happiness have arrived, yet what my future holds I do not know. What I do know, is the path that I have been lucky enough to find has given me hope.

Find your path.

About the Author

Steve Kind is a SMART Recovery facilitator, Certified Peer Recovery Specialist and a volunteer for Minnesota Recovery Connection.

After experiencing multiple failed attempts to get sober, Steve has dedicated his life to helping others find their pathway to a peaceful sobriety.

As a public speaker it is Steve's hope that his story may help others to avoid giving up hope for a better future.

www.ingramcontent.com/pod-product-compliance
Lightning Source LLC
Chambersburg PA
CBHW061420150726
47987CB00001B/33